New 5th Edition

NEW JERSEY DAY TRIPS

A GUIDE TO OUTINGS IN NEW JERSEY, NEW YORK, PENNSYLVANIA & DELAWARE

Revised and Updated

BARBARA HUDGINS

The Woodmont Press
P.O. Box 108
Green Village, N.J. 07935

This is the 5th revised and updated edition of New Jersey Day Trips. The first two editions were called Trips and Treks.

If a copy of this book is not available at your local bookstore, you may order one by sending $10.95 plus $1.50 shipping to:

The Woodmont Press
P.O. Box 108
Green Village, N.J. 07935

Library of Congress Catalog Card Number: 91-65333

ISBN 0-9607762-4-9
Printed in the United States of America

DEDICATION

To all the friends and family who trudged through countless amusement parks and reconstructed villages to help me with my book.

ACKNOWLEDGEMENTS

Much gratitude and thanks to:

All the driving companions who searched out New Jersey's nooks and crannies with me. In particular: Gail Davies, Sheila Di Marsico, Bill Mawhinney, Marilyn Kennedy, Linda Kimler, Alexandra Knox, Doug and Ralph Milnes, Pam Morse, Betty Murphy, Kathy Slack, and the Wemple family.

All those who shared their expertise with me, especially Ken Benson and Bonnie Lacey.

Those who helped with the book production beyond the call of duty, particularly: Mary Lou Nahas for copyreading, Jack Krug for editorial help, Kathy Hughes for book design of the first edition. Donna Chale and Cindy Kampf for proofreading, and Linda Kimler for pictures and general support.

And to Lani and Robert for their help and comments.

FOREWORD

There are several ways to put together a guidebook. One can do it regionally (e.g., all attractions in Sussex County are listed together), chronologically (everything open in winter is listed in one section) or by subject (all zoos are listed together, and all museums are listed together). There is no perfect way.

My book is set up primarily by subject. However, there are chapters that differ from this approach. The first chapter, "Unique Towns, Places to Browse" covers such towns as Atlantic City, New Hope, Princeton and various walking tours. Here I write about the town as a whole and include all the sites available. In the chapter "Museums of All Kinds," the listings proved to be so huge that I subdivided the sections geographically (N.Y., N.J. and PA.) and then subdivided New Jersey museums.

You will find some of my listings to be purely arbitrary. When a particular place could belong to more than one category, I simply chose the one I felt it fit in best. Pennsbury Manor, for instance, the reconstructed estate of William Penn, could fit in either the chapter titled "Homes of the Rich and Famous" or the one on restored villages.

The advantage of listing attractions by subject is that someone interested in a particular sport or hobby can easily find what is available at a glance. A newcomer wants to know what ski areas are near — a garden club president wants to know where to take her group on a trip — a parent asks a history teacher what Revolutionary War sites are around — and so forth. However, because many people want to know what is available in their immediate geographical area, I have included a regional index in the back of the book. Here the listings for New Jersey are under each county, and those for out-of-state are under a specific area (such as the Poconos, the Hudson Valley or New York City). One caution however — always check the main listings before you set out. There are many attractions that are open on a limited basis. For example, a well-done Colonial restoration — the Miller-Cory house — is open only on Sundays during the school year. Other places change guise with the season. Just as a weasel becomes an ermine in winter, summer action parks become winter ski areas, and August fairgrounds become September flea markets.

I wish you many hours of pleasurable day-tripping in and around New Jersey.

TEN AXIOMS OF DAYTRIPPING

1. Carry a map in your car — it's always best to check out your destination, even with the best of directions.

2. Take along a cooler filled with canned drinks and snacks — you never know what type of food (if any) lurks at the next stop.

3. Always have good walking shoes and sunglasses on hand — even if you're not wearing them. Extra towels too, in case of waterslides.

4. Take along more money than you expect to spend. Prices can change at any given time and some parking fees are not officially listed but nevertheless exist.

5. If you're taking a long trip best to telephone first. Some places may be unexpectedly closed.

6. Take advantage of free days. For example, New Jersey State parks waived their parking fees on Tuesdays for the past few years. The Philadelphia Museum of Art is free on Sunday mornings, etc.

7. Take advantage of coupons. Many amusement parks offer discounts through newspapers, Coke bottles, etc.

8. New York public museums have a "suggested donation" policy. You are under no oblication to pay the full amount according to the N.Y. Convention Bureau.

9. No matter how much they widen it, the Garden State Parkway will always be jammed on summer weekends, especially Saturday morning and Sunday evening.

10. Never order seafood salad at an unknown restaurant.

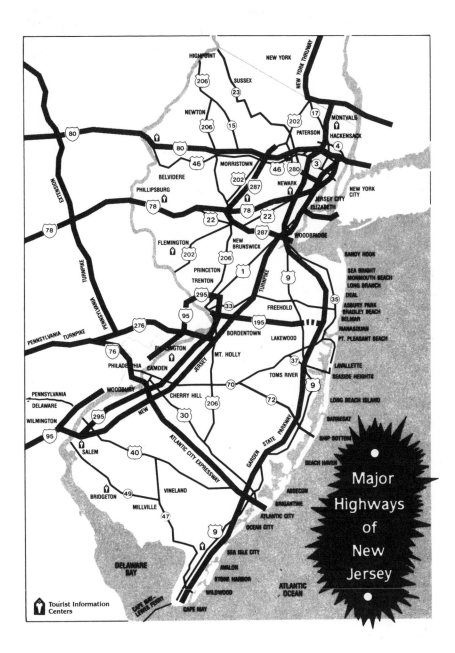

Major Highways of New Jersey

NOTE

Hours and prices listed in this book are as up to date as possible. However, changes occur constantly according to the whim of the owner or the budget cuts of state funds. Always telephone or check newspaper advertisements before you set out.

PHOTO CREDITS

Photographs were furnished by permission and courtesy of the following sources:

Page 1 and 210: Bucks County Chamber of Commerce. Pages 21, 28, 39, 61, 67, 167, 180, 185, 215: N.J. Div. of Travel & Tourism; Pages 133, 141, 149: Great Adventure; Page 85: Newark Museum; Pages 110, 123: N.Y. Convention & Visitors Bureau; Page 199: Linda Kimler; Page 221: Miniature Kingdom.

CONTENTS

UNIQUE TOWNS,
PLACES TO BROWSE,
GUIDED WALKING TOURS

Photo: Bucks County Chamber of Commerce

In This Chapter You Will Find:

Atlantic City, N.J.
Princeton, N.J.
New Hope, PA
Lahaska, PA
Cape May, N.J.
Chinatown, N.Y.

Guided Walking Tours for:
  Soho, N.Y.
  Other N.Y. Walking Tours
  Paterson, N.J.
  Bordentown, N.J.
  Burlington, N.J.
  Mount Holly, N.J.
  Other N.J. Tours
  Philadelphia, PA

ATLANTIC CITY

There are now twelve casino-hotels in Atlantic City and that's all there will be for a long time. The famed boardwalk is now a pastiche of sparkling hotels, monolithic parking lots, hole-in-the-wall concession stands and leftover buildings. In warm weather the place is alive with tourists, locals, musicians, and hand-pushed rolling chairs. The back streets combine jazz joints, new housing, new condos and areas that are still run down. But once you enter the casinos, you are in a world of plush carpets, mirrored glass, chorus girls and high-priced drinks - a little bit of Las Vegas swept onto the Jersey shoreline.

The casino-hotels have changed names more often than Hollywood stars change husbands. On the boardwalk they stretch from Bally's Grand on the south (formerly the Golden Nugget) to the Showboat on the north at Delaware Ave. Over at the marina (a few miles away) Harrah's and the Trump Castle overlook a flotilla of docked boats.

Here's a short run-down on what you will find:

Parking: Valet parking is available at the hotels if you are staying over or using the casino. Most offer free parking for a 3 or 6 hour stay. However, getting into town on a busy summer weekend can be full of traffic delays.

Transportation: Once you have parked your car, the best way to get around town is to take the small jitneys that operate along Pacific Avenue. They come frequently and cost $1.00. The tram no longer operates along the boardwalk, but you can walk on a nice day or take the push-along rolling chairs that cost about $5 for every six blocks. Cabs are plentiful if you want to get away from the boardwalk area. And NJ Transit buses serve the length of the island 24 hours a day. They run along Atlantic Ave.

Bus Tours: Still the favorite way for most people to make a one day visit — fares vary from point of embarkation. It costs $18 from north Jersey but the casinos give you quarters and other freebies when you arrive. You must stay 6 hours if you take a bus tour. Many people take a sandwich along on the bus trip down, then eat at the hotel buffet just before the return trip. These casino-subsidized buses travel to Atlantic City every day of the year. When groups charter their own buses, they often get a package which includes buffet and show.

The Hotels: Prices are high in the sparkling hotels. However, if you don't mind visiting A.C. when the chill winds blow, there are some very reasonable weekend packages available from the big hotels. These include room and dinner. Once the summer season hits, though, be prepared to pay through the nose. Actually, almost every shore resort in Jersey has a bus tour to A.C. several nights a week, so it is not necessary to stay in town in order to play in town. There are also many older motels along Pacific and Atlantic Avenues. Most of these have been refurbished. For a brochure listing hotels, restaurants and current shows, write to the Atlantic City Visitors Bureau, 2308 Pacific Ave., Atlantic City, NJ 08401 or call 609-348-7044.

The Casinos: If your idea of a casino is garnered from the movies and you expect evening dresses and tuxedos, leisurely gaming tables and James Bond types floating around, forget it. This is supermarket gambling, where little old ladies with shopping bags hover over the slot machines, longshoremen and bewildered bus groups from Delaware wander around in a vast hall of glass, chrome and green, and the hotel employees all seem to have taken a vow of silence. Roulette and blackjack and craps tables are placed cheek by jowl, and rows of slots glisten in the artificial light. It's all very confusing. However, minimum bets are posted at each table, and gaming guides are sometimes available at the hotel desks.

As for slot machines — you change your paper money into coins at the elevated change booths in the slot area. But to transform a bucketful of coins into dollars, you must hike over to the Coin Banks, usually located way across the room. The slots come in all varieties: from nickel and dime (not too many of these) to the one, five and ten dollar machines.

The casinos try mightily to keep their customers loyal. The gimmick of choice right now is a card (something like a credit card) which you get by joining a particular casino's "club". This card gives you back points every time you use the slot machines or tables, so that eventually, if you spend enough money, you get enough "comps" to eat in the fancy restaurants, buy in the gift shops or sleep in the hotel rooms. This allows the middle class to enjoy some of the privileges once reserved for the high rollers. It also keeps people pushing quarters into machines.

Food: There are many excellent restaurants in Atlantic City. From the old *Knife and Fork Inn* (outside the Boardwalk area) to the French, English and Japanese eating rooms in the large hotels. The better restaurants absolutely require reservations. However, the daytripper will more likely end up at the buffets (which vary in quality and price) at almost any hotel. Many bus tours offer coupons for these. There are also 24-hour coffee shops

4

that are mediocre and a few New York style delis that are good. And fast food courts are available everywhere, replacing some of the fancier (and prettier) lunchtime places of the 1980s.

Entertainment: First class shows, chorus girls and big name stars appear at the hotels, and this, above all, has brought a certain zing to the resort. Shortened versions of Broadway shows have become a favorite form of entertainment. Besides the big shows, there are lounges with brassy singers, lounges with tinkling pianos, big boxing matches and all sorts of tournaments. As for teenagers, they will find video game rooms in the hotels and some on the Boardwalk also. Families can enjoy the **Tivoli Pier** in the TropWorld Hotel which offers a miniature version of boardwalk amusements (including a ferris wheel) and the supersized bowling alley over at the Showboat hotel.

On the boardwalk, in warm weather, the old **Central Pier** still offers some rides, and there is often entertainment at the ampitheater at Indiana Ave. There is also a small art center at the Garden Pier. The giant shopping center called Ocean One (shaped like an ocean liner) includes shops and eateries and often hosts special events.

For those who want to venture beyond the Boardwalk, there are a few summertime attractions. One is **Lucy, the Margate Elephant**, an architectural oddity that is six stories high — complete with howdah. You can walk through Lucy (although the original rooms are gone) with a guided tour during the summer — for a fee. It is located at 9200 Atlantic Avenue in Margate — two towns down from Atlantic City. The wooden elephant is open weekends May and September and daily from late June to Labor Day.

On the inlet side, Atlantic City offers **Historic Gardener's Basin** which began life as a miniature fishing village in the manner of Mystic, Connecticut. But the square riggers and boutiques have disappeared. What is available now is the restaurant, The Flying Cloud, and a number of special events such as concerts and clambakes.

Other standard sidetrips from Atlantic City are the winery tours at Renault and Gross's Highland Winery, the Historic Towne of Smithville and Wheaton Village, all of which are mentioned elsewhere in this book. And of course, in the summertime, there is always the Atlantic City beach, which is free.

DIRECTIONS: Garden State Parkway to Exit 40 and 38S, or NJ Tpke. to Atlantic City Expressway.

PRINCETON

Shades of F. Scott Fitzgerald! Golden lads and lasses walk the well-clipped paths between venerable University halls while russet leaves flutter overhead from rows of sturdy trees. Time, scholarships, and the inclusion of girls have changed the atmosphere at this Ivy League bastion somewhat. But still, for a trip to a true University town that combines history, culture and typical collegiate Gothic architecture, nothing beats a visit to Princeton.

For many, the trip to Princeton means either a show at the popular McCarter theater or football at Palmer Stadium. For everyone else there is still plenty to do and see. And the best way to see the campus sights is to take the free tours offered by the *Orange Key Guide Service*. Just go to MacLean House on campus in time for the tours which leave at 10 AM, 11 AM, 1:30 PM, and 3:30 PM weekdays and Saturdays. Sunday tours are 1:30 and 3:30 P.M. The telephone number is 609-258-3603 but it is not necessary for individuals to reserve in advance. Here are some campus sights included in the tour:

1. **Nassau Hall:** Built in 1756, this Georgian stone structure has survived pillage and fire (by the British, not the students) over the years. It served as a barracks and hospital for troops of both sides during the Revolutionary War. In 1783 Congress met here and drafted the Constitution while Princeton was still the capital. It now serves as an administrative office for the University. A painting by Charles Willson Peale of Washington at the Battle of Trenton is to be found here.

2. **Firestone Library:** A beautiful two-million volume library built in 1948, it is the embodiment of the Collegiate Gothic style. Major collections include the papers of F. Scott Fitzgerald, Adlai E. Stevenson, John Foster Dulles, Woodrow Wilson and other famous graduates. A changing exhibit of rare books is also on display.

3. **Woodrow Wilson School of Public and International Affairs:** Guides will show you the outside of this striking building, one of the few modern structures on campus. Designed by Minoru Yamasaki, it includes a reflecting pool and the Fountain of Freedom by James Fitzgerald.

4. **The University Chapel:** Built in a Gothic design by Ralph Adams Cram in 1928, it is the third largest university chapel in the country, seating 1800. A 16th Century carved oak pulpit and some of the finest stained glass to be seen this side of the Atlan-

tic Ocean make the Chapel an outstanding part of the Princeton trip.

5. **The Putnam Sculptures:** These are a series of massive metal and stone sculptures scattered around the campus as if a giant had decided to distribute his toys among the college buildings. Almost all are abstract in design and they stick out like sore thumbs among the ivy-walled buildings. You can't miss them, so you might as well examine them. Sir Henry Moore, Jacques Lipchitz, Louise Nevelson and Pablo Picasso are among the biggies represented there.

6. **The Prospect:** A Tuscan villa built in 1949, it is now used as a Faculty Club and not open to the public. However, the formally designed garden to the rear is open for browsing and is very pleasant.

Not included in the tour, but an important stop, is the newly expanded **Princeton Art Museum**. This is a first rate museum and a wonder of wonders — it's free! Paintings include a generous sampling of Italian Renaissance and French Baroque. You'll find a good collection of Chinese bronzes as well as artifacts from Central and South America. A top collection of prints and a separate medieval room that includes part of the stained-glass window from the Cathedral at Chartes are also "must sees." Special changing exhibits are of a high order. Call 609-258-3762 for more information.

Besides the university, Princeton has pleasant shopping along Nassau Street and many good restaurants (among them *"Lahiere's," "The Nassau Inn"* and the *"Alchemist and Barrister"*). You might also want to look at the Princeton Cemetery at Wiggins and Witherspoon, which holds the remains of Aaron Burr and Grover Cleveland among its many notables. The Princeton Battle Monument, a fifty-foot structure, stands imposingly at Nassau and Mercer Streets, while a walking tour of the area will take you past many lovely old houses. Albert Einstein's former home, at 112 Mercer St., is not open to the public. However, many people take a photograph of it as they pass by. Several outstanding historic buildings, such as Morven and the Bainbridge House (which have separate listings in this book) and Drumthwacket, the present governor's mansion, are all within walking distance of the town center. A short drive away is Princeton Battlefield Park.

The **McCarter Theater** runs a full program of professional plays, movies, ballet and concerts from September to June. There are also a good number of fairs and community doings going on.

However, much of Princeton's activity is geared to the school season, so call first to see what's open if you're planning to visit during the summer or holidays (609-258-3000).

DIRECTIONS: Route 206 or 27 to Princeton. The University is on Nassau Street.

NEW HOPE, PENNSYLVANIA

There are a number of small towns in the United States that seem to survive simply by being picturesque. A combination of natural beauty, historical significance and the establishment of an art colony (followed inevitably by a writer's colony and a rustic theater) creates that certain atmosphere that brings the tourists out in droves. Whether the original tourist impetus was the antiques in the historical part of town or the artworks in the art colony, the more people arrive, the more craftshops, antique stores, boites, boutiques and charm-laden restaurants open.

New Hope, Pennsylvania has long been the cultural and picturesque capital of Bucks County. On any fall weekend the narrow sidewalks of this sophisticated oasis set in Pennsylvania farm country are simply jammed. People come to browse or just wallow in the atmosphere.

In the 1920's landscape painters settled here, bringing with them the excitement of the creative world. By the Thirties, Bucks County had become well known as a quiet weekend haven for novelists, poets and playwrights. And in 1939 a grist mill in the center of town was transformed into the **Bucks County Playhouse**. The opening program was "Springtime for Henry" with Edward Everett Horton, and the playhouse has remained a stalwart of the "Straw Hat Circuit" ever since. The season now begins in the late spring and extends well into the fall. Since the theater offers family musicals and matinee performances it is one of New Hope's biggest draws. (Telephone: 215-862-2041)

Another summer season attraction is the **New Hope Mule Drawn Barge Ride** which offers a one-hour ride down the old canal works. It is a slow and easy way to see the town. It departs from the barge landing at New Street, and usually several rides are offered during the afternoon. Call 215-862-2842 for details.

A popular pontoon ride is **Coryell's Ferry** which offers scenic rides on the Delaware. It loads behind Gerenser's Exotic Ice Cream Store, 22 S. Main St. And railroad enthusiasts will enjoy

8

the **New Hope 1890 Steam Railway** which operates between May and October. It leaves from Bridge and Stockton Streets. The schedule varies so call 215-862-2332 beforehand.

Historic house lovers will enjoy the **Parry Mansion** at South Main and Parry Streets. Guided tours of ten rooms that run the gamut from Colonial to early 20th century are available. The rooms were furnished by a professional interior decorator and each reflects a period—Federal, Victorian, etc.— in the history of the house. It's quite well done. The house is open from May to October on Friday through Sunday from 1-4 PM. Tours cost a small fee. Call 215-862-5652 for additional information.

But even without these extras there is plenty to see in New Hope. Stroll along the leaf-strewn streets and visit the shops if you are interested in antiques. There are plenty of shops featuring memorabilia in town, and if you collect old sheet music, military hats or miniature dolls, you'll find much to pick from. If you're tired there are horse-drawn carriage rides which leave from The Logan Inn.

Art galleries can be found on Main Street, Mechanic Street and Route 202. Phillips Mill, just two miles outside New Hope, hosts an art festival and has galleries too. Besides the standard landscape of Pennsylvania red barn country you can find modernistic sculpture and paintings also. The kids will be more interested in the toy shops, the knickknack shops and the candy shop (whence the aroma of chocolate-dipped strawberries wafts over town).

One of the charms of visiting a quaint, riverside town is eating in a quaint, interesting restaurant, and there are plenty of them in New Hope, most along the main drag. Whether you opt for the casual *Mother's*, the glossy *Hacienda*, or the cutesy *Picnic Basket*, you will be satisfied. The better places fill up on weekends, though, so you'd better make reservations as soon as you hit town. There's a variety of night spots in and around town also. Check the Information Center at 1 W. Mechanic Street.

Lambertville, on the Jersey side of the river, has a number of interesting restaurants also. Read more about Lambertville in the chapter on Flea Markets.

DIRECTIONS: Route 202 across Delaware River, Then 32S; or 179 to 29 to Lambertville and cross bridge.

LAHASKA, PENNSYLVANIA

Having gone as far as New Hope, you might as well go the extra four miles on Route 202 to Lahaska and the Peddler's Village. The road is dotted with antique shops which is what brought this area to prominence in the first place. **Peddler's Village** is one of those reconstructed shopping malls that combine the brick walls and lamps of the 18th Century plus very pretty landscaping with astute 20th Century commercialism. In fact, it is very similar to the Historic Towne of Smithville and a number of other Colonial style malls. This one has a great big waterwheel and lovely floral beds to give it the proper atmosphere. It even has its own Bed and Breakfast inn, one of the many in Bucks County.

Many people who visit New Hope like to go on to Lahaska to eat since Peddler's Village features one of those Colonial restaurants that has several different eating and drinking areas, at moderate prices. The Village also includes many shops which sell china, leather, children's clothes, handcrafts and so on, together with enough cheese, nut and candy shops to insure that you don't leave the grounds without buying something. There are special events here on special weekends — everything from a Strawberry Festival to a Teddy Bear Picnic.

A number of shopping areas have sprung up next to Peddler's Village. **The Yard**, with its California look and contemporary restaurant, a small discount mall and the flea market. More about that in the chapter on Flea Markets.

> **LOCATION:** Routes 202 & 263, Lahaska, PA.
> **HOURS:** 10-5:30 daily for shops. Fridays until 9. Some shops are Sunday 1-5. Restaurants are open later.
> **TELEPHONE:** 215-794-4000

CAPE MAY

When the Bed and Breakfast boom started in the 1970s, New Jersey was hardly mentioned in all those B&B books. But now, the Yuppies have discovered the Victorian summer homes of Cape May and have converted them into the latest thing in inns. Gone are the dull, old-fashioned guest houses whose porches always seemed to show peeling white paint. In their stead there is a whole array of Victorian homes, sporting the sprightly colors of pink, blue and maroon. Gothic cottages, Italian villas, Mansard and Stick style buildings have metamorphized into charming, whimsical Bed and Breakfast homes, restaurants, antique stores and art galleries. And the interest in this Victorian revitalization has led the town of Cape May to extend its season beyond the ten weeks of summer.

You can now take walking tours, house tours, and trolley tours on weekends from May through October. And a special Victorian Week, held in October, features ten days of antiques, crafts, fashion shows and tours. Another special is the Christmas candlelight tours. The group that runs many of these festivities is the *Mid-Atlantic Center for the Arts*, which operates out of the **Emlen Physick Estate**. The Physick house itself is the scene of a popular tour. This sprawling 1881 Stick Style home is typical of the Brown Decade both in its exterior and its somewhat somber furnishings. A trolley car tour that leaves from the estate travels to the more colorful beachfront area, where houses trimmed in carpenter's lace and fancy restaurants await the visitor.

Cape May has long been a part of the summer scene (see the chapter on the Jersey Shore). And the beachfront still has a few modern motels and video game arcades among the older hostelries. But the major ambience of the town is the restoration of its Victorian past. The Washington Street Mall is a focal point for shoppers and you can find any number of boutiques and outdoor cafes in this pleasant outdoor mall. For more information on the various tours and inns, contact: The Mid-Atlantic Center for the Arts, P.O. Box 340, Cape May, N.J. 08204, or telephone 609-884-5404.

DIRECTIONS: Garden State Parkway to Exit 1. Follow signs to historic area.

CHINATOWN, NEW YORK

There are many unique neighborhoods in nearby New York, but the one that stands out as the last of the true ethnic neighborhoods is Chinatown. Although there are some modern towers rising up in the area, most of Chinatown is still packed with six-story tenements that nestle within them a huge variety of shops and restaurants. Pagoda-shaped telephone booths, a Chinese movie, and Buddhist temples add touches of the Orient. But it is the smell of spices in the streets, the gnarled looking vegetables in the grocery shops and the tinkling brass bells in the curio shops that gives Chinatown its special flavor.

Most of all it is the restaurants that pull the crowds to Chinatown. You can find hot and spicy Northern cooking, the traditional (to New Yorkers) Cantonese cuisine, and the small tea shops that serve dim sum lunches. Sunday is the big day for tourists, so it gets awfully crowded, but weekdays it's just blah. Try Saturday, or get there early on Sunday if you want to find a parking space. This is the closest you'll get to a foreign country without leaving the United States.

DIRECTIONS: Use Holland Tunnel. Keep straight on Canal Street to Pell St. Chinatown lies in the general area between Pell & Mott streets in lower Manhattan.

GUIDED WALKING TOURS

There are two kinds of walking tours. One is the self-guided type where you begin with a map and a brochure (usually provided by the local historical society) and hoof it yourself. The other is the pre-arranged group tour wherein you reach your destination by bus or car and then proceed *en masse* down the street, following a highly knowledgeable leader who tells you what you are seeing. Group tours often include one or two private houses where you enter by special permission.

Here is a sampling of some of the many guided and self-guided tours available. While most group tours require a pre-arranged schedule and a group of at least ten, others are open to whomever shows up.

THE SOHO TOUR

This excursion is particularly popular with residents of New Jersey because Soho is comparatively new territory on the New York art scene. Soho is that section of Manhattan that is bounded by Houston, Sullivan, Canal and Broadway, with its boundaries ever widening. Although this basically industrial area has undergone a great transformation in the last fifteen years, there are still piles of garbage on the street and an occasional wino in the doorway, so traveling en masse is practical.

On a nice spring weekend, though, the streets of Soho are jammed with browsers. The art galleries have their doors open, (unlike Madison Avenue galleries where you must be buzzed in)

12

and many are on street level. The boutique shops and Art Nouveau restaurants are filled and the whole area has a carnival air. People with pink hair and black jackets or motley costumes roller skate, walk dogs or simply stroll around.

Enter into this colorful scene a group of thirty New Jerseyans dressed in suburban cloth coats and following a young man from the *Cast Iron Society* who is pointing out mansard roofs and wrought-iron grillework. Naturally, all eyes are riveted on this non-motley crew and many an arty bystander follows along. As a matter of fact, the particular group I was in stopped traffic several times as cars and passersby gaped at the intracacies of late 19th Century urban architecture, not knowing quite why. (The Cast Iron Society runs a limited number of tours. Call 212-427-2488 for information).

For groups who prefer gallery tours to architectural ones, there are several ways to plan them. One is through your local museum curator; another is through the many specialized art tour groups that operate in the New York-New Jersey area. In the galleries of Soho you can find Pop Art, Neon Art, Abstract, post-Modernism and whatever is the fad at the moment. Besides the galleries, the most popular stops are:

Urban Archaeology, 135 Spring St. - It's a store, not a museum, but it attracts browsers with its fascinating collection of old building remnants. Stone gargoyles, bathroom sinks outfitted with gold-plated fixtures and old doors and pediments are strewn around the place. Here is where you can find one of those turn-of-the century mirrored bars that are so popular in quaint local pubs.

Museum of Holography, 11 Mercer St. - Something new and exciting and popular with children. Holography is three- dimensional laser photography. The museum is open Tues.-Sun., 12-6. Adults: $3.50; Children & Seniors: $2.50. Telephone: 212-925-0526.

Dean & DeLuca, 121 Prince St. - Okay, so this is where our whole group ended up. The store sells a combination of gourmet kitchenware, gorgeous looking breads and a variety of cheeses and delicacies. You can probably find the same thing in New Jersey, but somehow it seems more exciting down here. Also more expensive.

OTHER NEW YORK WALKING TOURS

Since New York is a center for art and theater and New Yorkers are traditionally preoccupied with being "In", it is only natural that some of the most popular tours here are of the behind-the-scenes variety.

Lincoln Center, for instance, runs escorted tours through Avery Fischer Hall, the State Theater and of course, the Metropolitan Opera House. Call 212-877-1800 for reservations and information.

NBC Television Tours: these are extremely popular. Depending on the day and time of your visit you may get to see a program in progress. Anyway there is a lot of inside information on how TV really works. The tours run every fifteen minutes from 9:30 to 4:30 and leave from the main floor of the RCA Building. Tickets cost $7.25 per person and children under 6 are not permitted. It is best to get your tickets as early as possible, since the tours do fill up. Tickets go on sale at 9 A.M. For information on group tours call 212-664-4000.

For those interested in the backstage machinations of the Capitalist world, the **New York Stock Exchange**, 20 Broad St., in the Wall Street area, has been conducting free tours on a regular daily basis for years. Call 212-656-5167 for further information.

There are a number of private walking tour groups operating in the New York area, but they change name and number so frequently I hesitate to mention them. However, one tour guide who is extremely popular in my area is Lou Singer of **Singer Tours**, 130 St. Edward St., Brooklyn, NY 11201. Mr. Singer's "noshing" tours (where you stop and sample knishes, canneloni, Chinese dumplings and such fare during walks through the lower or upper East Side) and his architectural tours of Brooklyn are justly famous. Singer works primarily with groups. Telephone: 718-875-9084 between 7 and 11 P.M. Howard Goldberg's **Adventures on A Shoestring** walking tours are also very popular. Telephone: 212-265-2663 for this one. As for other groups, it's best to check in the most recent copy of the Manhattan Yellow Pages, to find groups that are operating at the moment.

14

PATERSON TOURS

Do-it-yourself tours, guided group tours, visits to the variegated ethnic churches or simply a walking tour of the public statues of Gaetano Federici—these are some of the many tour possibilities you find in the city of Paterson. This industrial city is proud of its history as one of the earliest manufacturing sites in the United States. Its tours emphasize the historic district of *The Society for Useful Manufactures*, a section of the city that was planned for commerce by Alexander Hamilton back in 1791.

The Great Falls of Paterson, a spectacular waterfall completely surrounded by concrete and urban landscape, is the focal point of the S.U.M. Tours. The Society for Useful Manufacture's Historic District covers the area of mills and plants the were once the heart and breath of the city. Paterson's Golden Age began early in the 19th Century when power from the falls created an industrial bonanza. **The Colt Mill** with its cotton duck sails for the Navy, the **Rogers Locomotive Works** building (which now contains the Paterson Museum and a host of interesting exhibits), and the silk mills that made Paterson the center of that industry are included in the tour. Many of these brick and stone edifices are in various states of rehabilitation.

The **Great Falls Development Corporation** runs tours that take you to the scenes of Paterson's industrial past, but they also will custom-tailor tours to the interests of the group. A popular stop on all the tours is the true Farmer's Market which offers vegetables, cheeses and other fresh items.

CONTACT: Grace George, Great Falls Visitor Center, 65 McBride Ave., Paterson, N.J. 07501. Telephone: 201-279-9587

BORDENTOWN WALKING TOUR

One of the most historical towns in New Jersey, Bordentown is no longer the Quaker enclave it once was. Nor is it the large metropolis (the major boat and coach stop on the route to Philadelphia) of yore. Several famous citizens once made their abodes here — among them Clara Barton, Thomas Paine, Francis Hopkinson (another Revolutionary notable) and Joseph Bonaparte, brother of Napoleon. There are many Quaker buildings still standing and the homes of the famous are here but are private for the most part. And even though the town - which depends heavily on the Ocean Spray cannery for income - is primarily working class, there is still an aura of quaintness and history here.

Self-guided walking tours begin with a brochure from the Historical Society which is located in the **Old City Hall**. The hall itself has many interesting rooms - among them a one-room courthouse upstairs and a four-cell jail downstairs. The jail demonstrates how economically space was used in the old days — a criminal was sentenced upstairs and jailed within the same building, right away. The City Hall is open to the public Tues.-Thurs., 9:30-11 & 12:30-3; Fri.: 9:30-11; Sat.: 10-3. For those individuals who take the brochure and proceed from City Hall it is mostly a matter of looking at the outside of the historic buildings. However, if you book a group tour (ten or more) you may get a peek inside.

The group tour I took had as our first stop the **Gilder House**. As we entered the front hall, we noticed an elaborate rendition of a family tree that traced the line from Samuel Bunting to the Reverend Gilder for whom the house is named. But it is the furniture from Joseph Bonaparte's estate that creates the most interest here. An elaborate buffet, a blue couch with eagles and a gold-trimmed tea set in the Empire style are some of the remnants the rich and proud French family left in this small New Jersey town. The guide also pointed out a painting of sheep by artist Susan Waters. She is another Bordentown native whose fame is growing with the stronger appreciation of American itinerant painters.

From the Gilder House we proceeded to the **Clara Barton Schoolhouse,** a prime historical site in the town. Actually Miss Barton taught here for a very short time but she made quite an impact on the town. Up until that time, middle class children went to private school while public schools were considered to be for paupers. Miss Barton has to persuade the local school-children to attend. There was no fee, but each child was required to bring a stick of wood to keep the woodstove going. The small red brick building has benches and a raised platform where the teacher sat (in the back of the room, not the front).

Other houses included on the self-guided walking tour are: The Friends Meeting House, Shippen House, Francis Hopkinson House, Thomas Paine House and the Joseph Borden House. While most of these are private they are often opened up for Bordentown's *"Open House Tour"* which takes place in mid-October.

CONTACT: Bordentown Historical Society, P.O. Box 182, 302 Farnsworth Ave., Bordentown, N.J. 08505. Telephone: 609-298-1740 (12-3 PM except Mondays).

BURLINGTON

Another town that saw its heyday years ago at a time when it was the capital of West Jersey and a stronghold of Quakerism is Burlington. Among the many buildings that still stand are the **Friends Meeting House,** the **Revell House,** and the **Ulysses S. Grant House,** plus several prominent churches.

A very active Historical Society operates a museum here comprised of five houses. One is the house once rented by the family of America's first novelist and is named, appropriately, the **James Fenimore Cooper House,** although the writer only spent the first thirteen months of his life here. The **Captain James Lawrence House** is right next door and is dedicated to pictures and memorabilia of the War of 1812 hero who is best known for his words, "Don't Give Up The Ship!" (You find out, during the tour here, that they did give up the ship, and the British won the battle, but what the heck, a good phrase is hard to find.) Although small, this is a well furnished and very interesting place.

These side-by-side houses are located at 457 and 459 High Street. **The Pearson How House** (453 High St.) the **Alice Wolcott Museum** and the **Delia Pugh Library** make up the rest of the museum complex. For hours of visitation or special arrangements call 609-386-4773. Usually, they are Mon. - Thurs., 1-4; Sun., 2-4.

Aside from its historical district, Burlington also offers the *Burlington Coat Factory* on Route 130, which is home base for a well-known outlet chain. There is also a small mall of outlet shops called The Burlington Mart. And down by the riverfront you can find an old-fashioned walk with a nice view.

A brochure for a self-guided walking tour of the historical district is available from City Hall. You can also make arrangements for guided group tours from there.

> **CONTACT:** Dr. Nicholas Kamaras, City Hall, Burlington, N.J. 08016. Telephone: 609-386-3993.

MOUNT HOLLY

The county seat of Burlington was a center of Quakerism in New Jersey. This quiet little town has several buildings of note on its walking tour. You may obtain a pamphlet for the self-guided tour from: Township Hall, 23 Washington St., Mt. Holly, N.J. 08060. Telephone: 609-261-0170.

Among the noteworthy buildings are: The **Burlington County Prison-Museum**, designed by Robert Mills, architect of the Washington Monument, the **Mill Street Hotel**, the **John Woolman Memorial** and a restored 1759 schoolhouse where Woolman, the famous Quaker abolitionist, once taught. Most of these are heavy old stone buildings that really set you back in time.

A few miles outside of Mt. Holly there stands the historic mansion of **Smithville** (not to be confused with the historic town of Smithville in Atlantic County). This large columned house includes a museum of bicycles and is open for tours Wed.-Sun. from April through November. Telephone 609-261-5068 for further information.

OTHER NEW JERSEY TOURS

SALEM TOUR: Salem was an early Quaker settlement in West Jersey in the county of the same name. The town boasts a large number of authentic 18th Century houses. The headquarters of the Historical Society at 79-83 Market Street is maintained as a museum and offers nineteen rooms of early American furniture and decorative arts. Living rooms, bedrooms, featherbeds, rooms full of dolls and much more are on view here Tues.-Fri. from 12-

4. There is a nominal fee for the museum. This is where you pick up the map for a walking tour of the local historic area. Among the important sights are the Old Court House and the ancient Salem Oak. *Telephone:* 609-935-5004.

GLOUCESTER COUNTY: For those who wish to see the many historical buildings in the small towns that dot the county of Gloucester, the County Historical Society has prepared a map which lists forty-eight of them and gives a short history of each. Many are privately owned, but the **Hunter-Lawrence House**, 58 North Broad St., Woodbury, is now a museum and open to the public. It is also headquarters of the Historical Society and you may write there for the map before you set out. *Telephone:* 609-845-4771.

BRIDGETON: Yet another southwestern Jersey town trying for a Renaissance of its heyday. The town includes New Jersey's largest historic district with over 2000 homes and buildings from the Colonial, Federal and Victorian eras all in various stages of repair. The strongest ambience here is Victorian with many large homes on hand. The Cohansey River runs through town and a new riverfront plaza has been built to host concerts, fairs and walking tours. A large park, which includes the Nail Museum and a good-size zoo is on the other side of the river. A few boutique shops have opened in the riverfront area, but the town has a long way to go to rival Cape May in interest. Maps, a slide film and arrangements for guided bus and walking tours are available at the Bridgeton-Cumberland Tourist Association at Routes 49 & 77, Bridgeton. *Telephone:* 609-451-4802.

SEASONAL TOURS: Many towns (including a few that used to run regular tours) now concentrate their efforts on a once a year "Open House" type of thing. Among these are **Plainfield**, which boasts many beautifully restored Victorian homes. Its hospital tour, usually in May, includes some old-style wrap-around porch houses that makes this town so distinctive. **Hoboken** celebrates its railroad station in October with festivities, tours of the Byzantine station and walks through some of the newly renovated brownstones. November is the season for **Sergeantsville's** "Thanksgiving In The Country" tour wherein the whole town makes soup for the church luncheon and runs buses back and forth to the various open houses. These tours are always highly publicized in the newspapers and are certainly worth checking out to see how the other half of the state lives.

PHILADELPHIA TOURS

Probably the best known self-guided tour is that of Indepen-dence National Historical Park (Independence Mall) which is treated in the chapter entitled "Classics". Other popular tours in Philadelphia are:

UNITED STATES MINT: Within the downtown historic area (it's located at Arch & 5th Sts.) is the building where the coins we use are produced. No, they don't give free samples, but you can buy special sets and commemorative coins from the sales counter in the lobby. Self-guided tours are continous and last about 45 minutes. Free. *Hours:* 9-4:30, Mon.-Sat. *Telephone:* 215-597-7350.

FAIRMOUNT PARK HISTORIC HOUSE TOURS: Fairmount Park cuts a wide swath through Philadelphia on both sides of the Schuylkill. It includes within its many acres, not only the usual playgrounds, pools and tennis courts, but such major attractions as the Philadelphia Zoo and the Philadelphia Museum of Art.

In the 18th Century, the park was a center for country homes of the gentry who wanted to escape the epidemics of the crowded city. Eight of these homes have been restored and are now open to the public. They include John Penn's Solitude, Robert Morris' Lemon Hill, and such Georgian classics as Woodford and Mount Pleasant. The houses, which are scattered about the park, are furnished with authentic antiques and hark back to the time when Philadelpha was the most important Colonial town in the world.

Guided tours for groups can be arranged beforehand to em-phasize history, decorative arts or gardens. In early December, a special Christmas tour features the houses decorated in the manner of the 18th and early 19th centuries. Individuals may also visit the homes although they will not get a guided tour. Public hours are Wed.-Sun., 10-4 and the fee is $1.00 for adults, and $.50 for children. There is also a special trolley tour of Fairmount Park which includes some historic homes. The trolley tour is available only on Wed. & Sun. at 1 P.M. and tickets are available at the Museum of Art and the Visitors Center for $5.00. Further information on the Fairmount Park house tours can be obtained by calling 215-787-5449.

For general information on Philadelphia Tours and other at-tractions write: Philadelphia Convention and Visitors Bureau, 1525 J.F. Kennedy Blvd., Philadelphia, PA 19102 or call 215-636-1666.

See Also: *Lambertville, Lahaska* and *Chester* in the chapter on "Flea Markets and Outlets".

WHERE WASHINGTON SLEPT, ATE AND FOUGHT

Photo: Courtesy N.J. Travel & Tourism

In This Chapter You Will Find:

JOCKEY HOLLOW

The winter of 1779-1780 was the coldest in a century. On December 1, 1779, General George Washington entered Morristown and took up residence at the home of Mrs. Jacob Ford, Jr.

Meanwhile, four miles away at Jockey Hollow, 10,000 men chopped down six hundred acres of oak, walnut and chestnut trees to build hundreds of huts along the slopes of the "hollow". Severe snowstorms hindered their work and delayed the supply of meat and bread they needed to survive. Starvation confronted the army, which also suffered from inadequate clothing, disease and low morale. So terrible was the winter of the Morristown encampment that many troops finally mutinied.

But the history books only tell you about Valley Forge. Why? Because New Jersey has simply never had a very good public relations man. Not until recently, anyway.

Today there are only a few reconstructed huts on the site which is administered by the National Park Service. However, the Visitor's Center at the parking lot area gives full information about the encampment. If you go beyond the main desk you find a mini-theater where an eleven-minute film begins at the touch of a button. The story of typical foot soldiers huddled in a simple hut waiting for the rations and money that took so long in coming is unfolded. After the film, you can move on to the mock-up of the soldiers hut and see the straw beds, muskets and clothing used at the time.

From the Information Center, proceed out the back door to the **Wick Farm** where a Park Service employee is always in residence. The farmhouse was occupied by both the Wick family (owners of the farm that included Jockey Hollow) and General Arthur St. Clair and his aide. A vegetable and herb garden, a well and a horse barn surround the wooden cottage.

Inside the smoky cabin, a Ranger dressed in Colonial garb will be cooking, melting down candles or just answering questions. A tour through the house shows the little bedroom of Tempe Wick, the General's office and bedroom. There are no signs, however, to tell you which is which.

From the Wick house, proceed to the open slopes called the Pennsylvania Line. There the simple soldier's huts and some hiking trails await. Special weekends there are often encampments or other doings. Free.

HOURS: 9-5 Daily. May be closed Mon. & Tues. in winter. Closed major holidays.
LOCATION: Take 202 to Tempe Wick Road (south of Morristown). Follow signs.
TELEPHONE: 201-543-4030

WASHINGTON'S HEADQUARTERS, MORRISTOWN

For another look at the details of military life, go to the **Ford Mansion** and **Revolutionary War Museum** which is part of the overall National Historic Site called Washington's Headquarters. It's a short drive away. You must enter through the museum and there you will find all the paraphernalia - surgeon's tools, mess kits, muskets and cleaning rods - that accompanied the troops. The display of 18th Century weaponry is considered one of the best in the country. There are also very graphic dioramas, sketches and audio-visuals that show the poor condition of the ragged army at Jockey Hollow. Some period costumes brighten the museum.

Don't miss the fifteen-minute movie shown periodically in the auditorium. A professional film which was shot on location both here and in Jockey Hollow, it contrasts the warmth and food available to officers at the mansion with the hungry, freezing men camped four miles away. A lively ball scene was filmed in the central hall of the Ford Mansion which is right next door to the museum.

The Mansion itself is a solid frame Colonial house - by no means a mansion in the modern sense. As you enter the long central hallway, you notice how well such halls were suited to the line dances such as the Virginia Reel. The Ford home was offered as headquarters to Washington by Mrs. Ford, a widow with four children. The Ford family lived in two rooms while the General and his staff occupied the rest of the house. The furnishings shown are authentic to the period and many are true Ford family pieces. Beds include the canopied master bed used by Washington. Highboys, chest-on-chests, wall maps and lots of straw mattresses are all to be noted. There are uniformed National Park Service people around to answer questions but no guided tours, except as pre-arranged for groups.

Despite the rigors of the Morristown encampment, the Ford Mansion looks like a warm, homey, yet comparatively elegant abode for the Chief of Staff. It was here, also, on May 10, 1780, that the Marquis de Lafayette was welcomed. He brought news that France would send a second expedition to help. And Alexander Hamilton, at that time Washington's aide-de-camp, used his time in Morristown to court Betsy Schuyler who was staying at the nearby Schuyler-Hamilton house.

HOURS: 9-5 Daily. May be closed Mon. & Tues. in winter. Closed major holidays.
ADMISSION: Adults: $1.00. Children and Seniors free.
DIRECTIONS: Route 287 to Exit 32A to Morris Ave. East. Follow signs to Washington's Headquarters.
TELEPHONE: 201-539-2016

DEY MANSION

A solid Dutch farmhouse built in the early Georgian style, the Dey Mansion was Washington's headquarters for three months during the summer and fall of 1780. Furnishings reflect the status of the Dey family who were quite well to-do. An unusual feature of this northern house is the separate kitchen. (There is a breezeway between it and the main house for use during the colder months.) According to the guide, the separate kitchen was practical, for if the hearth caught on fire, it would not take the rest of the house with it!

After an inspection of the well-stocked kitchen, you may tour the house which has two floors of well-kept furnishings and many family portraits. The third floor attic is a museum in itself with a hodge-podge of collectibles that range from Colonial antiques to 19th Century ice-skates.

Outside is a very pleasant garden and grape arbor with a few picnic tables placed about. You are so close to the neighboring golf course (for this historic site is part of a county park) that you might get a golf ball in your iced tea. There are also several outbuildings in various states of repair, including a spring house and a barn. A recent addition to the complex is the replica of a plantation house such as you would find in Colonial New Jersey. Inside this house there are displays of military and farming life, plus an 11-minute film on the Dey Mansion itself.

HOURS: Wed. - Fri.: 1-4:30. Sat.: 10-12 & 1-4:30. Sun.: 1-4:30
ADMISSION: Adults: $1.00. Under 10 free.
LOCATION: 199 Totowa Rd., Wayne, Passaic County, (in Preakness Valley Park).
TELEPHONE: 201-696-1776

WALLACE HOUSE

Washington's headquarters during the winter encampment at Middlebrook (1778-79) is a two-hundred year-old clapboard Colonial now hidden away on a back street in Somerville. Once you discover the back street, you will find that the guide who administers the Wallace House also takes care of the Old Dutch Parsonage across the street. So if you knock and nobody answers, wait a while — he might be at the other house. He will usually leave a sign advising you of the fact. On busy days, there are usually volunteers who help out.

The headquarters itself is a nine room, solidly built wood structure with wide plank floors that creak curiously under modern weight. Although the furnishings are not those actually used by Washington and his staff, they are all of the period. A four-poster bed with tatted canopy stands in the room where Washington probably slept. There are also campaign trunks and the typical toiletry articles there. The rooms for the aide-de-camp and lieutenants (among them, Alexander Hamilton) are furnished less handsomely with simple trundle beds and straw mattresses.

The dining room does not look large, but it is said up to thirty people ate there when General and Mrs. Washington entertained. It must have been awfully crowded. The Wallace House may have been the best home in the area, but the rooms are small and cramped compared to the high, airy drawing rooms at Mount Vernon. One can see why Washington was constantly pining for his old Virginia home. And although Martha spent part of the winter here she did manage to return to her Southern home once or twice. However, the house has an office, four bedrooms and a parlor, so there was ample room for entertaining.

The winter of 1778-79 was rather mild, much more pleasant than those at Valley Forge or Morristown, and the encampment at Middlebrook faced less disasters. Food, however, was never plentiful, so when the Washingtons entertained, they did so sparsely. Incidentally, Washington paid $1000 to rent this house - the only time he had to pay for his headquarters in New Jersey. Free. Reservations required for groups.

HOURS: Wed.-Sat.: 10-12 & 1-5. Sunday: 1-5.
LOCATION: 38 Washington Place, Somerville, Somerset County.
TELEPHONE: 908-725-1015

THE OLD DUTCH PARSONAGE

This house was the home first of Pastor Frelinghuysen, minister of the Dutch Reformed Church. The bricks that built the house were brought over as ballast from Holland. Later it became the home of Rev. Jacob Hardenburgh who married Frelinghuysen's widow. Hardenburgh was one of the "Fighting Pastors" of the Revolutionary War who condemned the British from the pulpit. He was a frequent host to General and Mrs. Washington when they lived close by during the Middlebrook Encampment. The house has since been moved so it is now across the street.

The parsonage was recently refurbished and now its displays emphasize the Dutch Colonial heritage. There are authentic relics, Colonial clothing to try on, exhibits on Dutch development, memoirs of the Frelinghuysen family and some handsome furniture, including a 1780 secretary, donated by that family.

HOURS, ETC., Check Wallace House entry.

ROCKINGHAM

A little beyond the quaint town of Rocky Hill, which in itself looks like it has slept since the Revolution, lies Rockingham. It was here that Washington stayed in 1783 while the Constitution was being hammered out at nearby Nassau Hall in Princeton. Actually, both George and Martha stayed here and entertained extensively. It is best known as the house where the "Farewell Address to the Armies" was composed.

A medium-sized Colonial with front porch, the house was once part of a fine estate of 360 acres with barns, stables, coachhouse

While the Continental Congress worked at Nassau Hall, Washington stayed at nearby Rockingham.

and granary. It has since been removed from its original site (because of dynamiting in a nearby quarry) and is set a little ways off Route 518 in such a way that it takes a hardy traveller to find it. However, you will discover that the pillared porch of this Colonial is in the back, and that the vista from that side is quite pleasing. A nice kitchen garden, flowering trees and some outbuildings skirt the house.

Although there is a guide, you may roam through the house yourself. There are two stories of period rooms and some historical exhibits. Of course rooms were never huge in these New Jersey Colonials, but the ten rooms in Rockingham are good sized. The furniture is handsome. Period pieces include Chippendale sets, burnished bureaus, canopied beds and antique tea services. The Blue Room study where the Farewell Address was composed is left with the ink stand and green cloth still on the table.

There are often special exhibits, such as a display of handmade quilts, on view here. Free.

HOURS: Wed.-Fri.: 9-12 & 1-6; Sat.: 10-12, & 1-6; Sun.: 1-6.
LOCATION: Route 518 (Off 206) Rocky Hill, Somerset County
TELEPHONE: 609-921-8835

THE OLD BARRACKS

If you are expecting an old, dilapidated military structure when you hear the name, "Old Barracks" you are in for a surprise. Outside, the fieldstone building with its narrow balcony that runs the length of the second story, looks in top-notch condition. The lawns and hedges are a gardener's delight. Not only are the Old Barracks well kept and well administered, but the building itself is well laid out and beautifully furnished. From the main room on, you will find china, Chippendale furniture and silver from the Colonial and Federal periods that are as good as any found in the many restored homes in New Jersey.

The Barracks have quite a history. Just before the building was saved from demolition, the rooms were being used as a "Home for the Relief of Respectable, Aged and Indigent Widows and Single Women". Before that, the building had been chopped up into a series of private dwellings. Before that it was a hospital for wounded American soldiers in the Revolutionary War. And before that - well, the famous crossing of the Delaware on Christmas Day was for the express purpose of surprising the Hessian mercenaries who were sleeping off their Christmas cheer in this self-same barracks.

Originally, the Barracks were built in 1758 during the French and Indian War because American colonists objected to the billeting of British troops in private households. Later, in 1776, the British and Hessian mercenaries used it until the Americans gained control. The building went through a series of ups and downs until the Old Barracks Association saved it in 1899. They persuaded the State to help and in 1902, the Association ceded their part of the Barracks to the State with the provision that the Association should control and manage the building forever.

And what a difference that has made. Unlike other State Historic Sites, they don't close down for lunch here, and you can be pretty sure they will be open when they say they're open. The tour guides are knowledgeable and well versed in their speeches. Also at the Barracks, you can view a magnificent dinner service, mementos of Washington, a collection of firearms (including a blunderbuss and early muskets) and a huge diorama of the Battle of Trenton. Gift shop, too, of course.

HOURS: Tues. - Sat.: 11-5; Sun.: 1-5. Closed major holidays.
ADMISSION: Adults: $2.00; Seniors: $1.00; Children: $.50
LOCATION: Barracks St. at West Front St., Trenton.
TELEPHONE: 609-396-1776

WASHINGTON CROSSING STATE PARK (N.J.)

This popular park, covering 807 acres that stretch from the banks of the Delaware in Titusville, commemorates the crossing that led to the most important victory of the war's early years. On Christmas night 1776, General Washington crossed the icy Delaware with 2,400 men, plus artillery and supplies. The crossing took nine hours and the men and officers converged on this spot on the Jersey side. The ensuing surprise attack gave a sweet taste of victory to the discouraged American troops.

Now at the park, you find a Visitor Center filled with information on the battle, the uniforms and muskets of the times. There are a variety of exhibits and some audio-visuals.

Outside there are open fields for frisbee throwing, a nature center (you must take a rocky road to get there), and an open air ampitheater for summer shows. There are many picturesque picnic groves here also. Near the Delaware River there is a monument marking the spot and two historic houses. One of these, the **Ferry House**, a refurbished building set up as an inn, offers guided tours at specific times. Admission to the park, the center and the houses is free, but there is a parking fee on summer weekends.

HOURS: Wed. - Sun.: 9-4:30. Shorter winter hours. Park open all the time.
LOCATION: Routes 29 & 546, Titusville, Mercer County.
TELEPHONE: 609-737-2515, 609-737-9304.

HISTORIC WASHINGTON CROSSING PARK (PA)

Across the river the site of the embarkation is the focus for a large park that stretches up the Delaware River and includes several sections. In the first section, a modern Visitor's Center offers brochures, a theater for a film about the crossing and tickets for three historical buildings within the park. Two of these buildings are within easy walking distance. The first is the **McKonkey Ferry Inn** where Washington and his staff met and ate just before the crossing. It is fixed up as a travelers' inn with tables set with pewter and bar a and grill. Quite close to it is the **Durham Boat House** with a reproduction of the famous boats that were used to ferry the troops. Across the street, **Homewood** is another reconstruction, this time of an 1816 house with fine quality Federal furnishings.

Traveling north you come upon another section of the park which includes a wildflower preserve, the high observation tower on Bowman's Hill and the **Thompson-Neely House** (which is an original structure built of Delaware River ledgestone and looking as authentic as all get out). Tickets for all three historic houses are reasonable and of course you get a guided tour through each. One thing about Pennsylvania, they are very exact about what is a true historic house and what is a replica. One guide even told me it took them twenty years to get New Jersey to stop calling that white clapboard house across the river the McKonkey House.

Lots of picnic pavilions, walking paths and driving roads throughout the park.

HOURS: Daily 9-5.
ADMISSION: Guided Tour: Adults: $1.50; Seniors $1.00; Children: $.50; Under 6, free.
DIRECTIONS: Take bridge from Titusville, N.J., drive north on Pa. 32 for other sections of park.
TELEPHONE: 215-493-4076

VALLEY FORGE

It is known as "The Crucible of Victory" because the 10,000 men who emerged from the harsh winter had coalesced into an efficient, well-trained fighting force. The encampment lasted from December 19,1777 to June 19, 1778. It is now commemorated at this huge 2200 acre park which is so vast you must start with a map or a bus tour.

The Visitor Center, where you can procure both, also offers a slide show and a small museum of Revolutionary swords and military equipment. It is here that you can board the buses ($5.00 for adults, $4.00 for children) which operate during the warm weather only. The bus tour, which stops at key sites, features a taped narration as you go along. Even better, you can rent or buy a tape for use as you drive along yourself. Among the important sites you will pass on the scenic drive are: the Memorial Arch, the earthen fortifications, statues of Anthony Wayne and Von Steuben, and of course, the soldiers' huts.

When staffing permits, costumed soldiers are at hand to welcome you at **Washington's Headquarters, The Isaac Cotts House** and **General Varnum's Headquarters**. There is a small admission fee for adults at these houses. There are often costumed personnel stationed at the soldier's huts also. They help to point out the hardships the soldiers endured. A friend's child was properly awed by the sacrifices of the Revolutionary soldiers when he saw one of the simple huts reconstructed here. "They didn't even have portable radios!" he told his mother.

For modern day visitors there are picnic grounds, bicycle trails, a snack bar and souvenir shop and lots of beautiful scenery. The park is free, but there is a fee for bus tours, tapes and certain houses.

HOURS: Daily except Christmas 8:30-5. For buses: Memorial
Day- Labor Day several times a day. April, May, Sept.
Oct.: 3 times a day.
LOCATION: Visitor Center: Junction of PA 23 & 363, Valley Forge,
PA.
TELEPHONE: 215-783-7700

MONMOUTH BATTLEFIELD STATE PARK

Although it was not a complete victory, still the Battle of Monmouth proved that American troops, honed by the winter at Valley Forge, could hold their own against British soldiers. Today's park was the scene of a hot day's battle with a general who ordered a retreat (and was later reprimanded by Washington) and a lady named Molly "Pitcher", who became a heroine according to legend.

The fields of close-cropped rolling hills are empty at Monmouth Battlefield, but a large new Visitors Center gives you the necessary information. Three audio-visual screens offer the story of the battle from the night before to the day after. And a relief map, set with tiny lights, displays the position of the opposing forces. Press a button and the lights move and "shoot" each other to the sound of rifle fire on the accompanying audio track. So much for the show.

Here at the center you can also pick up a map of the battlefield and other historic sites in the area. Also a refreshment counter and a picnic area are part of the building. If you drive around following the map you will find the **Craig House** (which may or may not be open, depending on volunteer staffing) where the wounded were cared for; **Tennant Church**, a good-looking, shake-sided Colonial edifice which was close to the battle; and **Molly Pitcher's Well**. Free.

HOURS: Daily 8-4 Winter; 8-6 Summer.
LOCATION: Route 9 to Route 33, just west of Freehold, Monmouth
County.
TELEPHONE: 908-462-9619

COVENHOVEN HOUSE

One of the four historic houses administered by the Monmouth County Historical Association, it is significant for its role in the Battle of Monmouth. Henry Clinton, commander of the British troops at the battle, stayed at the home from Friday, June 26 until Sunday, June 28, 1778. After the battle, he and his troops left Freehold and returned to New York.

The main section of the home is in Georgian style and is furnished according to a 1790 inventory of William A. Covenhoven, the well-to-do farmer who owned the property. A mural depicting a sea-battle and walls decorated in a blue-and-white Delft pattern were discovered in one bedroom during the restoration of the house. Extremely authentic and well-done — an interesting house to visit.

> **HOURS:** May-Oct.: Tues., Thurs., Sun.: 1-4; Sat.: 10-4.
> **ADMISSION:** Adults: $2.00: Seniors: $1.50; Children: $1.00; under 6 free.
> **LOCATION:** 150 West Main St., Freehold.
> **TELEPHONE:** 908-462-1466

RED BANK BATTLEFIELD

A small but decisive battle to defend Fort Mercer took place here on October 19, 1777. The Hessian army received many casualties at the hands of the American Army, which, up until this point had known mostly defeat. Since the Fort guarded the Delaware River and prevented British ships from entering occupied Philadelphia, the freedom of Fort Mercer was quite important. Although British ships eventually went through, the Red Bank victory helped France decide to join America in her fight against the British. The site is not to be confused with the town of Red Bank in Monmouth Country on the ocean side of New Jersey. The park contains old cannons and an historic house that is open for tours when guides are available (usually Memorial Day to Labor Day). Picnic areas. Free.

> **HOURS:** Daily, 9-5.
> **LOCATION:** 100 Hessian Ave., National Park, Gloucester County.
> **TELEPHONE:** 609-853-5120

INDIAN KING TAVERN

Set in the little town of Haddonfield, which looks as if it stepped out of the past, this public house, or tavern, was the site of frequent meetings of the New Jersey State Legislature during the Revolutionary War. Among the rooms the guide shows off are the Colonial kitchen, the toy room, and the bedroom where Dolly Madison slept. (Her uncle was a one-time owner of the tavern). Groups by appointment only. Children under 12 must be accompanied by an adult. Guided tours for individuals are ongoing. You must wait at the door for the next tour if there is one in progress at the moment.

HOURS: Wed.-Fri.: 9-11:30 & 1-5:30. Sat.: 10-11:30 & 1-5:30. Sun.: 1-5:30.
ADMISSION: Donation ($1.00 suggested)
LOCATION: 233 Kings Highway, Haddonfield, Camden County.
TELEPHONE: 609-429-6792

BOXWOOD HALL

Also known as the Boudinot Mansion, this very nicely furnished Colonial house is not far from the main drag in Elizabeth. Built in 1750, it was the home, during the Revolution, of Elias Boudinot, president of the Continental Congress. George Washington had lunch here on the day he embarked for New York and his inauguration as President. House furnishings include both the Colonial and later Empire style. State Historic Site. Free.

HOURS: Wed.-Fri.: 9-12 & 1-6. Sat.: 10-12 & 1-6. Sun.: 1-6.
LOCATION: 1073 East Jersey St., Elizabeth.
TELEPHONE: 908-648-4540

BUCCLEUCH MANSION

A handsome Georgian mansion in various states of repair (the surrounding gardens far outshine the physical exterior of the house at this point in time). The house is set inside Buccleuch Park on a tree-lined street that is practically part of the Rutgers Campus in New Brunswick. Originally built in 1793, White House Farm, as it was then known, was sold to an English army officer in 1774.

The house was confiscated by the Americans in 1776, but by December the British troops re-occupied New Brunswick. The bannister still retains the marks of the soldiers' musket barrels from the time of this occupation, which lasted until 1777. After the war, Colonel Charles Stewart, Commissary General of the Revolutionary Army, became the owner. At this time, White House Farm was visited by Washington, Hancock and Alexander Hamilton, who all loved the setting.

Much of Buccleuch Mansion's furnishings today are of 19th Century origin. Of particular note is the striking wallpaper in the the downstairs and upstairs hallways. Rooms include a Victorian parlor and a drawing room with Queen Anne pieces. You can also inspect the bedrooms (including the one where Washington slept), a toy room, a craft room with spinning wheel, and an attic filled with assorted "significa", including side-saddles, hoops for hoopskirts and two centuries of whatnots. Free (donations accepted). Group tours by appointment.

HOURS: Last Sun. in May - last Sun. in Oct.: 2-4.
LOCATION: Easton Ave. to Buccleuch Park, New Brunswick, Middlesex County.
TELEPHONE: 201-846-1063 (Curator); 201-745-5094 (House)

VON STEUBEN HOUSE

A Dutch Colonial home built in 1695 and further added to in 1752, this home is an example of early architecture in New Jersey. The house was confiscated by the Americans during the Revolutionary War because the owners (the Zabriskie family) were loyal to the British crown. Its position on the Hackensack River made it a strategic prize for both sides. (The house literally sits on the river's edge). It was later presented to Baron Von Steuben for his aid during the war.

One thing you notice in the furnishings here is the emphasis on local craftsmen. Some fine specimens of the local Colonial craft include a New Brunswick kas, a Hudson Valley kas, an old settle, etc. The upstairs garret is maintained as a museum by the Bergen County Historical Society and includes Indian artifacts, dolls and toys.

HOURS: Wed.-Sat.: 10-12 & 1-5; Sun.: 2-5
LOCATION: 1209 Main Street, River Edge, Bergen County (take River Edge exit from Route 4).
TELEPHONE: 201-487-1739

OTHER REVOLUTIONARY WAR SITES

Among the many other historic sites and buildings associated with the Revolutionary War are:

PRINCETON BATTLEFIELD STATE PARK: A short, decisive battle was fought here on January 3, 1777, just a week after the famous crossing of the Delaware. General Hugh Mercer was mortally wounded during this battle. Free. *Hours:* 9 AM to dusk. *Location:* Mercer St., Princeton.

BRANDYWINE BATTLEFIELD STATE PARK: This battle was a defeat for Washington's forces. It took place on September 11, 1777, and is commemorated by dioramas and audio-visuals at the Visitors Center. There are also two historic houses within the park. One was Washington's headquarters and the other was used by the Marquis de Lafayette. Free. *Hours:* Daily May 30-Labor Day. Weekends thereafter. *Location:* Route 1, Chadds Ford, PA. *Telephone:* 215-459-3342.

DRAKE HOUSE: During the battle of the Watchung Mountains, Washington used this house as his command headquarters. Although there is a Colonial bedroom where he is supposed to have rested, the house was later remodeled. It now reflects the Empire and Victorian styles as well as the basic Colonial. *Hours:* Sat.:2-4. *Admission:* $1.00; *Location:* 602 West Front St., Plainfield, Union County. *Telephone:* 908-755-5831.

FORT LEE PARK: Features a view of the Hudson and a bevy of reconstructed gun batteries on the site of an old fort built to defend the river against invasion. Only 33 acres here, but there are guides and a Visitor Center with museum, maps, audio-visuals, etc. Observation tower with view of George Washington Bridge. $2.00 parking fee. *Hours:* March-Dec., Wed.-Sun.: 10-5 (for Visitor Center). *Location:* Hudson Terrace, Fort Lee, Bergen County. *Telephone:* 201-461-3956.

HANCOCK HOUSE: Scene of massacre of American troops by attacking British Rangers, this 1734 house has period furnishings. Free. *Hours:* Wed.-Fri.: 9-12 & 1-6; Sat.: 10-12 & 1-6; Sun.: 1-6. *Location:* Route 49, 5 miles south of Salem, Salem County. *Telephone:* 609-935-4373.

CANNONBALL HOUSE: Named for the cannonball that struck it during the Battle of Springfield, 1780. Information and mementos of the battle are present. *Hours:* 1st & 3rd Sun.: 2-4, Sept. - June. *Admission:* $.25. *Location:* 124 Morris Ave., Springfield, Union County. *Telephone:* 908-467-3580.

SCHUYLER-HAMILTON HOUSE: Colonial home where Alexander Hamilton courted Betsey Schuyler. *Hours:* Tues. & Sun., 2-5. *Admission:* Adults: $1.00; Under 12 free. *Location:* 5 Olyphant Place, Morristown, Morris County. *Telephone:* 201-267-4039.

ALLEN HOUSE: Since this 1750 house was operated as the Blue Ball Tavern during the Revolutionary War, two major rooms here have been furnished in that manner. Tables are set with pewter, there is a bar and grill with whiskey jugs and so forth. Upstairs, changing exhibits *Hours:* April-Dec.: Tues., Thurs., Sun., 1-4; Sat. 10-4. *Admission:* Adults: $2.00; Children: $1.00; Seniors: $1.50. Under 6 free. *Location:* Route 35 & Sycamore Ave., Shrewsbury, Monmouth County. *Telephone:* 908-462-1466.

See Also: *Nassau Hall, Morven, Independence Hall* and several of the colonial homes mentioned in the chapter "Restored Villages and Homes".

HOMES OF THE RICH
AND FAMOUS

Photo: Courtesy N.J. Travel & Tourism

In This Chapter You Will Find:

Nemours, DE
Hyde Park, N.Y.
The Vanderbilt Mansion, N.Y.
Edison Labs —Glenmont, N.J.
Historic Speedwell, N.J.
Grover Cleveland Birthplace, N.J.
Ballantine House, N.J.
Lambert Castle, N.J.
Ringwood Manor, N.J.
Skylands, N.J.
Lyndhurst, N.Y.
Sunnyside, N.Y.
Boscobel, N.Y.
Maccoulloch Hall, N.J.
Morven, N.J.
Bainbridge House, N.J.
William Trent House, N.J.
Kuser Farm Mansion, N.J.
Walt Whitman House, N.J.
Pennsbury Manor, PA
Andalusia, PA
Green Hill Farm, PA

NEMOURS

The fabulous homes of the super-rich are America's equivalent of the palaces and castles of Europe. And no home is more palatial than Nemours, the former residence of Alfred I. DuPont. Located outside Wilmington in the increasingly popular Brandywine Valley area, Nemours is the latest in a series of DuPont Estates now open to the public.

The mansion, built in 1909, is a modified Louis XVI French chateau. The landscaped gardens are in the French formal style and include marble statues, cascading fountains and a series of terraces and stairways to please the eye. In fact, the hand of Louis XVI seems to lie everywhere in Nemours — a tribute as much to the Gallic origins of the DuPonts as to the possibility that American millionaires in 1910 must have known the era of conspicuous consumption was about to end. A few years later the income tax and World War I helped destroy any notion of an American aristocracy. Like the French kings before them, the DuPonts may have realized this was the last chance to flaunt their riches.

There was also Alfred's desire to outdo his cousin Pierre's Longwood Gardens. A schism had developed in the family over a marriage, a mad love affair, a remarriage — this is the stuff that best-selling novels are made of. I heard about it on the tour bus going down; at Nemours they don't breathe a word of scandal. And actually it was the third wife — a beautiful young woman whose portrait enhances many of the rooms — who was mistress at Nemours.

Once you enter the chateau, you are led by a tour guide into a home of vast elegance. The gold and white dining room boasts ornate moldings on walls and ceilings, Rococco style paintings and a chandelier worthy of the Phantom of the Opera. The reception room, living room and other public rooms are equally fabulous with inlaid ceilings, marble tiled floors, rich oriental rugs and carved walls. Furniture includes both genuine antiques like George Washington's chair and fine copies of Louis XVI furnishings.

You rarely see the kitchens of "great homes," but at Nemours there's a downstairs tour of the restaurant-sized cooking area with its empty pantry and huge pots. A dumbwaiter is set up with a breakfast tray of Spode china as if ready to be sent up to the bedroom of Mrs. DuPont. Also, downstairs is the bowling alley (no, it's not automatic, they used real pin boys), the billiard room (with a table the size of a bowling alley) and the furnace room (ingeniously set up by Alfred himself, who was an engineer).

The guides who escorted us through had an almost proprietary air about Nemours. When a man asked about the cost of all this, the guide sniffed, "We don't discuss money here." And I made the social gaffe of mentioning the second wife. I was told sternly that the only Mrs. DuPont mentioned at Nemours was the third Mrs. DuPont. However, our group was treated to orange juice on the terrace, a tray of rosebuds and a free packet of postcards.

After the house tour you may either board a mini-bus for a tour of the gardens or walk around yourself. Fountains and pools, colonnades and balustrades, marble Cupids and Dianas, velvet lawns and clipped hedges create a mini-Versailles here.

Nemours doesn't exactly admit hordes of people. Numbers are limited and there are only four tours a day. Reservations are suggested for individuals and required for groups. No children under 16. No picture-taking inside the mansion. And mind your manners — this here is DuPont territory!

> **HOURS:** May-Nov.: Tues.-Sat.: tours at 9, 11, 1 & 3. Sunday tours: 11, 1 & 3.
> **ADMISSION:** $8.00
> **LOCATION:** Rockland Road (inside Alfred I. DuPont Institute) Wilmington, Delaware.
> **TELEPHONE:** 302-651-6912 or write: Reservations Office, Nemours Foundation, P.O. Box 109, Wilmington, Delaware 19899

HYDE PARK

For people who lived under Franklin Delano Roosevelt's administration, there is either a deep love for the man who dominated the White House from 1932 to 1945 — or an abiding hatred. As president during the great Depression and World War II Roosevelt was both blamed and praised for cataclysmic changes in American life. And Roosevelt's charming boyhood home has always been identified with the man.

Now a National Historic Site, the Hyde Park complex consists of the family home, the beautiful grounds on a high, green hill overlooking a clean Hudson River and the **Roosevelt Library and Museum**. Starting at the home, you enter from a parking lot which is lined with apple trees still bearing fruit. The white, classically proportioned country house is not overly large and can accommodate only 50 people at a time. However, there is an easy traffic flow since you do not have to wait for a tour guide to take you through. Instead, you may move about as you like, using the cassette tape recording as your guide. The cassette was recorded by Eleanor Roosevelt and gives you an interesting insight into family life in the inimitable accents of that voice.

Upon entering the main hall, you see the heavy furnishings that characterized a country home of the 1890's. Further on, the pretty Dresden Room is brightened by the colorful floral drapes and upholstery picked out by Sara Roosevelt in 1939 shortly before the King and Queen of England visited. The whole house, in fact, shows much more the influence of Franklin's mother, Sara, than of his wife.

Upstairs, the boyhood bedroom and FDR's bedroom contain the memorabilia we expect. Favorite pictures, the leash and blanket of the scottie Fala on his own chair, and books and magazines that were scattered there in March, 1945, are still present in the room.

Next to the house is the FDR Library. The museum section contains gifts from foreign rulers, cartoons, photographs, and a passing picture of both the Depression and World War II. Special exhibits on both Franklin and Eleanor are here, plus the wooden wheelchair Roosevelt used. Outside on the quiet green lawn next to the rose garden are the graves of both FDR and Eleanor. And, in another section of the estate, **Val-Kill**, residence of Eleanor, is open to viewers on a limited basis.

HOURS: Daily 9-5. Closed Tues.& Wed., Nov.-Mar.
ADMISSION: Adults. 16-61: $3.50; Others free.
LOCATION: Hyde Park, N.Y. Take Garden State Parkway to NY Thruway to Exit 18. Cross Mid-Hudson Bridge, then Route 9N for 7 miles. Follow signs.
TELEPHONE: 914-229-9115

VANDERBILT MANSION

If the Roosevelt home radiates quiet wealth, the Vanderbilt Mansion exudes conspicuous consumption. A marble palace in the style of the Italian Renaissance, it is set on large estate grounds where swans paddle about in a meandering stream. Inside, the mansion's furnishings are closer to French Rococco than Italian Renaissance. The huge marble reception hall opens to both the dining room and drawing room. The dining room, which seated thirty, and the beautifully furnished drawing room were the scene of gala balls. A small side room called the Gold Room was the gathering place for guests to sip sherry before dinner. This room attracts tourists to its gold leaf decoration. The ceiling painting depicts scantily clad maidens floating in the azure sky.

If the downstairs chairs all look like thrones, then the upstairs bedrooms of Mr. and Mrs. Vanderbilt were certainly fit for a king and queen. Walls of embroidered silk and a bed with a marble gate around it are features copied from a French queen's bedroom to outfit the one Mrs. Vanderbilt used. As for Mr. Vanderbilt — he merely had a canopy with a crown above his bed and true Flemish tapestries hanging on the walls. It all goes to show what you could do if you had money in the pre-income tax days.

The mansion with its marble and finely turned Circassian walnut and the quiet, heavily treed grounds all help to recreate the splendor of a bygone era. Tours begin at the Visitors' Center where you can also buy tickets and pick up brochures and postcards. A film about the mansion is shown here and then a guide will accompany you over to the house. Once there, you are allowed to inspect the opulent rooms at your own pace. Tours usually take between 30 to 45 minutes.

HOURS: Daily 9-5. Closed major holidays. Closed Tues., Wed.,Mar.-Nov.
ADMISSION: Adults 16-61: $2.00; Others free.
LOCATION: Use Hyde Park directions.
TELEPHONE: 914-229-9115

THE EDISON LABS

For many area schools, a trip to the Edison Labs is *de rigeur* around the 4th or 5th grade. Therefore, parents get the idea that this is strictly a children's tour. So while troops of camera-toting Japanese and Germans tramp through the facilities at West Orange, there are still local residents who have never set foot inside the laboratory where Edison worked for 44 years.

Indeed, if a visiting scientist hadn't dragged me there when we first moved to the Garden State, I never would have troubled to go. The second time around, I was under the influence of an Architectural History course, and insisted we see Glenmont,

Edison's elegant Victorian home. After all, where else can you find a perfectly intact sample of Haute Victoriana for a small fee?

Actually both buildings comprise the **Edison National Historic Site**. Headquarters are on a busy commercial area of West Orange. You buy the tickets there, and make reservations for Glenmont (on days when entrance is available). Then you can begin your tour of the Labs (which takes about an hour and a quarter.) Tours are usually by National Park Service personnel.

Among the rooms you will see is the phonograph room which displays various models of Edison's prized invention. Naturally, our group was treated to audio effects — from Edison reciting "Mary Had A Little Lamb" in tinfoil to a 1922 comedy routine on an inch-thick wooden record.

From audio, one goes to visual. In the next room we watched the first feature motion picture — "The Great Train Robbery". A few years ago this movie was shown in the **Black Maria** (a replica of the original tarpaper studio which is on display outside). But in order to accomodate the large number of tourists, the film is now shown in a large central room, along with a movie about Edison. "The Great Train Robbery", by the way, is of interest not only because it is the first Western. This early 1900's silent picture was filmed locally, using the talents of laboratory workers and the trains of the Erie Lackawanna. (You will probably recognize the Essex County terrain, if not the old railroad cars).

The chemical labs, the machine shop and junk storage bins are also part of the extensive tour. Grand finale is the golden oak library where Edison's desk, cot and 10,000 volumes still stand. Even the six-foot wall clock remains stopped at 3:27 — the time on October 18, 1931 when Edison died.

> **HOURS:** Wed.-Sun., 9-5. Tours start at 9:30. Last tour is 3:30.
> **ADMISSION:** Adults 17-61: $2.00; Others free.
> **LOCATION:** Main St. & Lakeside Ave., West Orange, Essex Couty
> **TELEPHONE:** 201-736-5050

GLENMONT

Tickets to Glenmont, the newly refurbished home of Edison, are sold on a first come, first served basis to visitors to the National Historic Site at the main office. Visiting days are limited, so its best to call first if your main object is to see the elegant Victorian house set on a sweeping lawn in the private development called Llewellyn Park (about 2 miles from the Labs). Tours are guided.

Glenmont is a rambling, stick-style house, where Edison resided with his second wife, Minna, after he moved north from Menlo Park. Here he entertained visitors from around the world — but it is also a warm family home where his children grew up. The house is filled with carved oak woodwork, oriental rugs, wild animal skins, stained glass windows, and a large, sunny Conservatory that is worthy of an English manor house. One finds rich fabrics and tile foors, paintings and of course a gentleman's library filled with leather-bound tomes. There is a pipe-organ and a grand piano that was used both by the children and by musicians auditioning for Edison's phonograph company.

The upstairs bedrooms and sitting rooms are less ornate, obviously meant for family life although the furniture is still of the monumental variety. After the house tour, one may visit the greenhouse, potting shed and other outbuildings on this 13 1/2 acre estate. It is a pleasant glimpse not only of a famous man's home, but of an unhurried, elegant era.

HOURS: Sat., Sun.: 11-4:00. Call first as hours may change.
ADMISSION: (For Labs and house) 17-61: $2.00; Others free.
LOCATION: Lewellyn Park, West Orange (Buy tickets at Labs)
TELEPHONE: 201-736-5050

HISTORIC SPEEDWELL

Every 19th Century technological breakthrough led to further inventions. And Historic Speedwell in Morristown is the scene of one of the most important American achievements. It was here that Samuel Morse and Alfred Vail spent years perfecting the electro- magnetic telegraph. And that invention gave rise to the later inventions of radio, television and more. Perhaps some inventor today will find inspiration from the exhibits here.

One thing you learn from a visit to this green and pleasant compound: you do not have to be a scientist to be an inventor. Samuel Morse was a portrait painter by profession. At the **Vail House** (the main building of the complex), you can see the portraits Morse painted of the senior Mr. and Mrs. Vail. These were painted in 1837. Although Morse did not live here, he was a frequent guest.

The original Vail money came from their Iron Works. Many of the buildings are devoted to artifacts concerning the making and molding of iron machinery. In the *Homestead Carriage House* there is a collection of wooden patterns. The wet sand molds formed by these patterns were used to create the iron gears, waterwheels and parts for locomotives that were the main industry here. The foundry was best known for its early steam engines. In fact, the first trans-Atlantic steamship was built here.

At the *1849 Carriage House*, you will find a one-horse open sleigh (without the horse, of course) and a number of butter-churns on display. *The Granary* has hand-crafted wooden tools and an exhibit of ice-harvesting equipment. And the *Vail House* itself is a fine example of a comfortable mid-19th Century home.

But it is at the *Factory*, originally built for cotton weaving, that you will find the most information about the telegraph. Vail and Morse held the first public demonstration of this new wonder here in 1838. An exhibit of documents, models and instruments illustrates the invention and development of the telegraph. A slide presentation tells you story if you just push the button next to the screen.

The story, by the way, is that Alfred Vail, a student of the ministry at NYU came back to visit his Alma Mater and saw Fine Arts Professor Samuel Morse demonstrate the electro-magnetic invention. Alfred became entranced and offered Morse space and money (which came from his father and brother) to perfect the telegraph. Vail became Morse's junior partner, but by prior agreement, he received very little credit and no share of the future earnings of the Western Union Company.

Historic Speedwell is situated on an old homestead of the Vail family across from a picturesque dam where a Vail factory once stood.

HOURS: Apr.-Oct.: Thurs., Fri.: 12-4; Sat., Sun.: 1-5.
ADMISSION: Adults: $2.00; Seniors: $1.00; Children 6-12: $.50
LOCATION: Route 202 (Speedwell Ave.) at Cory Road, one mile north of Morristown Green, Morris County.
TELEPHONE: 201-540-0211

GROVER CLEVELAND BIRTHPLACE

Grover Cleveland, the only United States president to be born in New Jersey, spent his first year in this pleasant Manse. The clapboard house was built in 1832 for the pastor of the First Presbyterian Society. Two years later, Reverend Richard F. Cleveland obtained that position. Grover was born in 1837, but by the following year the pastor had retired and moved his family to Buffalo.

The house, which is a State Historic Site, therefore boasts a melange of furniture. The open hearth kitchen reflects the earlier 1830 period when life in the country was fairly simple. However, a number of later pieces from Cleveland's presidency reflect the richer, more ornate world of the 1880's. A large chair and rocker from the White House term plus several other pieces show both Cleveland's girth and his station in life.

The caretaker of the Manse is happy to act as guide and to point out the photographs, medals, sheet music, etc. that have been collected about Cleveland. A portrait of Mrs. Cleveland, a beautiful young woman whom he married when she was 21 and he 49 adorns the house and the guide bubbles with anecdotes about her. No heavy history here. No talk of Pullman strikes and gold panics and oppressed workers. What you learn is good presidential gossip. Frances was Grover's ward, and she turned down his marriage proposal several times before she finally said yes. She was the youngest First Lady ever; their first baby, Ruth, became the namesake of a still popular candy bar, etc., etc.

After his second term (Adlai Stevenson was his Vice-President), Cleveland retired to Princeton where he served as lecturer and trustee. He became friends with Woodrow Wilson, then president of the university. They are both buried, incidentally, in Princeton Cemetary.

All the downstairs rooms of the "Old Manse" are open to the public and include the well-filled living room; a bedroom with high-backed bed, cradle and quilts; a den with lots of memorabilia and the earlier, pre-Victorian kitchen. My companion, herself the daughter of a minister, was impressed with the house as a pastor's residence. So was the original congregation that bought it in 1832 and thought the construction price of $1490 a little steep. The house, by the way, is set on a busy street in Caldwell and is easy to miss since it's not really very large despite its phenomenal 1832 price. Free.

HOURS: Wed.-Fri.: 9-12 & 1-6. Sat.: 9-12 & 1-5.; Sun.: 1-6. Call first.
LOCATION: 207 Bloomfield Ave., Caldwell, Essex County.
TELEPHONE: 201-226-1810

THE BALLANTINE HOUSE

One of the pleasures of visiting the Newark Museum is the presence of the Ballantine House right next door. You enter this opulent late Victorian townhouse from an interior passageway in the museum proper. The house was restored to its original lustre only a few years ago. And while you cannot go into the rooms, you can see perfectly through the glass walls and you can enter partially. It is a marvelous job of restoration with the colors brighter and the furniture cleaner than it probably ever was in its heyday.

On the way in, you read about the Ballantines, a Scotch family who rose from poor immigrants to wealthy beer barons within a span of two generations. Since a townhouse on Washington Park was the sure sign of success in Newark, John Ballantine commissioned this spacious, seventeen room, three-story Renaissance Revival house to be built in the mid-1880's.

In the high Victorian period, the term "interior decoration" was taken literally and every inch of space is covered, plastered, panelled, draped, ensconced or otherwise prettified. The dining room, for instance, features oak and cherry parquet floors, mahogany woodwork, a ceiling of molded papier mache panels between painted plaster beams, and walls of leather-looking paper. Add to that a brick and wood fireplace, small stained glass windows, tapestried chairs and a table sparkling with white linen and you get a scene of solid bourgeois luxury that was meant to impress the guests.

Other rooms on view are the rich, red-toned library, the delicate French-style drawing room and the somber reception room. The large hallway where you walk also serves to show off special exhibits of Tiffany glassware or Belleek ceramics. And at Christmas time, a tree full of ornaments and holly decorations are added to this already richly decorated home. A magnificent stained glass window with its rising sun presides over the stairwell leading to the second floor. The Ballantine House provides not only insights into Victorian highstyle living, but an understanding of why later generations opted for bare, modern, unadorned lines in rebellion against all this decoration. Free.

> **HOURS:** Tues.-Sun.: 12-5.
> **LOCATION:** (Enter through Newark Museum) 49 Washington St., Newark.
> **TELEPHONE:** 201-596-6550

LAMBERT CASTLE

Situated high on a bluff in the Garrett Mountain Reservation overlooking Paterson, Lambert Castle is more impressive from the outside than from within. Built by silk manufacturer Catholina Lambert in the heyday of 19th Century opulence, it appears as a brownstone Medieval castle with rounded towers and crenelated turrets — just perfect for longbow archers to repel the invading hordes.

However, it was not the invading hordes that undid Lambert, but the silk strike of 1913 together with a decline in the American silk trade. Bankruptcy loomed and many of Lambert's prize possessions — European paintings and fine furnishings — were sold to pay debtors. He retained the house, though, until his death in 1923.

The view from Lambert castle is spectacular, encompassing both the city of Paterson with its many church domes and spires and the mountains beyond. But once inside the Castle you find that only the first floor is open to the public. The place is run by the *Passaic County Historical Society* and is half museum, half historic house. The ballroom has been cut down in size because a new ceiling now covers the high-domed original. There are photographs showing how the home once looked, plus an interesting 13-foot clock in the shape of a woman, a giant walnut sideboard and a stained glass window. New furnishings are constantly being added to remind you of the grand past. A dining room of opulent dimensions gives one some vision of what this house was once like.

There is also the everything-but-the-kitchen-sink historical museum memorabilia here — somebody's collection of spoons (including what must be the largest tablespoon in the world), pictures of the Great Falls, details on famous sons of Paterson and so forth.

HOURS: Wed. — Sun. 1-3:30 (for museum).
ADMISSION: Adults: $1.50; Seniors: $1.00; Children free.
LOCATION: Valley Road. Garrett Mountain Reservation, Paterson, Passaic County.
TELEPHONE: 201-881-2761

RINGWOOD MANOR

If they ever film a Chekov play in New Jersey, Ringwood Manor would make a perfect setting. This rambling manor house set on a rise overlooking a small lake where ducks paddle about is a prime example of the Victorian country house. Actually the house was originally the residence of Martin Ryerson, an ironmaster, and relics of the old iron forge days still dot the landscape. Short cannons and iron chains are placed about at intervals. The grounds are either well kept or dingy depending on whether the Manor park got its funding from the State for the year.

But it is the expanded manor with a porte-cochere designed by Stanford White, that gives Ringwood its high Victorian look. As the country home first of Peter Cooper, the industrialist and philanthropist who founded not only Cooper Union but the short-lived Greenback Party as well, and then of his son-in-law Abram S. Hewitt, Ringwood became a pleasant haven filled with antiques, and cottage furniture. Approximately 30 rooms are open to the public (the house contains well over 50) and bedrooms with lace curtains, parlors filled with paintings, heavy oak stairways and bronze chandeliers create a pleasant ambience. The walls are also hung with mementos of the Cooper-Hewitt family: newspaper articles and cartoons on politics both national and local, for Peter Cooper ran for President when he was 85, and Hewitt was Mayor of New York.

Outside on the grassy lawn and beyond, visitors picnic or meander around the wide grounds with its gardens and playgrounds. The manor is one corner of a huge state park high in the Ramapo mountains. Each section of the park has its own toll gate and parking fee ($3 weekdays, $4 weekends) although Tuesdays are usually free in New Jersey state parks. Shepherd's Lake has a lovely swimming, canoeing and picnic area and therefore is by far the most popular area of the park, filling up early on weekends. Another historic section of *Ringwood Manor State Park* is:

SKYLANDS

A 44-room mansion in the Jacobean style that looks like an English castle. No furnishing inside but there are handsome carvings on the walls, the ceilings and the fireplace. Skylands is best known for its gardens (see Garden section) but it is also the scene of weddings for brides who like a touch class in their nuptials. At the moment the mansion is not open to the general public but can be used for groups.

HOURS: Park — daily. MANOR HOUSE: May 1 — Oct. 31: Tues. — Sun.: 10-4.
ADMISSION: Parking fees $3 weekday, $4 weekend each section, during warm weather.
LOCATION: Route 17 past N.Y. State line to Sloatsburg Road
TELEPHONE: 201-962-7031 or 7047

LYNDHURST

Just a few minutes south of the Tappan Zee Bridge and run by the National Trust for Historical Preservation, this Gothic "castle" was the summer home of Jay Gould. The crystal greenhouses were once the foremost indoor gardens in America although they are now empty. The house, with its turreted towers and manicured lawn, is often used in commercials and advertisements as an example of the good life.

Visitors are taken through the home by tour guides and are shown, among other things: an ornate dining room with enough carved woodwork to fill a Gothic church; the butler's pantry which reminds one of the "Upstairs, Downstairs" days when people really had butlers; and the huge drawing room with its many landscape paintings, its stained glass windows and view of the Hudson. Much of the interior is wood or plaster painted to look like stone to enhance the Medieval effect. This is not unusual in homes built in the Gothic Revival style, although it seems to disappoint many tour groups who expect more of Jay Gould.

HOURS: Apr.-Oct.: Tues.-Sun. 10-5 Nov.-Apr.: Weekends 10-5.
ADMISSION: Adults: $6.00; Seniors: $5.00; Children: $3.00
LOCATION: U.S. Route 9, Tarrytown, N.Y., 1/4 mile south of Tappan Zee Bridge.
TELEPHONE: 914-631-0313

SUNNYSIDE

Home of Washington Irving, America's first internationally famous author. Built in a whimsical manner to suit Irving's individual taste, the early 19th Century house is a cross between the Dutch and the quaint. It is built on the banks of the Hudson with lovely grounds, swan ponds and a Visitor's Center where a film on the Sleepy Hollow Restorations (of which this is one) is shown. Guided tours only. Because the rooms and hallways are small, and the tour takes time, there are long lines here on summer weekends. Best to go during the week. Sleepy Hollow Church and graveyard are nearby.

HOURS: 10-5 Daily. Closed major holidays.
ADMISSION: Adults: $5.00; Children: $3.00; Seniors: $4.50
LOCATION: Take Tappan Zee Bridge to New York, then Route 9 south to Sunnyside Lane.
TELEPHONE: 914-631-8200

BOSCOBEL

A stately Federal mansion set on the banks of the Hudson River (it was moved 15 miles from its original location), Boscobel was begun by Morris Dyckman in 1804. Dyckman, who made his money as an arms dealer, was able to afford the best furnishings. Although he died before it was finished, his wife moved in and furnished it most elegantly. The house is completely restored and refurbished (in fact it was refurbished twice!) and reflects an authenticity of period.

A large central hall, sweeping stairway, patterned wallpaper, Duncan Phyfe furniture, china, glass, silver and a bevy of whale oil lamps reflect an era of early and gracious wealth. The wide lawns, the rose garden and the view of West Point across the river all add to the ambience of quiet gentility. Guides take you through the home, but you may peruse the outdoor scenery on your own. A small gift shop is located in a separate building.

HOURS: Daily except Tues. Closed Jan. & Feb. Tours: 9:30-5 Nov., Dec., Mar., 9:30-4 Closed major holidays.
ADMISSION: Adults: $5.00; Children 6-14: $2.50; Seniors: $4.00
LOCATION: Garrison, N.Y. on Route 9D, 8 miles north of Bear Mt. Bridge.
TELEPHONE: 914-265-3638

MACCULLOCH HALL

Unfortunately, this 1908 Federal structure has very limited public hours because the furnishings within are quite handsome. Oriental rugs throughout, huge Waterford crystal chandeliers brought over from the millionaire Twombly estate (now Fairleigh Dickinson campus), and an original portrait of Washington by Rembrandt Peale are among the eclectic collection of the mansion's last owner.

There is no attempt to furnish each room according to a specific period but you will see quality cupboards, china, and crystal of the 18th and 19th Century throughout the house.

Macculloch Hall also houses two small rooms dedicated to Thomas Nast, the famous cartoonist whose vitriolic cartoons helped to topple the corrupt Boss Tweed regime. Nast was a Morristown resident (his home is practically across the street) whose drawings became classics. His depiction of Santa Claus is the one we now use as the standard and he also created the donkey and the elephant as symbols of the political parties. The Nast room includes cartoons, paintings, drawings, and awards.

The house is shown by guided tour (allow a half-an-hour at least) but you may wander through the pleasant garden by yourself. The mansion is specially decorated for Christmas and offers extended hours the first week in December.

> **HOURS:** April-mid Dec.: Sun. 2-4:30 PM. Open to groups by appointment.
> **ADMISSION:** Adults: $3.00; Seniors: $2.00; Students: $1.00
> **LOCATION:** 45 Macculloch Ave., Morristown, Morris County (2 blocks west of South Street).
> **TELEPHONE:** 201-538-2404

MORVEN

Until December 1981, this lovely Georgian mansion was the official home of New Jersey's governor. Now that Drumthwacket has taken over the honor, Morven is administered by the *N.J. Historical Society* as an historic house and museum.

Morven is not really a large house and one feels that previous governors must have had trouble accomodating their guests here. The dining room is only of moderate size and one cannot imagine state dinners here. That is probably why the surrounding five acres with those verandas and gardens were often used for summer parties.

The Stockton family whose portraits dominate Morven, owe this grand colonial house to Richard Stockton the Elder who began building it in 1701. His grandson, known as Richard the Signer (because he signed the Declaration of Independence) and his wife Annis, named the residence Morven. Morven was the home of the King Fingal, a character in the tremendously popular, and absolutely fake, "The Lays of Ossian".

In 1777, General Cornwallis seized Morven, used it as his headquarters, then looted and burned it. In 1783, Elias Boudinet, a Stockton brother-in-law, used it as his residence. It was here that American leaders came to celebrate the signing of the Peace Treaty of Britain.

Burned twice, enlarged over the years, the house was finally rehabilitated in 1955 by the New Jersey State Legislature to be used as a Governor's mansion. The high calibre of its furnishings and the clean look of wallpaper and paint made Morven one of New Jersey's outstanding historical homes. Now, however, most of the Queen Anne furniture has been removed. So, also, has the beautiful silver service that once graced the dining room. The paintings, mantels and wallpaper are all intact, though. Upstairs, you will find an interesting small museum with changing exhibits.

HOURS: Call for available hours.
ADMISSIONS: Adults: $2.00; Seniors, children: $1.00.
LOCATION: 55 Stockton Street, Princeton.
TELEPHONE: 609-683-0169

BAINBRIDGE HOUSE

This small brick building is wedged between stores and movie houses on the well-traversed Nassau Street and stands practically opposite the iron gates of Princeton University. The one-time home of Captain William Bainbridge, a hero of the War of 1812 and a commander of the U.S.S. Constitution, it serves now as headquarters for the Princeton Historical Society. Luckily, this particular historical society keeps its house open to the public much longer than most. A typical small home of the well-to-do family of the late 18th Century, it features period furnishings in the downstairs rooms plus changing exhibits.

There is also a surprisingly well-stocked souvenir and book shop here. The Historical Society here also conducts tours of Princeton, which should be reserved beforehand.

> **HOURS:** Tues.-Sun.: 12-4; Jan, Feb: weekends only. Closed major holidays. Jun. - Aug. also open Mon.
> **ADMISSION:** Free (donations accepted)
> **LOCATION:** 158 Nassau Street, Princeton, Mercer County.
> **TELEPHONE:** 609-921-6748

WILLIAM TRENT HOUSE

The founder of Trenton, so to speak, because his house and property were known as "Trent's Town", William Trent built his stately home in 1719. It was later the residence of four governors. "A genteel brick dwelling house, three stories high, with a large, handsome staircase and entry", according to an early observer, it is one of the best restorations in New Jersey. In Georgian style with 18th Century English furniture and many early American pieces. Some of the William & Mary and Queen Anne furnishings here are equal to what you would find in Colonial Williamsburg, and the old-fashioned kitchen is really worth the tour. Guided tours by knowledgeable volunteers.

> **HOURS:** Daily 10-2
> **ADMISSION:** Adults: $1.50 Children: $.50
> **LOCATION:** 15 Market Street, Trenton.
> **TELEPHONE:** 609-989-3027

KUSER FARM MANSION

The country home of the Kusers was built in 1882 as both a vacation home and a working farm. The family had financial interests in hotels, beer, cars and more, but are best known for their connection with 20th Century Fox. The elder Kuser had helped William Fox start his motion picture company with a $200,000 loan. The connection continued for years with the Kusers showing movies at a specially constructed screen in their dining room well into the 1960s.

While the house here is not a place of super luxury (it was meant for casual summer entertaining and family get togethers) it is one of meticulous craftmanship. Specially trained German craftsmen worked on the ornately carved mantelpieces throughout the house. Double floors, heavy woodwork, stained glass windows and a bedroom featuring a Delft tile fireplace are among the details to be noted. The 45-foot dining room features the heavily ornate table and chairs that were the hallmark of the Victorian age.

The Kuser Mansion and surrounding farm were sold to Hamilton Township in the late 1970s to be used as a public park. The outdoor area includes a gazebo and many picnic tables, and has a pleasant, quiet atmosphere. Last tour begins one half-hour before closing. Free.

HOURS: (House) May-Nov., Thurs.-Sun.: 11-3
LOCATION: 390 Newark Avenue, Hamilton Twp., Mercer County
take Kuser Road exit from 295 just before Trenton.
TELEPHONE: 609-890-3630

WALT WHITMAN HOUSE

A narrow row house in Camden contains the rooms where the poet who sang of America lived out the last eight years of his life. Accumulations of furniture (much of it the landlord's which Whitman took over along with the house), photographs and memorabilia are here. Whitman had had a paralytic stroke and much of what is in the house was given to him by friends during this invalid period. A bathtub kept in the upstairs bedroom is typical of the many gifts his friend collected for him.

Four rooms are open, two downstairs, two upstairs. The downstairs rooms, and a new library section that recently opened up next door, are filled with books, manuscripts and photographs. (Whitman was the most photographed writer in America in his time.) A painting by Thomas Eakins, hats, locks of hair, etc. are just a portion of the memorabilia. A guide will show you around. Since this is a State Historic Site, it is always a good idea to call first —state houses are sometimes closed for renovations or because the guide is on vacation. Free.

HOURS: Wed.-Fri.: 9-12 & 1-6; Sat.: 10-12 & 1-6; Sun.: 1-6
LOCATION: 330 Mickle Street, Camden.
TELEPHONE: 609-964-5383

PENNSBURY MANOR

Here is a complete recreation, on the original site, of the beautiful Manor House built by William Penn on the banks of the Delaware. Located 25 miles above Philadelphia in what was then a wilderness, the estate includes many outbuildings such as a bake and brew house, a smoke house, ice house and stable. Although everything was built from scratch in the 1930s, great care was taken to follow the letters and journals of Penn regarding this self-sufficient estate.

There are two striking things about Pennsbury Manor. One is the earliness of the period. The house was built in the late 17th Century (Penn lived there only from 1699 to 1701), so the furnishings reflect the heavy Jacobean hand. And the tour guides look as if they came from the pages of Mother Goose with their tunics and high black hats — quite different from the ubiquitous mob caps and wool shawls of the typical colonial reconstruction.

The other is the surprising elegance of this Quaker household. Although nothing is lavish, still the furnishings are richer than one would expect of a Quaker leader.

As the guide points out, although William Penn was a great believer in the equality of men, he was still the Proprietor, entitled to receive an annual fee from each settler for each parcel of land sold. He had, after all, received the Charter of Pennsylvania from King Charles II. He also came from a wealthy background and apparently relished good furniture.

After a tour through the bedrooms, parlors and countingrooms of the Manor, a tour through the grounds is in order. First to the barge-landing where a handsome replica of the ornate barge that Penn used to travel down to Philadelphia is moored. (Actually it looks more like a large gondola than a modern-day flat barge.) Then there is the herb garden, the barnyard with its peacocks and hens, and the brew house where it is supposed great vats of ale were mixed and where huge ovens held the bread to be baked for the estate.

The grounds include orchards and gardens. Walnut, hawthorn and hazel trees, fruit trees and rosebushes created a little corner of England in the new wilderness of America.

> **HOURS:** Tues.-Sat.: 9-5; Sun:12-5 Last tour at 3:30 Jan & Feb Tours at 11 & 2.
> **ADMISSION:** Adults: $2.50; Seniors: $1.75; Students: $1.00; Under 6: Free.

LOCATION: Bordertown Road, near Levittown, Bucks County, PA.
TELEPHONE: 215-946-0400

ANDALUSIA

Nicholas Biddle was one of America's first millionaires, and the Biddle name still connotes a sense of grace, polish and "old money" in the Philadelphia area. Andalusia was the country seat of Nicholas, although the house came to him through marriage. He transformed it in 1834 from a Regency mansion to its present form — one of the outstanding examples of Greek Revival architecture in the Northeast. Indeed, its facade of startling white pillars and "Greek temple" architrave will remind you of the many antebellum Southern mansions built in the same style.

The house faces the Delaware River and its large sloping green lawn runs down to the edge of the water. On this lawn you will find both a billiard room and a Gothic "ruin". The "ruin", a crumbling tower, was built that way. This was not uncommon in the 1830s, when the romantic novels of Sir Walter Scott, plus tales of excavations in the mid-East, had Americans crazy over anything Medieval, Greek, Turkish or Egyptian.

Inside the mansion, furniture varies from splendid, polished Regency buffets to odd shaped Greek-style chairs. The music room, with its delicate pianoforte and whale oil lamps brings visions of genteel ladies offering an evening musicale to an assemblage of local gentry.

Outside again, there are extensive grounds which include tennis courts, a swimming pool, a hedge walk, a grape arbor and another huge house which is not open to visitors. Tours of Andalusia are for groups only, but one can go through with a minimum of five people. These tours are booked through the historic house, *Cliveden*, in Philadelphia. Groups can also book a package tour run by Pennsbury Manor called "Mansions on the Delaware" which includes two or more houses plus lunch.

HOURS: By reserved tour only.
LOCATION: Bensalem Twp., Bucks County, PA.
TELEPHONE: Cliveden: 215-848-1777; Pennsbury Manor: 215- 946-0400.

GREEN HILL FARM

Bucks County, Pennsylvania, was a haven for writers in the 1930s. Most of the literary celebrities of that time moved on to other pastures. But Pearl S. Buck, who reached the zenith of her fame during the pre-World War II period, (she won the Nobel Prize in 1938) remained here in her lovely country home until her death in 1963.

The stone and wood house seems to typify the Hollywood picture of a writer's country retreat: a huge floor-to-ceiling brick fireplace, great expanses of polished wood flooring, overstuffed sofas and walls lined with books. Add to this a collection of Oriental lamps and tables, screens and sculptures, and you get a picture of Pearl S. Buck, author and admirer of Chinese culture. At one point there were also nine adopted Amerasian children in the house which explains the generous dimensions and open spaces of the home.

Visits to Green Hill Farm are by guided tour only. The tour includes a look at the commemorative room where all the awards and prizes are displayed and the study where Ms. Buck wrote her works (sitting in a most uncomfortable looking straight backed Chinese chair). Outside there is a lovely old-fashioned patio, lots of green rolling hills, and a separate shop where you may purchase Oriental pieces and other souvenirs. The Pearl S. Buck Foundation, dedicated to helping Amerasian children abandoned by their fathers, is located in the big red barn not far from the house.

HOURS: Tours are given Tues.-Sat.: 10:30, 1:30 & 2:30. Mar. 1 - Dec. 31.
ADMISSION: Adults: $5.00; Seniors, children: $4.00; Under 6: Free.
LOCATION: Perkasie, PA Take 202S to 313W to town of Dublin, PA. Turn left at Maple Ave. (which becomes Dublin Road) then one mile.
TELEPHONE: 215-249-0100 or 800-242-2825

See Also: *Winterthur* (Restored and Reconstructed), *Longwood* and *Duke Gardens* (The Garden Variety) and specific homes of the prominent in the chapter on "Walking Tours".

RESTORED AND RECONSTRUCTED COLONIAL, FEDERAL & VICTORIAN VILLAGES, FARMS, MILLS & HOMES

Photo: Courtesy N.J. Travel & Tourism

In This Chapter You Will Find:

Waterloo Village, N.J.
Van Cortlandt Manor, N.Y.
Philipsburg Manor, N.Y.
Clinton Historical Museum Village, N.J.
Historic Towne of Smithville, N.J.
Wheaton Village, N.J.
East Jersey Old Towne, N.J.
Batsto, N.J.
Millbrook Village
Allaire Village, N.J.
Historic Cold Spring Village, N.J.
Longstreet Farm, N.J.
Fosterfields, N.J.
Howell Living History Farm, N.J.
Israel Crane House, N.J.
Miller-Cory House, N.J.
Other Historic Houses in New Jersey
Winterthur, DE
The Hagley Museum, DE
South Street Seaport, N.Y.

WATERLOO VILLAGE

The largest restoration in New Jersey, Waterloo offers homes and mills scattered along the woodsy terrain next to the Musconetcong River. Over the years, Waterloo has become known not only as a restored village, but as the setting for a summer music festival as well. Concerts range from Classical to Bluegrass to well-known pop stars and are featured on weekends from June through August.

The village complex covers over 5000 acres and includes buildings ranging from a tiny 1740 duplex to a solid 1870 mansion. Since Waterloo prospered both during the Revolutionary War and the later era of the Morris Canal and Sussex Railroad, the houses reflect the Colonial, Federal and Victorian styles. When you tour the village, however, you find that most guides are dressed in the doublets and skirts of the late 18th Century working class.

The speeches the guides give regularly to school and scout groups are often the most interesting thing about a restored village. The hostess in the *Canal House*, for instance, demonstrates the wooden-knobbed weasel that used to draw the wool yarn into a skein. Every time the weasel made a full skein, it would go "pop", thus explaining the childhood song about thirty years too late for me. I found you are more likely to hear these anecdote-filled speeches if you latch onto some group going through.

A favorite for children is the gristmill where huge stones grind the corn which the guide upstairs pours between the stones. Then you troop downstairs where the waterwheel is creating a loud whoosh. Here you discover the cornmeal pouring out the spout, while another guide explains the process.

There's a lot of walking to do here — several homes, the General Store (where you can buy the clay candlesticks the potter makes), the Canal Museum (explaining the works of Morris Canal), and all the various craft buildings. Bring good shoes. A further walk up the hill takes you to a complete Indian village as it would have been when the first settlers came. A long house, animals skins drying, clothes, and the accoutrements of tribal life are here, together with a guide who explains the customs.

There are now several eating places, including a food tent, a restaurant for concert night buffets, a hamburger grill and a quaint stone tavern for cheese and crackers. Concert-goers often come an hour or two early, tour the village, and picnic on the grass before they take their seats. Concert tickets are priced separately. Guided tours may not be available on concert or special days, but the houses will be open.

HOURS: Mid-April-Oct.: 10-6; Nov.-Dec.: 10-5 daily. Closed Mondays.
ADMISSION: Adults: $7.50; Seniors: $5.00; Children: $3.00; Under 6 Free. Concert prices vary.
LOCATION: Byram Twp., Sussex County. Take I-80 to Route 206N. Left at Waterloo Road.
TELEPHONE: 201-347-0900

THE VAN CORTLANDT MANOR

Ever wonder why they call it "Bar and Grill"? Or why a small whiskey glass is referred to as a "shot glass"? You'll find the answer to these and other questions you may or may not have asked at Van Cortlandt Manor, an 18th Century restoration on the New York side of the Hudson, where guides combine anecdotes and demonstrations in their tours.

Set on a rise overlooking both the Hudson and Croton Rivers, Van Cortlandt Manor is a prime example of the strong influence of the Dutch in the New York-New Jersey area. At one time in the late 1700s, the estate extended from the Hudson River to Connecticut. The Manor House is now one of the better Colonial restorations in the area.

Tours begin at the reception center where accurately costumed guides take groups of fifteen people through several buildings. Our group stopped first at the *Ferry House*. The ferry once plied the Croton River and travelers would stop here for food, drink, and lodging. The building is not large, but travelers would sleep three or four to a bed so they all managed.

At the other end of a long brick walk, lined with rows of tulips, is the *Manor House* itself. While not as elegant as the Southern Colonial mansions, it is impressive for this area — three stories high with a two-story porch wrapped around it. A heavy Dutch door opens to the main floor where the atmosphere is one of burnished wood and quiet elegance. Delft tiles line the fireplaces. Chippendale and Queen Anne furniture fill the rooms, and English china rests in the practical Dutch cupboards whose doors could be closed at night.

The ground floor kitchen was a magnet for our group. Here the guide, still flushed from baking two rhubarb pies in the massive hearth fireplace, answered endless questions. She showed us the original Dutch oven (a heavy iron kettle with a closed lid), the beehive oven in the back of the fireplace and the gridiron for baking steaks. She did everything, in fact, but share the rhubarb pie with us. Those, I assume, are eaten by the employees when the last tourist departs.

Van Cortlandt Manor, also includes a smokehouse, ice house, and blacksmith forge. The tours are geared for adults and schoolage children.

HOURS: 10-5. Closed major holidays.
ADMISSION: Adults: $5.00; Children: $3.00; Seniors: $4.50.
LOCATION: Croton-on-the-Hudson, N.Y. Take Tappan Zee Bridge to Route 9N to Croton Pond Ave., one block east to South Riverside Ave., turn right and go 1/4 mile to entrance.
TELEPHONE: 914-631-8200

PHILIPSBURG MANOR

A large farm and gristmill, a wood-planked bridge that spans a tranquil stream, an old stone manor-house and a huge modern reception center filled with exhibits are all a part of this "Sleepy Hollow" restoration. The estate is set up as it would have been in 1750, with authentic furnishings and authentically garbed guides. You begin with a movie about the Philipse family who once managed 90,000 acres and shipped flour and meal down the Hudson. Unfortunately, they backed the losing side during the Revolutionary War and lost their holdings as a result.

Guided tours of the manor, a demonstration of the gristmill, and a walk around the large property and through the barn are part of the outing. You can see sheep and lambs gamboling about as you traverse the property. Administered in a highly professional manner.

LOCATION: Upper Mills, North Tarrytown, N.Y. Take Tappan Zee Bridge, then Route 9N for 2 miles. Look for signs.
HOURS, ETC: Same as Van Cortlandt Manor.

CLINTON HISTORICAL MUSEUM VILLAGE

An old red mill with a churning water-wheel sits by a 200-foot wide waterfall to create the picturesque environment for this museum village. In fact, the red mill is one of the most photographed structures in New Jersey. It is this mill that is the hub of the "village". However, the entire inside of the red mill is being refurbished and new exhibits will be on hand when it re-opens. The other buildings are smaller and scattered along the banks of the river. You can find a log cabin, a little red school house, a general store/post office, a blacksmith shop, a stonecrusher and an information center in the small complex.

The museum also runs a series of specials to attract the crowds. These include summer concerts, craft days and a harvest jubilee. The place is run, by the way, by a private, non-profit educational organization. Guided tours for groups are given at no extra cost but must be arranged in advance.

Across the river, the large stone building facing the mill houses the **Hunterdon Art Center** (closed Mondays), which is certainly worth a visit. Exhibits of prints, painting, and sculpture are always on hand. In the interim, some historic exhibits may be shown here.

From the art center you can walk up the main street of the small country town of Clinton. Some nice boutiques and a fern-hung luncheon spot make for pleasant browsing.

HOURS: April- Oct. 31: Tues.-Sun.: 10-4. Gift shop always open.
ADMISSION: Adults: $3.00; Seniors: $1.50; Children: $1.00; Under 6 Free.
LOCATION: 56 Main Street, Clinton, Hunterdon County (Off Rte. 78).
TELEPHONE: 201-735-4101

HISTORIC TOWNE OF SMITHVILLE

Only twelve miles from Atlantic City, the Historic Towne of Smithville was at one time half a reconstructed Colonial village and half a boutiquey shopping center in Colonial disguise. Now the whole area has become a quaint shopping town. Gone is the

Working craftsmen are at hand at some restored villages.

oyster boat in the lake. Gone are the farm animals and the weavers and spinners. In their stead there are even more boutique shops on the other side of the lake.

The mainstay of Smithville is still the Smithville Inn, a bustling restaurant with nine dining areas. It is the only genuine historic site in the town, and it started life as a stagecoach stop in 1787. It is set up in Colonial style and the anterooms, halls and dining areas are chock full of antiques such as hutches, bedwarmers and farm implements.

The Quail Hill Inn is now a huge antique center. As for the shops — there are plenty of them (plus a garden-style restaurant) on the winding roads of the village. "Everything you never needed" (as one friend summed it up) all on a pleasant green with brick walkways lined with flower beds. Candles, plants, shells, gourmet foods, scented soaps, chocolates, etc. It will remind you of Peddler's Village, Lahaska, or New Hope or Cape May — where you may find unique items or the latest fad. At least these places are a pleasant change from the concrete shopping malls we usually frequent. During summer there are often special events here.

HOURS: Vary for shops. Restaurants daily for lunch and dinner.
LOCATION: Smithville on Route 9, Atlantic County.
TELEPHONE: 609-652-7777

WHEATON VILLAGE

A Victorian Village set around a green with houses styled in 1888 gingerbread, Wheaton Village is a nice, clean spot in the middle of a small industrial town called Millville about 35 miles west of Atlantic City. The village is dedicated to the glass industry that still flourishes in this corner of New Jersey and its main attraction is the **Museum of Glass**. The museum is housed in an elegant Victorian building and includes glass items that go back as far as 300 B.C.

Glass collectors will probably enjoy this museum with its flower-embedded paperweights, medicine bottles, cut glass and door-knobs. You learn everything you ever wanted to know about bottles, including the origin of the word "booze" from the Booz bottle. The foyer boasts the chandeliers from the old Traymore Hotel in Atlantic City and the original brass sconces from the Waldorf Astoria.

Another attraction is the glass factory where visitors can watch from a gallery above while gaffers plunge their gathering rods into the blazing furnaces and then shape them into wine glasses, bottles and paperweights. Three times a day there are "shows" which means an announcer with a mike explains just what the gaffer is doing. This is hot work and even from the gallery you can feel the intensity of the furnace. And nowadays, Wheaton Village allows visitors to make their own paperweights. For $35.00, you (and a qualified gaffer) make an individual creation. Call to reserve for this offer.

Other buildings in the Village include a craft arcade where you can see weavers, potters and printers going about their work. The craftsman's handiwork plus lots of glass vases and paperweights can be purchased in the stores that line the village green.

For kids there's a small play area, an 1876 schoolhouse to peek at and an 1880 Train Station (with a miniature train ride for an extra fee).

The General Store sells penny candy from an old-fashioned glass jar and the drugstore features an ice cream parlor. All in all, Wheaton Village is not a bad place to visit, especially for glass fanciers, although many buildings on the village green are actually stores.

HOURS: Daily, 10-5 (Reduced schedule Jan.-Mar.)
ADMISSION: Adults: $5.00; Students:$2.50; Seniors: $4.50; Under 6 Free. Family Rate: $10.00. Reduced winter rates.
LOCATION: 10th & "G" Street, Millville, Cumberland County. Take Routes 47, 49 or 55.
TELEPHONE: 609-825-6800

EAST JERSEY OLDE TOWNE

A reconstructed Colonial village has been growing in Johnson Park, Piscataway, for lo, these many years. A good number of small, sturdy houses are there, set on a pleasant village green meant to resemble an 18th Century settlement in the Raritan Valley. Several of the buildings have been moved from other sites. One can find a church, a farmhouse, a tavern, a blacksmith shop, among others, and there are picket fences and tiny garden plots and brick walkways.

Most of the time these houses are not open, but you can walk around the green and inspect the outside. Luckily, one of the wooden houses includes a well-stocked gift shop which is open weekdays.

There are also special events at the village at which time guides are available for the houses. These events usually take place on major holidays such as Memorial Day and the Fourth of July weekends. Group tours are available on a pre-arranged basis and may include lunch at the tavern. Another popular activity is weddings at the quaint, but small, Three-Mile-Run Church, a structure that dates back to 1703. Now that the Middlesex County Park system has taken over, things may change.

HOURS: (Gift shop) Mon.-Fri.: 10-3.
LOCATION: River Road (Route 18) at Hoes Lane, Piscataway, Middlesex County.
TELEPHONE: 201-463-9077 ·

BATSTO

What was once a self-contained community lies within the Wharton Tract (a huge State preserve within the section known as the Pine Barrens). Tall trees, open lowlands, lakes with clusters of campgrounds are all part of this unusual region which reminded me of the North Carolina tidelands.

As for Batsto Village itself, it was once the center of the bog iron industry in New Jersey. Later, glass was manufactured here, then lumbering and cranberry farming were tried. As you approach, you find a handsome farm surrounded by split rail fences with horses, chickens and ducks in view. The huge farmhouse has a late Victorian tower rising eight stories from its center, giving the place a "haunted mansion" look. The rooms inside are filled with the furniture of the well-to-do families that lived there, and the wall-to-wall library of James Wharton, the financier who once owned the place, is most impressive. The tour takes 45 minutes and is very comprehensive.

The first stop at Batsto is the Visitors Center. If you want the mansion tour buy your tickets immediately for they admit only 15 people at a time to this once-an-hour inspection. But there are other things to see at Batsto. A General Store, a barn with several barnyard animals, a large lake where fishing is allowed, a sawmill, and some refurbished workers houses. During the summer these houses usually have some craftsmen inside — a weaver, a potter and a blacksmith will be at work and will answer your questions if you have any. One of the homes is a museum set up as an ironworkers house to give you some feel for the community life that existed here.

The farm with its unusual main house, surrounding barns and wide swept fields all in the middle of the untouched pine barrens has the true look of the haunting past. It also has the attraction of a horse and carriage ride which is usually available on summer weekends.

> **HOURS:** Mem. Day-Labor Day: 10-6; rest of year: 11-5. Closed major holidays.
> **ADMISSION:** (to Mansion) Adults: $1.50; Children 6-11: $.75.
> **LOCATION:** Route 9 to 542 West. Or Garden State Parkway New Gretna Exit to 9S to 542.
> **TELEPHONE:** 609-561-3262
> **PARKING:** $4.00 weekends.

MILLBROOK VILLAGE

One of New Jersey's best kept secrets is this authentic 19th Century village set in the Kittatiny Mountains. It is run by the National Park Service as part of the Delaware Water Gap Recreation Area. Surprisingly, there were several guides in and around the village's clapboard buildings on the day I visited. (The number of guides at most National Park Service installations are few and far between because of severe budget chopping). These guides, dressed in period costumes of the 1860-1880 era, lead tours through several houses and engage in such crafts as woodworking and blacksmithing.

The original Millbrook Village was a small enclave of houses and stores clustered around a grist mill that opened in 1832. Since the mill served grain farmers in the surrounding countryside, the town became the social and commercial center of the community. In this way it mirrored much of America's agricultural life. A hotel with taproom, a smithy, a general store and a simple white-steepled church are among the buildings that surrounded the original mill by the brook.

Millbrook reached its zenith between 1870 and 1885. The village declined after 1900 and by mid-century it was a ghost town. What you see here now is a re-creation of Millbrook at its height. A village green, busy townfolk, lovely, well-kept homes and a church within walking distance are part of the scene. It could almost be

71

Kansas except for the mountainous terrain. Free and well worth tracking down.

HOURS: Late June — Labor Day: Daily, 9-5. Sept.- 1st wk. Oct.: Weekends, 9-5.
LOCATION: Sussex County. Take Route 80 west to the last exit in N.J. (Millbrook exit). Turn right, follow Old Mine Road 12 miles north.
TELEPHONE: 201-496-4458

ALLAIRE VILLAGE

Set inside the greenery of Allaire State Park, this complex is also known as the Deserted Village and the Howell Iron Works. The huge brick furnace is one left over from the bog iron days when James P. Allaire bought the ironworks in 1822 and sought to establish a sort of ideal, self-contained community. Since this was the age of Oneida settlements and Utopian communities, such a worker's paradise did not seem unusual. In fact, as long as the ironworks transformed local bog into pig iron, everything prospered. But after twenty-five years, competition from the high grade iron one brought economic ruin to the region. The village became deserted. A well documented display on the ironworks can be found in the clean, air-conditioned Visitors Center.

Nowadays the village is populated with craftsmen and guides. All during the summer a carpenter, a blacksmith and several hostesses inhabit the stores and shops here at the deserted village. Real bread is baked at the bakery and real goods (and plenty of them) are sold at the General Store. There are several other things going on in this park — particularly a railroad museum with old time trains and an operating railroad — which bring in the families with the kids. Nature trails, picnic areas, horse and buggy rides, and lots of special weekend summertime activities are contributing factors to the comparative popularity of Allaire.

HOURS: Park 8 AM-8 PM. Village: Daily; 10-5, Mem. Day-Labor Day. Shorter winter hours.
ADMISSION: Weekends: $4.00, Weekdays: $3.00 (Parking).
LOCATION: Allaire State Park, Monmouth County. Take Exit 98, Garden State Parkway, go 2 miles west.
TELEPHONE: 201-938-2371

HISTORIC COLD SPRING VILLAGE

A delightful little restored village has sprung up among the pine trees on a quiet stretch of road not far from the hubbub of the Wildwood motels. In operation since 1981, Cold Spring Village (not to be confused with the village of Cold Spring near Boscobel or Cold Spring Harbor in New York) has much of the charm that other restored villages aspire to. It's not so large as to be exhausting, nor so small that it might disappoint.

This is not a village set in a particular time — all the buildings are pre-1900, but they range from an ancient Colonial to the large Grange Hall which dates back to 1897. In between, you will find a tiny 1820 octogonal house and various forms of American Colonial. These houses are not empty — but each building has inside an authentic craftsman or interpreter. A genuine weaver, an old fashioned printer, and a furniture maker are some of the tenants here.

There are bits of country nostalgia here such as an old fashioned water pump (the water is undoubtedly from the cold spring), a small farm enclosure, and walkways made of crushed clamshells. A horse-drawn carriage, on hand the day I visited, was a big hit with the children. A new Marine Museum offers displays on the whaling industry and other fishy facts. For those who get hungry, the village also offers an ice cream store and bakery. Full meals are usually available at the Grange Hall where old style American fare is featured. Weekends there are often special events such as singers, contests and so forth. Two railroad stations add to the local color. The admission fee is the same for one day as for the season, so shore vacationers can visit more than once.

> **HOURS:** Memorial Day — Sept.: Daily 10-4.
> **ADMISSION:** Adults: $1.50; Children: $.75; Family: $4.00.
> **LOCATION:** 731 Seashore Road, Cold Spring, Cape May County. Take G.S.P. Exit 0 to Route 109 to Seashore Road.
> **TELEPHONE:** 609-898-2300

LONGSTREET FARM

For those who want to recapture the sights and smells of an era not so long past, a visit to Longstreet Farm quite fills the bill. Although the farm is kept to the 1890 to 1900 era, the machinery here was used well into the 1920s and may bring back memories

73

to those born on a farm. Old-fashioned combines and tractors, an apple corer, a machine that de-kernelizes corn (but only the hard corn meant for animals) and other antique contraptions are kept in a series of barns and sheds. Of course, animals are present, although not in profusion. There are lazy pigs lying in the mud, horses swatting flies, cows, chickens, and flies, flies, flies. In fact, if your children have ever asked why horses have tails,they can discover why here — they make the most efficient fly-swatters.

Open-slatted corn cribs that allow the air to circulate are on view. The milking shed is fitted out in the old way — with slots for the cow's head and buckets for hand milking. The carriage house contains a variety of buckboards. And they do have people here, too. Since Longstreet is a living historical farm, the workers dress in casual 1890s clothes as they go about their usual farm chores: feeding, seeding, plowing, milking — all in a day's work according to the season. And the eggs and milk are sold at market as are the hogs that are killed in the fall according to traditional farm custom.

No guided tours are given to individuals but groups may call ahead and arrange them. The main farmhouse is not open at this time, but the farm is open all year and follows the seasonal activities of plowing, harvesting, threshing, sheep-shearing and ice-cutting.

The farm is just one portion of the beautiful **Holmdel Park**, which provides much lovely scenery. Across the street, a sheltered picnic area offers tables and a snack bar. In a hollow below the shelter, a pond allows ducks to swim gracefully and accept breadcrusts from visitors. And beyond the pond, a cultivated arboretum presents a colorful view of flowering crabapples, rhododendrons and hundreds of shade trees. The park also provides a nature trail that winds among the beech, oak and hickory trees. Wildflowers and blueberry bushes are other plusses at this abundant county park. Free.

HOURS: 10-4 daily, Sept.-May. 9-5 daily, June-Labor Day.
LOCATION: Longstreet Road, off Holmdel Road. Take Garden State Arts Center Exit off GSP, follow Keyport Road, look for signs.
TELEPHONE: 201-946-3758

FOSTERFIELDS

Another old-fashioned farm that dates from the turn of the century in American agriculture, Fosterfields is run by the Morris County Park Commission. The large farm has many farm implements on display and a variety of farm animals visible in various enclosures along the walkway. There are also barns and various outbuildings. The main farmhouse, **The Willows**, has been restored and is open for tours and demonstrations on Thursdays and Fridays. A separate fee is charged.

On weekends, from the spring to fall season, a genuine farmer hitches up the horses, sows the seeds, threshes the hay and performs other seasonal tasks. Once in a while there is a special day during which the audience is allowed to get involved.

The handsome Visitors Center has displays on farming and also offers a short film on the history of Fosterfields. Here is where you can pick up brochures and information on any of the special activities — whether it's a Fourth of July picnic or a Saturday devoted to hay-racking.

HOURS: Apr.-Oct., Wed.-Sat.: 10-5; Sun.: 1-5. Jan., Feb.: Sat. 1-4.
ADMISSION: Weekends: Adults: $2.00; Children, Seniors: $1.00
LOCATION: Route 24 & Kahdena Rd., Morris Twp., Morris County.
TELEPHONE: 201-326-7645

HOWELL LIVING HISTORY FARM

Yet another active farm set in the turn of the century mode. What you find here is farm life that is pre-computerized. Various stages of mechanization are on show — the reaper reaps and binds mechanically, but it does not thresh. The wheat is bound by machine but the machine is pulled by a plodding draft horse, not a yellow Caterpillar. The wagon that picks up the bound sheaves is also available for hayrides. We were lucky enough to get a hitch in this wagon — great fun if you don't have back trouble or allergies.

There's plenty of acreage at the farm and you're part of the bucolic atmosphere from the moment you leave the parking lot and walk down the dirt road to the farmhouse. On the way you pass sheep and chicks and geese and cows — all safely behind fences, thank goodness. The farmhouse itself is in the process of being restored, and the volunteers need all the help they can get. School groups are welcome to weave burlap, make corn husk dolls, and help out in other ways. On weekends, a professional farmer is on hand to guide the draft horse in ploughing, sowing and reaping.

There are several Saturdays devoted to such things as a Spring Market and a Fall Festival. You might give Howell Farm a call before visiting to see if anything special is planned. Free (donations accepted).

HOURS: Apr.- July: Tues.-Sat.: 10-4; Aug.: Sat. 5-8 PM; Sept.-Dec.1: Sat.: 10-4; Sun.: 12-4.
LOCATION: Howell Twp., Mercer County. Take Rt. 29 to Belle Mtn. Ski Area turnoff (Valley Rd.) then 2 miles east.
TELEPHONE: 609-737-2399

ISRAEL CRANE HOUSE

A handsome house built in the Federal period and then remodeled in the Greek Revival style, the Crane house was moved from its original site to the present location by the Montclair Historical Society. The group also trains the docents who give guided tours throughout the three-story building.

Furnishings in the Federal and Empire style are evident in the main house. Upstairs in the garret, a full schoolroom exists. (One of the Cranes did run a school here.) An authentic blackboard (which is, incidentally, a large board painted black), an old-fashioned dunce cap and the elongated desks that accommodated several children at a time are part of the set-up here. Also in the garret are a full tool collection and a mass of dried herbs.

Behind the main house is a two-story kitchen building reconstructed to resemble the 1840 kitchen that once existed. One unique feature of the Crane House is that the docents do allow you to sample the cooking. Just a tiny piece, but you can taste bread from the beehive oven, while the chicken simmers over the open hearth. Docents are quite good at explaining about the cooking utensils (such as the lazy-back which eased cooking chores for post-Colonial wives). Beyond the kitchen building is a pleasant backyard planted with flowers and herbs in the 18th Century fashion. And beyond that, the *Country Store Museum* is housed in a small building erected by Nathaniel Crane in 1820. Although the items in the store are just wooden models and are not for sale, you do get the sense of an old-fashioned post-office/store as the social center for a town. A small gift shop here offers books and mementos for sale. And on the second floor there is a craft room where quilts, looms and a spinning wheel are displayed. Special classes in quilting and such are held here periodically.

> **HOURS:** Sept.-June: Sun.:2-5, Wed.: 1-4. Group tours weekdays.
> **ADMISSION:** Adults: $2.00; Children: $.50
> **LOCATION:** 110 Orange Rd. (Off Bloomfield Ave.) Montclair, Essex County.
> **TELEPHONE:** 201-744-1796

MILLER-CORY HOUSE

Every Sunday during the school season, volunteers cook, churn butter and perform seasonal tasks in and around this 1740 farmhouse. The everyday, humdrum tasks of Colonial life — from soap-making to herb-drying are emphasized here. The house, the adjacent Visitor Center, and a separate kitchen comprise a small enclave of Colonial life. In pleasant weather, wool spinners and other workers may be found outside and the separate kitchen is the scene of soup and bread making. Good idea, since there is often a line for a tour of the Miller-Cory house itself.

Guided tours of the house proper take about half-an-hour, with 15 people to each tour. Although three tours may go on simultaneously, there may be a wait on a busy fall afternoon. The tour is most thorough and includes everything from how to tighten the rope springs on a bed to how to make utensils from a cow's horn. School children and adults will find the house tour highly educational while pre-schoolers may be content to simply mosey around the grounds. They can tour the herb garden, the tool collection in the Visitor Center, or watch the outdoor volunteers at work.

HOURS: Sept.-June, Sun.: 2-5; Jan.-Mar., Sun.: 2-4.
ADMISSION: Adults: $1.00; Children: $.50.
LOCATION: 614 Mountain Ave., Westfield, Union County.
TELEPHONE: 201-232-1776

OTHER HISTORIC HOUSES (N.J.)

The number of historic houses in New Jersey is so large it would take an entire volume just to list them. Here are a few:

COOPER MILL: An 1826 mill where you can see corn ground into meal before your eyes. Guided tours upon request. Open Fri.- Tues., 10-5, July & Aug. Weekends only in spring and fall. Located on Route 24, Chester, Morris County, one mile west of Rte. 206. *Telephone:* 201-326-7645.

OSBORN CANNONBALL HOUSE: An 18th Century house with period furnishings. 1840 Front St., Scotch Plains, Union County. Open Sun.: 2-4, Sept.-June. *Telephone:* 908-889-1928

FORCE HOUSE: Next to Memorial Field in Livingston, the 18th & 19th Century homestead of a local family. Open on 2nd & 4th Sunday of the month except summer. 366 S. Livingston Ave., Livingston, Essex County.

OGDEN-BELCHER MANSION: A well-respected restoration on a historic street in Elizabeth and one that you can visit only by writing to: Elizabeth Historical Foundation, Box 1, Elizabeth, NJ.

MARLPIT HALL: A beautiful, refurbished Colonial that started life as a Dutch cottage in 1685 and was later enlarged in the English style. Located at 137 Kings Highway, Middletown, Monmouth County. Open April-Oct. Tues., Thurs., Sun.: 1-4; Sat.: 10-4. *Admission:* Adults: $2.00; Seniors: $1.50; Children: $1.00; under 6, free.

GREENFIELD HALL: Well-furnished, handsome Georgian building that features personal items belonging to Elizabeth Haddon, and a doll collection. Open Tues. & Thurs., 2-4:40. Closed summer. *Location:* 343 King Highway, Haddonfield, Camden County. *Telephone:* 609-429-7375.

MARSHALL HOUSE: One-time home of James Marshall who discovered gold at Sutter's Mill, California, but never made any money from the find. Built in 1816. Prize possession is a friendship quilt. Headquarters Lambertville Historical Society. Open May to mid-Oct., Thurs., Sun.: 1-4 PM. Adults $.50, Children $.25 *Location:* 60 Bridge Street, Lambertville, Hunterdon County. *Telephone:* 609-397-0770 or 609-397-2531.

VAN-RIPER-HOPPER HOUSE: Dutch Colonial farmhouse with period furnishings, local history display, herb garden. Open Fri.-Tues.: 1-5. Free. *Location:* 533 Berdan Ave., Wayne, Passaic County. *Telephone:* 201-694-7192.

SOMERS MANSION: Oldest house in Atlantic County has unusual roof shaped like upside-down ship's hull. Local memorabilia. A State Historic Site. *Hours:* Wed.-Fri.: 9-12 & 1-6; Sat.: 10-12 & 1-6; Sun.: 1-6. *Location:* Route 52 to Shore Rd., Somers Point. *Telephone:* 609-927-2212.

ACORN HALL: Mid-Victorian home in the Italianate style with many original furnishings in its two parlours. Children's toys and gadgets. Well-kept lawn with huge oak and Victorian garden with gazebo. Open Thurs. 11-3; Sun.: 1:30-4, spring through fall only. Adults: $2.00; Children: $.50. 68 Morris Ave., Morristown, Morris County. *Telephone:* 201-267-3465.

THE OLD MONROE SCHOOLHOUSE: Hand-hewn stone schoolhouse with wooden desks, hand slates and pot-bellied stove. Picnic facilities. Open 1st Sun. May-Oct. Adults: $1.00; Children: $.75. *Location:* Route 44 between Hamburg and Newton, Sussex County. *Telephone:* 201-827-4459.

THE HERMITAGE: Handsome Gothic Revival building filled with Victorian furnishings. 19th century clothing exhibit from June to Sept. Special craft shows before Thanksgiving and Easter. Open for guided tours 1st & 3rd Wed. & Sun. 1-4. *Location:* 335 North Franklin Tpke., Ho-Ho-Kus, Bergen County. *Admission:* Adults: $2.00, children under 12, free. *Telephone:* 201-445-8311.

TOWNSHIP OF LEBANON MUSEUM: A white 1823 schoolhouse with all its desks, textbooks and inkwells in place. Reserved school tours are booked and classes taught. *Hours:* Tues., Thurs.: 9:30-5. Sat.: 1-5. Free. *Location:* Musconetcong River Road, New Hampton, Hunterdon County. *Telephone:* 908-537-6464.

BARCLAY FARMSTEAD: Old fashioned Quaker farmhouse furnished with 19th century pieces. Interprets life of the period. Free. *Hours:* Tues., Thurs., 1-3:30. *Location:* Barclay Lane, Cherry Hill, Camden County. *Telephone:* 609-795-6225.

DR. WILLIAM ROBINSON PLANTATION: Restored 1690 farmhouse with artifacts, maps and pictures in its museum section. Guided tours by costumed docents. *Hours:* April-Dec., 1st Sunday 1-4. *Location:* 593 Madison Hill Road, Clark, Union County. *Telephone:* 908-381-3081.

WINTERTHUR

The *creme de la creme* when it comes to American decorative arts, Winterthur is Henri DuPont's version of hundreds of restored homes rolled into one. The main mansion contains 175 rooms, each one decorated in a pre-1840 style. In many cases the rooms are more than merely decorated — whole dining rooms, kitchens, etc. (including walls, ceilngs and fireplaces) were transported panel by panel and placed inside the mansion. Six style periods are shown: Seventeenth Century, William and Mary, Queen Anne, Chippendale, Federal and Empire

Each piece is documented, so that the Duncan Phyfe room, for instance, had its architectural elements removed from a specific house in New York where Phyfe furniture was used. You can find a striking plantation dining room removed in its entirety from a South Carlina home, a New England kitchen, a Shaker bedroom, a New York parlour, and a flying staircase copied from the Montmorenci estate in North Carolina. One oft-photographed room features authentic 18th Century Chinese wallpaper that covers both the walls and the ceilings.

There are more than rooms at Winterthur. The Cobblestone Court, right inside the building, looks like a movie set for an 18th Century film. This courtyard features the facades of four different buildings, including The Red Lion Inn and a typical Connecticut home.

However, there are several different tours and things get a little tricky here. The 16-room *Winterthur in Spring* tour includes some of the best rooms but is available only during spring and summer. The *Reserved Tour* is two hours long and includes many upstairs rooms and the cobblestone courtyard. It is not offered during spring or Christmas. *The Yuletide Tour*, also very popular, features some of the top rooms, dressed for Christmas. The American Sampler Tour is available all the time, but it takes place in the new wing, not the main house, and somehow, the rooms are not of the same quality.

Besides the main museum, there are extensive gardens at Winterthur — sixty acres of greenery, dotted with woods and copses. During spring, flowering displays include azaleas and dogwoods. A special tram takes you through the gardens. The main Visitors Center (where you get the garden tram and tickets) offers a luncheon buffet and a marvelous book and gift shop. Also here are the free maps and brochures you will need for your tour. And for those who want to do some serious shopping, there are rugs and chairs and china for sale at the Gallery and Plant Shop, a luxurious little building located adjacent to the main house.

For lovers of 18th Century architecture and furnishings this is the premier place to visit. Only a multi-millionaire could lavish this attention to detail on his "collection".

HOURS: Tues.-Sat.: 9:30-5. Sun.: 12-5. Closed Mondays & major holidays.
ADMISSION: (General) Adults: $8.00; Seniors, students: $6.50. Under 12 free. (Reserved Tour) Adults: $12.50; Children 12-16: $6.00. Under 12 not admitted.
LOCATION: NJ Turnpike to 295 & Delaware Mem. Bridge, then north on I95 to Route 52 (Exit 7). Left on 52 to Winterthur.
TELEPHONE: 302-888-4600. Reserved Tour: 800-448-3883 Mon.-Fri.

HAGLEY MUSEUM

Another DuPont complex and a huge one at that. The acreage includes homes, offices, barns and the black powder apparatus of the original gunpowder mills that was the foundation of the DuPont fortune. The "museum" section offers exhibits that trace industrial development throughout the 19th Century. From there you take a small bus to visit the other sections such as the original DuPont home. The bus goes through a steep wooded area along the banks of the Brandywine River, passing machine shops, roller mills and other stops of interest.

At the original DuPont residence, called *"Eleutherian Mills"* you find a handsome Georgian structure surrounded by gardens. Nearby is the office where the company began. It still contains the old desks and ledgers. There are guides posted at both these places, but you are free to roam around the gardens, the barn (which contains both a Conestoga wagon and antique carriages and cars) and the cooper's workshop.

Also on the premises, along the bus stops, are an early school-house where children of the workers could learn their ABCs and a coffee shop. A picnic area and several vending machines are on the grounds also, while the gift shop is near the Visitors Center.

HOURS: Apr.-Dec.: Daily 9:30-4:30. Jan.-Mar. Tues.-Sat.; Sun.: 1-5.
ADMISSION: Adults: $6.00; Seniors, students: $5.00; Children 6-14: $2.50; Under 6 free. Family rate: $17.00
LOCATION: Greenville, Delaware, off Route 141
TELEPHONE: 302-658-2400

SOUTH STREET SEAPORT

Boston has its Quincy Market. Baltimore has its Inner Harbor. It was only a matter of time before New York jumped on the bandwagon and restored its own quaint seaport area. The South Street Seaport has been years in the making. But now there is enough holiday atmosphere about the place to make it one of New York's most popular tourist spots. Busloads of New Jerseyans come in every day to walk the broad plazas, shop, eat, and vie for elbow space with Wall Street executives.

The "museum" (as it is called) is actually the entire restoration of several blocks around New York's earliest seaport. Schermerhorn Row, Water Street, Fulton Street and South Street boast some of the few remaining Federal style townhouses to be found in the big city. These gracious rowhouses have been beautifully restored and now house shops and restaurants. At the water's edge there are several ships available for touring. These are of a later vintage than you might expect — the one I visited was the 1911 four-masted vessel, The Peking — but photos and displays emphasize the rigors of the sea even in the early 20th Century. A more fanciful view of the sea may be obtained from a ride on the side-wheelers, *The Andrew Fletcher* and the *Dewitt Clinton*, which offer tours of Manhattan's waterways. These narrated boat tours which depart from Pier 16 have proved vastly popular. There are now music and dance tours and special group charters. The sailings start at noon during warm weather, and depart every two hours.

Ship tours and rides cost extra, of course, as does entrance to the formal exhibit galleries, the Children's Center and the guided tour of the historic area. Tickets may be purchased at the Pier 16 ticketbooth or the Museum Visitor Center.

But the main attraction is the food and shops, so on to the Fulton Market (built on the site of the old Fulton Fish Market), where you can enjoy the latest craze — ethnic fast food! Sushi, moussaka, bagels and lox, tortillas, pizza, empanadas, etc., are sold from stands and niches everywhere in this three-story building. For better seafood there is a good restaurant on the top floor plus Sloppy Louie's and Sweets (both about a block or two away). Reservations are required for these unless you happen to luck into very dull day.

For those who don't eat, there are plenty of cute and quaint (and expensive) shops around. The latest section to open up at South Street is Pier 17, yet another pavillion devoted to food and fancy goods.

There are wide open walking spaces here and on a sunny day, with the wind off the river, it is New York as we would like it to be. No cars, no muggers, (no place to buy an aspirin or a Band-Aid or a box of tissues either, should you need them) but after all, you can't expect everything.

HOURS: Daily for shops and restaurants.
ADMISSION: (Museum): Adults: $6.00; Seniors: $5.00; Students: $4.00; Children: $3.00. Boatride and combination tickets extra.
LOCATION: Fulton & South Sts. just off FDR Drive, NYC.
TELEPHONE: (Museum): 212-669-9424; (Boat Ride) 212-385-0791

See Also: *Pennsbury Manor* and *Historic Speedwell* (Homes of the Rich and Famous), *Jockey Hollow/Wick Farm* (Where Washington Slept, Ate and Fought), *New Jersey Historical Museums* (Museums of All Kinds) and such tours as *Bordentown* and *Mt. Holly* in the "Walking Tours" chapter.

MUSEUMS OF ALL KINDS

In This Chapter You Will Find:

New Jersey — Art & Science Museums

New Jersey State Museum, Newark Museum, Montclair Art Museum, Morris Museum of Arts and Science, Bergen Museum, Monmouth Museum, Other Museums of Art and Science.

New Jersey — Specialty Museums

Franklin Mineral Museum, The Golf House, Bell Labs Exhibit, Squibb Headquarters, Windmill Museum, Doll Castle Doll Museum, Aviation Hall of Fame, Campbell Museum, Edison Memorial Tower and Museum.

New Jersey —Historical Museums

Museum of Early Trades and Crafts, Schoolhouse Museum, Ocean County Historical Museum, Hopewell Museum, Ocean City Historical Museum, Spy House Museum, Cape May Historical Museum, New Jersey Historical Society, Monmouth County Historical Association, Camden County Historical Society, Paterson Museum, American Labor Museum.

New York Museums

Metropolitan Museum of Art, American Museum of Natural History, The Cloisters, The Frick Collection, Museum of Modern Art, Forbes Galleries.

Pennsylvania Museums

Franklin Institute, Philadelphia Museum of Art, Pennsylvania Academy of Fine Arts, Rosenbach Museum and Library, University of Pennsylvania Archeology Museum, Barnes Foundation, The Mercer Mile, Brandywine River Museum.

NEW JERSEY STATE MUSEUM

It stands in Trenton, pristine and white against the backdrop of the Delaware River, the very model of a modern, well-kept museum. There is no admission charge. The separate Museum Theater, just adjacent, offers a well-proportioned stage and comfortable seating for movies and live performances. The Planetarium, housed in its own section, seats 150 people and offers two weekend shows. There is a large lunchroom ringed by vending machines that is perfect for school children and families who bring their own lunches. The restrooms are clean, well maintained and plentiful. The State Museum at Trenton seems to have everything — except enough visitors. Nowadays, there are many weekend specials to attract customers.

Set up as a family museum, with exhibits to interest both children and adults, the museum offers a balance between the art and science sections. The addition of several new galleries of paintings and decorative arts, which range from 17th century urns to 20th century cubist canvasses, brings a new dimension to the Jersey collection. The natural science section offers an excellent collection of stuffed animals posed within their natural habitats. Another large display is devoted to life around the seashore with relief dioramas depicting the chain of tidal life from worms to higher life. There are also full exhibits on insects, minerals and the solar system. The first floor is devoted to changing exhibits of art and sculpture and special items.

As for the **planetarium**, which costs $1.00 extra, shows are given two or three times on weekends and during the week also during summer. Children under seven are not admitted, although there are special "Stars for Tots" shows once in a while. The shows vary, the seats are comfortable and the simulated sky has great depth once the stars get moving around. Laser concerts are scheduled here also. There is a gift shop outside the planetarium with lots of science items. Another gift shop upstairs has a larger selection.

For people living within easy driving distance of the New Jersey State Museum, it is a bargain not to be missed. For those of us farther away, it is a worthwhile stop when you are down in the Princeton-Trenton area. Parking is a problem on weekdays, so try for a weekend visit. Free.

HOURS: Tues.-Sat. 9-4:45. Sun. 12-5.
LOCATION: 205 West State Street, Trenton. Use Route 29 along Delaware River or Route 1 into State Street.
TELEPHONE: 609-292-6464

THE NEWARK MUSEUM

Recently expanded, the Newark Museum is not only twice its previous size, it has also been completely redesigned so that it is open, airy, convenient (yes, there are now elevators) - a first class museum that is worth every penny that was put into it. There is now room to show off the collection - American paintings, Tibetan statues, African masks, - plus plenty of space for the special exhibits that come and go. A center court allows for lunches and lectures, and the well designed corridors make for easy walking.

The Asian Galleries on the third floor include not only the museum's fine Tibetan collection but Indian, Chinese and Korean treasures as well. Here, as in the other galleries, the exhibits are well mounted and the explanatory material easy to read. The second floor includes both 19th Century American art and lots of contemporary painting.

In another wing of the second floor is the completely revamped Junior Gallery and mini-zoo. The terrariums and aquariums found here are a far cry from the strange funnel-like enclosures they used to have for the small animals. Nearby is the Native American Gallery with its large collection of costumes and artifacts. And of course there is a program hall for all the school classes that come to the museum.

It may be a little confusing at first, moving from one wing to another, but floor plan guides are available. The small Dreyfuss Planetarium is on the left hand side of the garden entrance. This 50 seat facility offers sky shows to the general public on week-ends and holidays for $1.00. The museum also includes a pleasant garden complete with a lifelike sculpture of George Segal's Tollhouse. A tiny one-room schoolhouse that dates back to 1784 and a Fire Museum are also part of the garden scene.

There are two museum shops - one for kids, one for adults. And attended parking is available in the adjacent parking lot, corner of Central & University Avenues. Have your parking ticket stamped at the Information Desk.

The Ballantine House (which has a separate listing in this book) is next door. You enter through the museum. Free.

HOURS: 12-5 Tues.-Sun., except major holidays.
LOCATION: 49 Washington St., Newark (facing Washington Park)
TELEPHONE: 201-596-6550

THE MONTCLAIR ART MUSEUM

A true art museum nestled in a town that was once an artists' center, the Montclair Museum reflects a high level of community support. Built in 1912, this is not somebody's leftover mansion but a solid, stone neo-Classical edifice dedicated to the showing of painting and sculpture. The major collection is of American paintings covering a period of three centuries. Many familiar names — Edward Hopper, Mary Cassatt, Benjamin West — are represented here, along with a host of other American artists. Two large rooms are reserved for the special exhibits which are often of important American painters of various schools.

Additional collections include prints, tapestries and needlepoint, the Whitney silver collection, Chinese snuff bottles, and American costumes and accessories. And upstairs, a permanent Indian collection is of interest to the kids. Costumes and artifacts go beyond New Jersey's Lenni Lenape — the Plains and Southwest Indians are given equal treatment here with good displays of Sioux and Navajo dress.

This is quite an active museum what with lecture series, morning coffee hours, gallery talks, Saturday night movies and an ongoing art school downstairs.

HOURS: Tues., Wed., Fri., Sat. 10-5; 2nd & 4th Thurs. 2-9; Sun. 2-5. Closed major holidays.
ADMISSION: Adults $4.00; seniors & students $2.00; under 18 free. Thurs. free.
LOCATION: Bloomfield Ave. & South Mountain Ave., Montclair, Essex County.
TELEPHONE: 201-746-5555

MORRIS MUSEUM OF ARTS AND SCIENCES

On rainy days, empty weekends or just any day, there's nothing like a quick trip to a local bastion of culture to uplift the spirit, educate, and get the kids out of the house all in one fell swoop. The Morris Museum of Arts and Sciences is one of these dependable bastions. Housed in a lovely old mansion surrounded by great trees, it is small enough not to be to exhausting to young children. It is also varied enough to appeal to children of all ages, plus their parents. Science and technology exhibits have included displays on computers, sound waves and fibers.

There is also a rock and mineral exhibit. (This one comes complete with a dark room for viewing fluorescent rocks.) The natural sciences are represented by glass-encased exhibits of stuffed animals in their natural environments, plus a live zoo downstairs. The children usually trek down to this room with its lazy alligator and turtles safely inside glass cases. And since it is called a museum of arts and sciences, there is always at least one major art exhibit on display that is changed every few months. Recent major expansion allows for extra space for these art shows and traveling exhibits, plus a nice view of the outside.

Social Sciences are found on the second floor. Here, 3rd, 4th and 5th graders can see graphic examples of their studies of both North American Indian and colonial life. Besides the colonial kitchen and everything you'd ever want to know about the Lenni Lenape Indians, the second floor also offers a special "touch and feel" room for two-to-seven year olds.

Other popular exhibits are the model railroad in the basement and the tiny dinosaur room, also downstairs. And last, but not least, is the Museum Gift Shop where my son has bought at least thirty rocket erasers at 35 cents each, only to lose them mysteriously as soon as we get home. The museum also includes a comfortable 300 seat theater which is the scene of many special events and shows.

HOURS: Mon.-Sat. 10-5; Sun. 1-5.
ADMISSION: Adults $2.00; seniors and children $1.00
LOCATION: Route 24 to Normandy Parkway, Morristown, Morris County
TELEPHONE: 201-538-0454

BERGEN MUSEUM

Here is another local museum that offers both the arts and sciences, with a nice balance between the adult and children's exhibits. Although much of the gallery area in this 25-year-old private institution is given over to changing exhibits, the permanent collection includes the Hackensack Mastodon and the newer Dwarskill Mastodon and several other natural history displays.

For children there is the Discovery Room with touch and feel exhibits and a small "shadow" room a la Franklin Institute. Another room displays snakes, frogs and fishtanks and of course the inevitable Indian collection is placed about. Changing exhibits include photographs, invitational paintings and technological displays. And there is always some family activity offered at 2 P.M. on Saturdays. The museum is located (or should I say, hidden) in the right wing of the Bergen County Community Services Building, a huge brick building in the typically bureaucratic style of architecture.

> **HOURS:** Tues. - Sat.: 10-5: Sun.: 1-5.
> **ADMISSION:** Adults: $2.50; Children, Seniors: $1.00
> **LOCATION:** Corner of E. Ridgewood and Fairview Aves. Paramus, Bergen County
> **TELEPHONE:** 201-265-1248

THE MONMOUTH MUSEUM

This handsome, modern building, set in the middle of a community college campus, offers two distinct sections. One is for adults, and the other, a new, enlarged wing is devoted to children. Each section offers a single exhibit devoted to a specific theme. The exhibit in the children's wing is changed every two years. A recent exhibit concerned America's westward expansion and included everything from frying pans to wagon wheels to desert snakes, all with a touch and feel emphasis. The newest show has to do with fossils and dinosaurs and again, the single theme will take up the entire space of the wing.

The adult section is also changed completely every so often. The exhibit I saw depicted seaside life in the late Victorian era, complete with wooden carousel and turn of the century costumes. Very well done. There was a good balance between the written information, the old photographs and newspapers and the costumed mannequins.

The children's section was quite popular with school groups and hence the expansion so that there is more space for both sections. As for individuals, it's quite a nice place to visit, but call first to make sure an exhibit is on, since it takes some time to change from one complete theme to another. And be aware, that although the Monmouth Museum is located inside a public college campus, it is a private institution and is not free.

HOURS: Tues. - Sat. 10-4:30. Sun. 1-5.
ADMISSION: Adults: $2.00; Children, Seniors, Students: $1.00
DIRECTIONS: Exit 109, Garden State Parkway, then west on Newman Springs Road (Route 520) to entrance of Brookdale Community College, Lincroft, Monmouth County.
TELEPHONE: 908-747-2266.

OTHER N.J. MUSEUMS OF ART AND SCIENCE

JERSEY CITY MUSEUM: Located on the top floor of the Jersey City main library, the museum is a combination of rotating exhibits of contemporary art (usually one-person shows) and a permanent gallery of 19th Century paintings and furnishings. Free. *Hours:* Wed.: 10:30-8, Tues. - Sat.: 10:30-5. Closed Saturdays in summer. *Location:* 472 Jersey Ave., Jersey City. *Telephone:* 201-547-4514.

RUTGERS GEOLOGY MUSEUM: A super-large room ringed by a balcony comprises this science museum located on the second floor of the Geology building on the Rutgers campus. A reconstructed mastodon, charts of geological periods, small fossils, mineral display, etc. Interesting lectures and demonstrations for school groups. The small gift shop has small rocks and minerals for sale at very reasonable prices. Free. *Hours:* Mon.: 1-4; Tues.-Fri.: 9-12, Sept.-June. Call for summer hours. *Location:* College Ave., Queens College, Rutgers, New Brunswick. *Telephone:* 908-932-7243.

JANE VOORHEES ZIMMERLI ART MUSEUM: Housed in modern Voorhees Hall, on the Rutgers campus, the art gallery includes a permanent collection of American artists with many well-known names, such as Winslow Homer, among the exhibits. Prints, sculpture and changing displays. Free. *Hours:* Weekdays except Wed.: 10-4:30; Weekends: 12-5, Closed Sat. & Aug. in summer. *Location:* Voorhees Hall, Hamilton St., Queens Campus, Rutgers Univ., New Brunswick. *Telephone:* 908-932-7237.

PRINCETON ART MUSEUM: Mentioned in the section on Princeton but worth another mention here since it is one of the nicest art museums in New Jersey. Recently expanded and now beautifully laid out; modern, well-lit, and with a collection that encompasses European and Oriental art as well as American. Free. *Location:* Princeton Campus, Nassau St. & Washington Road, Princeton, Mercer County. *Telephone:* 609-452-3788.

NOYES MUSEUM: A striking modern museum set on the edge of the Brigantine Wildlife Refuge which specializes in changing exhibits of contemporary painting and sculpture. A well-mounted collection of duck decoys is also on display. The building overlooks a lilypad lake and is quite pleasant. *Hours:* Wed.-Sat., 11-4; Sun., 12-4. *Admission:* Adults: $2.00; Seniors: $1.00; Children: $.50; Free on Fridays. *Location:* Lily Lake Road, Oceanville, Atlantic County. *Telephone:* 609-652-8848.

MIDDLESEX COUNTY MUSEUM: Set in a handsomely restored 1741 Georgian mansion (known first as Ivy Hall and then as the Cornelius Low House) the museum offers changing exhibits of art, local history and special themes. A one-theme exhibit often takes up the entire house. Entrance is most easily attained through the Busch Campus of Rutgers University. Free. *Hours:* Tues.-Sun., 1-4. *Location:* 1225 River Road, Piscataway. *Telephone:* 908-745-4177.

TRENTON CITY MUSEUM: Housed in the Victorian Italianate building known as Ellarslie, which was recently restored, the museum offers a combination of changing art exhibits and a permanent collection of local historical material. Ellarslie is set inside of Trenton's Cadwalader Park, which was designed by Frederick Law Olmstead. Free. *Hours:* Tues.-Sat.: 11-3; Sun.: 2-4. *Location:* Cadwalader Park, Parkside Ave., Trenton. *Telephone:* 609-989-3632.

New Jersey Specialty Museums

FRANKLIN MINERAL MUSEUM

New Jersey is both the zinc mining and fluorescent rock capital of the world. While this may not be on the same level as a financial or entertainment capital, it does provide one mecca for rockhounds — Franklin Borough in Sussex County. Here, in a small building nestled in the green-clad mountains you will find the Franklin Mineral Museum.

Children seem to have a fascination with rocks — as any mother who has ever dumped odd-sized stones out of her darling's pockets can attest. At the Franklin Mineral Museum you can dig for rocks with pick and shovel at the adjacent Buckwheat Dump. The museum itself is divided into three sections: a fluorescent rock display, a general exhibit on zinc and other minerals, and a replica of an actual mine.

Once you enter the unprepossessing building and pay the reasonable entrance fee, you are ushered into a long, narrow room by the genial guide. There you face a row of gray, ordinary rocks of varying sizes behind a glass case. The guide flicks off the lights, and lo and behold — the rocks turn into an extraordinary array of shining colors. Green, purple, blue luminous rocks, many with unusual patterns, glow behind the glass while the guide explains their names and properties. The guide flicks on the light and it's all over. The rocks are back to their old pedestrian form.

Next on the agenda is a tour of the mine replica. Zinc mines, it seems, were much safer than coal mines, and the plaster labyrinth we entered was not so much scary as claustrophobic. We passed ore cars and plaster miners while our guide assured us that the walls were friendly and that miners only fear the large excavations. Once the tours are over, you are free to examine the exhibits in the third room which include unusual rocks and zinc mining materials. A gift shop in the main lobby also sells a very good selection of rocks, gemstones and necklaces at non-inflated prices.

But for many, the highlight of the trip is the chance to go prospecting in the rock dump at the back of the museum, although chances of finding a true specimen are slim. You must bring your own equipment — pickaxes, hammers, shovels (or just your own hands since many of the rocks are loose) plus a bag to carry your specimens. Those who hope to find a fluorescent rock need a special lamp to determine whether then have a genuine article. School age children love the dumphunting, but they must be accompanied by an adult until they are fourteen.

> **HOURS:** July, Aug.: Wed. - Sat.: 10-4; Sun.: 12:30 - 4:30. Spring & Fall: Fri., Sat.: 10-4; Sun.: 12:30-4:30. Tours take about one hour.

ADMISSION: Adults: $2.00; Children: $1.00; Under 5 free. Same rate applies for dump.

DIRECTIONS: Route 80 to Route 15 Sparta, then Route 517 to Franklin then one mile north on 23. Museum is on Evans St.

TELEPHONE: 201-827-3481

THE GOLF HOUSE

Set among the posh country estates of Far Hills, the Golf House is a combination of museum, stately house and working headquarters of the United States Golf Association. It is truly a mansion in the grand manner with well-placed spruce, pine and dogwood trees framing the landscape. A circular driveway leads you up to the white portico where you might almost expect a butler to take your bags. However, you simply park in the adjoining lot and enter the massive doors. In the front lobby you will find a combination information stand and gift shop. You can pick up brochures and proceed around the mansion from there.

There are two floors of exhibit space and among the most popular rooms are those with hands-on displays. You can practice putting, take a video quiz, trace the history of the game and compare the swings of various players. There is even a golf video game which you can play (using joysticks) with one or two players. If you like it well enough you can buy a copy at the gift shop.

Other exhibits include a history of the game itself, plus rooms devoted to golfing costumes, golf clubs, and the evolution of the golf ball (from feathery to gutta percha to rubber). There is even a whole exhibit devoted to turf and how to keep the greens well maintained. Other traditional exhibits include pictures and information on golf greats (such as Bob Jones) as well as famous people who happened to play golf. Some of the well-prized momentos are the golf clubs of presidents Woodrow Wilson, Franklin Roosevelt and of course Dwight Eisenhower. Also on view is the Moon Club used by Alan Shepard to play on the lunar surface and the special clubs used by trick-shot artist Joe Kirkwood.

The house also contains a magnificent flying staircase, paintings and sculpture and a library of 8000 volumes. One of New Jersey's nicest freebies (donations are accepted of course) and a great place to take visitors who enjoy the game.

HOURS: Mon. - Fri. 9-5; Weekends: 10-4. Closed holidays.
LOCATION: Route 512, east of Route 202, Far Hills, Somerset County
TELEPHONE: 908-234-2300

THE BELL LABS EXHIBIT

One result of the breakup of AT&T was the disassembling of a very nice science exhibit in the huge lobby of Bell Labs. Not that many people came to see it, but occasional visitors did ogle the talking computer and the bouncing ball molecules. Now, all that is gone.

However, there is still the historical exhibit over at the right hand side of the lobby. Some display cases and you can see the original receiver and hear Alexander Graham Bell shouting "Mr. Watson, come here, I need you!" You can also hear a 1933 stereophonic recording of Leopold Stokowski conducting symphonic music (kids love this — I don't think they ever hear good orchestra music nowadays). Another recording you can hear is the original soundtrack of the first talking picture, "The Jazz Singer," with Al Jolson coming over rather tinnily through the receiver. There are models of computer chips and a mock-up of a communications satellite. Bell Labs never promoted the exhibit very much, and you may feel peculiar tiptoeing around the exhibit cases, but for those in the area, this is a nice place to visit. Free.

HOURS: Weekdays: 8:15-5:30. Weekends: 1-5:30.
LOCATION: South St. & Mountain Ave., Murray Hill, (New Providence) Union County.
TELEPHONE: 908-582-3000.

SQUIBB HEADQUARTERS

The company is now called Bristol Myers Squibb, by the way. There are really two museums here. One is a small pharmaceutical exhibit that traces the history of Squibb products from their humble beginnings and includes old-fashioned microscopes, old patent medicine bottles, etc. The other is the adjacent art gallery which rotates its shows. Because new artists are often shown here and reviewed by art critics, the galleries have achieved a certain importance in the New Jersey art world. Another "show" you get here is the spectacular gathering of waterfowl that come by the hundreds in fall and winter to stay at the pond that fronts the complex. Free.

HOURS: Mon. - Fri.: 9-5, Thurs. until 8. Weekends: 1-5
LOCATION: Route 206 between Princeton and Lawrenceville, Mercer County

THE WINDMILL MUSEUM

Designed and built by the late Poul Jorgenson and his wife, the sixty foot Volendam mill is a seven story structure with sail arms that measure 68 feet from end to end. Although the sail arms can turn, the windmill is not used as such but as a museum. Old milling tools, ancient millstones, and wooden shoes are on display. The windmill is set way out in a rustic area of the state. Best to call first, for an appointment. Group tours given.

HOURS: May - Sept.: Weekends, 12-4
ADMISSION: Adults: $2.00; Children: $1.00
LOCATION: Adamic Hill Road, near Milford, off Route 519, Hunterdon County
TELEPHONE: 908-995-4365

DOLL CASTLE DOLL MUSEUM

No, this is not a collection of doll princesses set inside a lifesize doll castle. Rather, it is a museum run by the editors of Doll Castle News (a magazine devoted to information for and by doll collectors), and is housed upstairs over the printing office. Over 2000 dolls and stuffed animals are on display, plus miniatures, dollhouses and such. The collection includes corn husk, cloth and soft-sculpture dolls as well as the traditional kind. The emphasis is not so much on antique dolls as on the variety of 20th Century creations. The museum is meant for both children and doll enthusiasts (and according to the owner here, doll collecting is the second most popular hobby in the United States).

HOURS: June - Oct.: Wed., Thurs., Fri.: 10-4 and by appt.
ADMISSION: Adults: $2.25; Children $.50.
LOCATION: 37 Belvidere Ave., Washington, Warren County.
TELEPHONE: 908-689-6513; 689-7042

AVIATION HALL OF FAME

Aviation achievements from balloon voyages in 1850 Perth Amboy to modern day flights are commemorated in this interesting museum which is actually in two separate sections. One section is located on top of the stairs at the old Teterboro Airport Control Tower where views of the runway and a short film on aviation history await. Most of all, you can listen in to pilot-control tower conversation over the radio. They even offer birthday parties up here for those who love the atmosphere. Kids can use fake telephones to make believe they are bringing in the aircraft.

The larger museum section is on the other side of the airfield. Here you will find a house filled with aviation memorabilia and displays (which include a small, hands-on helicopter.) Outside, in the back, you can climb aboard an old-fashioned propeller plane, and see how the folks in the Forties and Fifties used to ride. (At least the seats were wider then — and only two across!).

For those who remember when a Sunday afternoon outing with the kids was a jaunt to the airport, and for Air Force veterans, this is a fun place to visit. But it's best to call first, since much of the work force here is volunteer, and there may be unexpected closings.

HOURS: 10-4 Daily
ADMISSION: Adults: $3.00; Children: $2.00; Seniors: $2.00.
LOCATION: Atlantic Aviation Hangar, Teterboro Airport, off Route 46, Bergen County. Look for sign.
TELEPHONE: 201-288-6344

CAMPBELL MUSEUM

For America's biggest soup company what else but a collection of soup tureens, bowls and ladles? However, since the decoration of tureens was considered high art in the 17th and 18th centuries, the collection here is quite dazzling. Porcelain, silver, pewter — the most extensive collection in the world is found here and includes pieces used by European royalty. Because part of the collection always travels, what is shown will vary. However, such stellar pieces as a huge silver tureen crafted into a warship (from Catherine the Great's table) makes a visit here well worth the trip. You will also find cows, boar's heads, rabbits, and chickens fashioned in clay and used for serving soup. A movie depicting how tureens are fashioned is shown in the Visitor Center, by appointment. Light snacks are often served. And during the Christmas period a display of antique toys are on view. The museum, by the way, is housed next to the Campbell Administration building which is easily accessible from Route 30. Free.

HOURS: Mon. - Fri. 9-4:30. Closed holidays.
LOCATION: Campbell Place, Camden.
TELEPHONE: 609-342-6440.

EDISON MEMORIAL TOWER AND MUSEUM

The tower is shaped like an electric light with a bulb on top and commemorates the site of Edison's Menlo Park laboratory, birthplace of the incandescent bulb. The original laboratory was moved to Greenfield, Michigan, by Henry Ford for his Americana Museum, but there is a small museum here with lightbulbs, phonographs, and other mementos of Edison's achievement. Free.
HOURS: Tues. - Fri.: 12:30-4; Sat., Sun.: 12:30-4:30.
LOCATION: Christie St., Menlo Park, in Edison State Park, Middlesex County.
TELEPHONE: 908-549-3299

New Jersey: Historical Museums

MUSEUM OF EARLY TRADES AND CRAFTS

Created in 1970 to preserve the life and times of early settlers, this small museum shows the labor of love of its creator and curator. Thirty-eight years of collecting and research went into the exhibits. Diaries, ledgers, advertisements, broadsides, and newspapers were scoured for details of everyday life in the Colonies — most particularly life in the New Jersey colony. The exhibit on brooms, for instance, is based on the business of one particular broommaker in Florham Park. He started out with one broommaking machine, used local cattails for the brush, and did business as a sideline to farming. Later, as times prospered, the broommaker had several employees and a full time business. This information and much, much more is imparted by the curator and docents who greet each visitor at the door.

For the first generation of settlers, home meant a one-room shack with a dirt floor. Furniture was crudely made from the wood of surrounding trees. You ate what you grew or what you bartered. Mother was the family doctor and every household had an herb garden that was used for medicine as well as flavoring.

Major exhibits of the museum change every few months but each one takes a particular trade or craft and follows it through three generations. The exhibit I encountered emphasized shoes. Shoes were made by the father of the family in the first generation. Cobblers came in later. Leather was taken from the hides of cows that were slaughtered for food. Shoes which were made at night by candlelight had neither right nor left feet. Both halves of the pair were exactly the same. Just imagine — a colonial mother didn't have to stand there in the morning and repeat, "No, the left shoe goes on the left foot," as I do.

Besides the changing exhibits, there is a permanent room set up as a colonial kitchen. The museum also contains a complete set of tools for the 34 trades that existed in New Jersey at the time of the Revolution. Although the museum is not very large, the lectures are so comprehensive that you should plan to spend at least an hour here. Special craft demonstrations on first and third Saturdays.

HOURS: Tues.- Sat.: 10-4; Sun.: 2-5. Closed major holidays.
ADMISSION: Adults: $2.00 Children: $1.00
LOCATION: Main Street (Route 24) and Green Village Road, Madison, Morris County
TELEPHONE: 201-377-2982

SCHOOLHOUSE MUSEUM

Although this historical museum is set inside an 1873 schoolhouse, only one section of the vast paraphenalia collected here is devoted to the little old schoolroom. Besides the teacher's platform, desks, maps and schoolbooks, there is also a colonial and Victorian kitchen and sections set up as typical rooms of the 19th Century. Over 3,000 items are jammed into the one huge room — everything from bobbin lace to beaver hats. Upstairs, the attic has even more with lots of 19th Century dresses, firemen's uniforms, etc. Memorabilia of the church, early Dutch settlers and local celebrities (including a well-known actor), tools and harness and more are all to be found in this well-stocked museum. Free. (Donations accepted).

HOURS: Mid-April - Mid-Nov.: Sun. 3-5. Wed. by appt.
LOCATION: 650 East Glen Ave. right off Route 17, Ridgewood, Bergen County.
TELEPHONE: 201-445-1778 (Director): 201-447-3242 (Museum).

OCEAN COUNTY HISTORICAL MUSEUM

Basically a historic house with rooms set up in comfortable 19th Century fashion. A music-library room, and a well-set dining room set the tone. The Victorian kitchen is of particular interest since it is chock full of useful gadgets that have since been deemed non-essential. A gizmo for softening corks had the curators mystified until a tourist told them what it was.

Upstairs a child's bedroom is all set up and a small school-house impresses the youngsters. Downstairs, in the basement, there are museum-type memorabilia including a machine for harvesting cranberries and pictures of Lakehurst during the age of dirigibles.

HOURS: Tues. and Thurs.: 1-3; Sat.: 10-12
ADMISSION: $1.00 (donations)
LOCATION: 26 Hadley Ave., Toms River, Ocean County
TELEPHONE: 908-341-1880

HOPEWELL MUSEUM

Again, a combination historic house/museum with rooms done up in particular periods. The house itself is Victorian, but the rooms display Colonial, Empire and Victorian furnishings. An 1880 organ and a Joseph Bonaparte sideboard are prized possessions here. In the back of the mansion, an addition houses a large Indian collection and a great many costumed mannequins. The costumes include ballgowns, wedding dresses and other finery worn in the 19th Century. Upstairs there are even more decorated rooms since this house is much larger inside than it seems from the exterior. Guided tour. Free. (Donations accepted).

HOURS: Mon., Wed., Sat.: 2-4:30
LOCATION: 28 East Broad St. (Route 518) Hopewell, Mercer County
TELEPHONE: 609-466-0103

OCEAN CITY HISTORICAL MUSEUM

Life in the 1890's is graphically depicted in this historical museum which harks back to the heyday of the Jersey shore. Ocean City, the quiet and sober neighbor of Atlantic City, has attracted families to its beaches since 1879. Costumes, furnishings, Indian artifacts and mementos of the wreck of the Sindia are all here. Free.

HOURS: Mon.-Fri.: 10-4; Sat.: 1-4. Closed holidays, and possibly winter.
LOCATION: 409 Wesley Ave., Ocean City, Cape May County.
TELEPHONE: 609-399-1801.

SPY HOUSE MUSEUM

A combination of historic site and two museums make up this unusual complex by the seashore. One section is a cottage erected in 1663 and called "The Spy House" because it was a favorite meeting place of Revolutionary War spies. The Shoal Harbor Marine Museum and the Penelope Stout Museum of Crafts of Man comprise the rest of the complex. You can find lobster pots, eeling equipment, and a variety of furniture in this tripart museum. Many special weekend events, from colonial baking to military encampments, are planned from spring to fall.

HOURS: Mon. - Fri.: 2-4; Sat.: 1-4.
ADMISSION: Donation
LOCATION: 119 Port Monmouth Rd., Port Monmouth. (Take Exit 117 off Garden State Parkway to Route 36E to Port Monmouth.)
TELEPHONE: 908-787-1807

CAPE MAY COUNTY HISTORICAL MUSEUM

Housed in a well-preserved 18th Century home, the museum includes an 1820 dining room all set up, a children's room with antique toys, and much glassware and china. Across the yard the well stocked barn features harpoons from Cape May's whaling past, Indian artifacts and farm implements. Here also is the huge glass prism top to the old Cape May lighthouse. Visits are by guided tour and take about an hour. The adjacent Genealogy Room is of interest to many historians because of the number of Mayflower descendents in the Cape May area. There is also a small gift shop in the museum proper.

> **HOURS:** Summer: Mon. - Sat., 10-4; Spring & Fall: Tues. - Sat., 10-4. Jan. - Mar. Sat. only
> **ADMISSION:** Adults $2.00; Under 12 free.
> **LOCATION:** Route 9 at Cape May Court House, Cape May County
> **TELEPHONE:** 609-465-3535

NEW JERSEY HISTORICAL SOCIETY

One of the most extensive collections of books, manuscripts and other material about the Garden State is found in the library of this 4-story building. The museum section consists of rooms set up with colonial, federal and Victorian furnishings, and smaller rooms relating to specific interests such as music and printing. Artifacts of everyday life, plus rotating exhibits on quiltmaking, shipbuilding, etc. are featured here.

> **HOURS:** Wed.-Fri., 3rd Sat.: 10-4
> **ADMISSION:** $2.00
> **LOCATION:** 230 Broadway, Newark.
> **TELEPHONE:** 201-483-3939

MONMOUTH COUNTY HISTORICAL ASSOCIATION

Another combination of museum and society headquarters is housed in a handsome, 3-story Georgian colonial not far from the scene of the battle of Monmouth. Impressive collections of mahogany furniture, old china, glassware and paintings furnish the historical rooms of the "mansion" (it was actually built in 1931). You can also find specialty rooms devoted to dolls, old boxes, and so forth, plus an attic filled with bicycles, pony carts, and other leftovers from the 18th and 19th centuries. A new "hands-on experience" appeals to children. The Association also administers several historic houses in Monmouth County.

HOURS: Tues. - Sat.: 10-4; Sun.: 1-4.
ADMISSION: Adults: $2.00; Children: $1.00; Seniors: $1.50.
LOCATION: 70 Court St., Freehold.
TELEPHONE: 908-462-1466

CAMDEN COUNTY HISTORICAL SOCIETY

Three sections include: a museum with early American glass, fire-fighting equipment, military artifacts and the tools of early handicrafts set up in "shops" of cobblers, carpenters, coopers, etc.; a library with 18,000 books and pamphlets, manuscripts and newspapers; and Pomona Hall, an excellent example of early Georgian architecture furnished in both 18th and 19th Century fashion. Pomona Hall is a separate house, connected by a breezeway to the museum section. The guided tour will take you through many well-furnished rooms.

HOURS: Mon. - Thurs.: 12:30-4:30; Sat.: 1-4; Sun.: 2-4:30. Closed Aug. & major holidays.
ADMISSION: Adults: $2.00; Seniors: $1.00; Students: $.75; under 16 free.
LOCATION: Park Blvd. & Euclid Ave., Camden.
TELEPHONE: 609-964-3333.

THE PATERSON MUSEUM

Located a block and a half from Paterson's Great Falls, in the one-time factory building of the Rogers Locomotive Company, the Paterson Museum takes up part of the huge first floor of the imposing red brick building. The museum contains a fascinating compilation of photographs, factory machines, old posters and early inventions. Although primarily a historical museum, there are exhibits devoted to arts and science, including a mineral exhibit.

Paterson seems to be the only community in New Jersey that does not equate the historical with the quaint. The great silk spinning machines, the pictures of grim, immigrant workers, the metal shell of the first submarine all testify to the fact that the dominant thrust of the 19th Century was the Industrial Revolution. The Rogers locomotive that stands outside the building was the Iron Horse that opened up the plains.

HOURS: Tues.- Fri.: 10-4:00: Sat., Sun.: 12:30-4:30. Closed holidays.
ADMISSION: Adults: $1.00; Children free.
LOCATION: 2 Market St., Paterson, Passaic County.
TELEPHONE: 201-881-3874

AMERICAN LABOR MUSEUM (BOTTO HOUSE)

A combination historic house/museum with an emphasis, for a change, on the working class. This family home of an Italian immigrant worker became a rallying place for striking union members during the 1913 Paterson Silk strike. Since Haledon had a Socialist mayor at the time, and Paterson itself had banned group assemblies, workers gathered here to hear the likes of John Reed and Big Bill Hayward during the bitter strike.

The Botto House is a sturdy, well-built wooden structure smack-dab in the center of a middle-income neighborhood in a suburb of Paterson. Although it was once modernized, it has been transformed back into its earlier self. In fact, the nice new kitchen floor was ripped up and replaced by those dull linoleum sheets of 1903 vintage —and new ovens were replaced by huge old black stoves. Ah, history. The guide will show you how the family lived in the old days. Vegetables were grown in the garden, rabbits and chickens were kept for food, canned goods went into the root cellar and nothing was thrown away. The outdoor garden is kept just as it was at the time when Italian immigrants lived here and worked in the nearby mills.

Aside from the homey artifacts, several rooms in the Botto House are devoted to pictures and displays about the early American labor movement. These include photographs of the unsafe and unsanitary working conditions in turn-of-the century factories. As both a museum and a historic home, the Botto House offers a nice change from the usual historical fare in New Jersey.

> **HOURS:** Wed. - Sun.: 1-4.
> **ADMISSION:** Adults: $1.50; Children under 12, free.
> **LOCATION:** 83 Norwood St., Haledon, Passaic County. Call for directions.
> **TELEPHONE:** 201-595-7953.

OTHER NEW JERSEY HISTORICAL MUSEUMS

There are dozens of other small historical museums dotted about the state. These reflect the past highlights of a particular region, as do many of the ones mentioned in this chapter, and are no less important. However limitations of time and space make it impossible to visit or even list the many historical museums available. Since these museums are usually of local interest they are often mentioned in local newspapers and special events are always written up. Readers interested in history should also check the listings of historic houses in this book. They are very similar in scope and content to the historical museums and may be found in such chapters as *"Where Washington Ate, Fought and Slept"*, *"Homes of the Rich and Famous"*, *"Walking Tours"* and *"Restored Villages, Mills, Farms and Homes."*

METROPOLITAN MUSEUM OF ART

This huge Palladian building that covers several blocks of New York's Fifth Avenue is still the Grande Dame of museums this side of the Atlantic. It is the repository of a European culture wafted to our shores by millionaires whose art collections were donated for reasons of either generosity or tax exemptions. At one time the Museum was so old-Europe centered that it admitted neither American nor "Modern" art. However, all that has changed.

With the addition of the American Wing you now get a museum and a half at the Met. The "wing" is, in fact, equal to most medium-sized museums. The three floors encompass American furniture and decorative arts, recreated 17th and 18th Century rooms, paintings and sculpture. To view it chronologically you must take an elevator and start at the top with the William and Mary chairs, descend through the restored rooms, the many paintings of George Washington (including the original "Crossing the Delaware"), pass the Frederic Remington sculptures and end up on the first floor with large well-lit canvasses by Whistler and John Singer Sargeant. To get back to the main museum you cross the *piece de resistance:* the Englehard Garden Court. This immense courtyard contains purple willowed Tiffany screens, Louis Sullivan stairs and a complete bank facade. The glassed-in courtyard offers potted palms, garden chairs and a wonderful 1900s ambience.

But to begin at the beginning — when you first enter the Metropolitan's huge marble lobby you may feel as if you've entered Grand Central Station by mistake. Milling crowds, a central information booth, several ticket booths, coat-check areas, signs for the restaurant and rest-rooms, a bookshop and a jewelry counter doing booming business — this is a museum? Well, one traditional feature of the Museum is that from the front lobby it's Greeks to the left, Egyptians to the right and Europeans upstairs.

If you are with young children you might as well go for the mummies and the Temple of Dendur. Great stone sarcophagi and ancient sphinxes have a fascination for children that roomsful of paintings simply don't. The Medieval armor on the first floor is another child's favorite.

107

The second floor houses the European paintings which start with the Medieval period. From there you wander through Italian and Northern Renaissance, Dutch Masters, English portraits and French landscapes.

There are so many rooms to see — a Renaissance patio and a medieval tapestry hall, rooms devoted to gilded musical instruments and whole wings devoted to modern art, New Guinea artifacts and costume design.

For the exhausted, there's always lunch at the Fountain restaurant. You can wait on line for cafeteria food, or sit in elegance at the center restaurant and pay New York prices for a plate of chicken salad. (Reserve for the restaurant at the Information Booth when you arrive.) They are both in a large marble hall and the din of two hundred people and clanking silver can become a bit much. But it's a unique place and both children and little old ladies like it.

HOURS: Tues.-Thurs., Sun.: 9:30-5:15; Fri., Sat.: 9:30-8:45.
ADMISSION: Suggested donation: Adults: $6.00; Students, seniors: $3.00. Children under 12, free.
LOCATION: Fifth Ave. between 81sth and 84th Sts., N.Y.C.
TELEPHONE: 212-879-5500; 535-7710

AMERICAN MUSEUM OF NATURAL HISTORY

Best known for its dinosaur collection, with the carefully reconstructed bones of Tyrannosaurus Rex and other prehistoric animals looming overhead, the museum offers plenty more. The huge collection includes over 34 million artifacts and specimens. Although the building dates back to the 19th Century the insides have been spiffed up and modernized. Special lighting and piped in music enhance some of the recent displays.

Part of the museum is dedicated to Anthropology with special halls recreating life, costumes, tools and instruments of the American Indian, the Asian people, Pacific people and so forth. Great stone heads from Mexico, the smell of the South American jungle, tribal music from Africa are all included. And then there are all those dioramas with mannequins depicting the different types of cave men.

Three floors of stuffed cheetahs and elks and elephants and a new display that shows just how they are created are part of the permanent exhibit here. And the Gem and Mineral collection has a sparkling setting where huge sections of quartz and amethyst glow behind modernistic lucite cases in a darkened room. For kids, the giant blue whale and stuffed penguins in the Discovery Room are always popular.

The Information Desk not only has floor plans (a must in this two-section museum) but the free "highlights" tour leaves from here also. For those who want to rest their feet and see something overwhelming at the same time there is the Naturemax theater (extra price) where a 40 foot screen full of volcanos or waterfalls gives an almost 3-dimensional effect.

As for eating, first you find the basement (and you practically have to be a member of the Explorer's Club to accomplish that) and then you decide between a fast food eatery and a trendy little glass-enclosed restaurant where you can eat sun-dried tomatoes and wonder when the heck this museum became chic.

The **Hayden Planetarium** is right next door but you can gain entrance through the museum proper — although you must pay a hefty separate fee. The planetarium is one of the largest in the country and runs both regular star shows and specials for children on Saturday morning. There are also Laserium concerts here, a lunar landscape, and a nice big meteor chunk to inspect.

HOURS: Daily: 10-5:45 (Wed., Fri., Sat. til 9).
ADMISSION: (Suggested) Adults: $4.00; Children: $2.00. Free 5-9. Fri.& Sat.
LOCATION: Central Park West and 79th St., New York.
TELEPHONE: 212-769-5100; Planetarium: 212-769-5900.

THE CLOISTERS

High on a tree-covered bluff just minutes from the bustling streets of Manhattan's Washington Heights, there stands a world apart. The Cloisters, a museum built in the style of a 14th Century monastery, displays the art and architecture of the Middle Ages in a setting completely devoted to that single age. Unlike its mother museum (for the Cloisters is a part of the Metropolitan Museum of Art) which tries to cover the span of art from antiquity to the 20th Century, this monastic replica covers only the

Courtyard of the Cloisters — a unique museum devoted to the culture of the Middle Ages.

12th to 15th Centuries in Europe. But the Cloisters includes both religious and secular art and geographical variety. The red tile roof and campanile of the building reflect the style of a Southern European monastery. But inside you will find the actual stones, colonnades and worn steps of a Romanesque Chapel, a Spanish apse and a Gothic hall complete with arched ceilings and flying buttresses.

The Cloisters gets its name from the covered walkway surrounding an enclosed garden that was typical of the Medieval monastery. The main cloister at the museum is the large central one on the first floor. Completed before 1206 and taken stone by stone from a Benedictine abbey in southern France, this cloister with its rounded arches and peaceful interior garden sets a tone of otherworldliness for the entire museum.

There are several other cloisters downstairs which one can walk through. Of particular interest to gardeners is the herb garden here. Two hundred species of plants grown in the Middle Ages sprout among the espalier trees and arcades of a Cistercian cloister. Here you will find not only the Physick herbs, but quite a few poisonous plants as well.

Every museum has its star attractions and certainly one of the stellar crowd-pleasers at the Cloisters is the *Hall of the Unicorn Tapestries*. Remarkable in their color, preservation and realism, these several panels of tapestries tell a story which you read by moving from one to the other (they are not hung in consecutive order). The story of the hunt, killing and resurrection of the Unicorn was commissioned by a lord and shows the life of the Medieval aristocracy as well as the symbolism of the age. The *"Belle Heures of the Duc de Berry"* and the *Chalice of Antioch* are two other attractions in the downstairs treasury.

Of course no visit to a museum is complete without a stop at the gift shop. At the Cloisters you can find books, records of medieval music, posters, jewelry and replicas of statues and artworks. You can even find a do-it-yourself needlework kit for the famous unicorn in the garden.

Since the Cloisters is built on a bluff overlooking the Hudson, be sure to drink in the view of Fort Tryon Park and the wild Palisades across the river in New Jersey. John D. Rockefeller Jr. paid for it all — the Cloisters, the park and the view, when he donated the whole shebang in 1938.

HOURS: Tues. - Sun. 9:30-5:15. Closes 4:45 in winter.

111

ADMISSION: Suggested donation: Adults: $6.00; Seniors, students: $3.00. Includes admission to the Met. Museum.
DIRECTIONS: George Washington Bridge to Henry Hudson Parkway North. Take first exit off Parkway to Fort Tryon Park. Follow signs.
TELEPHONE: 212-923-3700

THE FRICK COLLECTION

This little jewel of a museum, housed in the former mansion of the coke and steel magnate is a must for art lovers. The European paintings and furniture display a heavy emphasis on both the Renaissance and Eighteenth Century. The Fragonard Room with panels painted for Madame Du Barry and the Boucher Room with panels commissioned by Madame de Pompadour have the appropriate French furniture and ambience to take you back to the reigns of the various Louises. Medieval paintings, enamels, Rembrandts and lots of 18th Century British portraits and landscapes abound.

Since this was once a home, the paintings are hung much as they would have been in the days of opulence. Gainsborough ladies and Turner landscapes decorate the comfortable halls, and a lovely inner courtyard provides the sort of atrium for rest and contemplation cultured people once thought necessary. There is also a lecture hall for the free talks which are given at eleven o'clock certain weekdays.

Only the first floor is open, but this is a formidable collection, so allow at least an hour to browse through. Children under ten are not admitted and those under 16 must be accompanied by adults — they are serious about art in this place.

HOURS: Tues. - Sat.: 10-6; Sun.: 1-6.
ADMISSION: Adults —$3.00. Students, Seniors: $1.50.
LOCATION: One East 70th St. (At Fifth Ave.) N.Y.C.
TELEPHONE: 212-288-0700

MUSEUM OF MODERN ART

A newly remodeled MOMA opened in 1984. It may look more like an airport terminal than a museum, with its walls of glass and escalators, but it reclaims its crown as arbiter of taste for the modern world. The collection ranges from Henri Rousseau and early Impressionists to the latest works. A leader in the collecting of photographs and films as art, the museum has also a section on industrial design which lets us all know what is good design and what isn't. An ice cream scoop featured here becomes the ice cream scoop to use. The Industrial Design section is now on the top floor and features a helicopter hanging from the ceiling. And in the basement there are two movie theaters. Outside there's the sculpture garden, but the cafeteria is now a huge indoor space featuring very ordinary food. The popular museum shop has its own entrance next door.

HOURS: Fri. - Tues.: 11-6; Thurs.: 11-9; closed Wed.
ADMISSION: Adults: $7.00; Students, Seniors: $4.00. Children with adult, free.
LOCATION: 11 West 53rd St. (between 5th & 6th Aves.), N.Y.C.
TELEPHONE: 212-708-9480.

FORBES GALLERIES

Since Malcolm Forbes was one of New Jersey's most colorful residents, many Jerseyans enjoy a peek at the toys of this fabulous millionaire and his family. And toys they are - literally. For in one of the sections of this museum you will find 12,000 toy soldiers set up in dioramas or vignettes that include Indians circling cowboys, jousting knights, marching bands and so on.

In another section, called *"Ships Ahoy"*, there are 500 toy boats on display. These are intricately wrought boats done in all sorts of materials. You will also see the glass panels from the grand salon of the old ocean liner, *The Normandie* along with other art deco designs.

Other galleries include *Presidential Papers* (with documents emphasizing the personal side of the presidents) a Trophy Room full of tributes to forgotten moments and a picture gallery that rotates exhibits. And of course, since the Forbes collection is famous for them, you do get to see twelve of the jewelled Easter Eggs created by Faberge for the Russian Czars. These are among many other objects de luxe in a separate room.

The galleries are housed inside the Forbes Magazine building in Greenwich Village. Admission is free but entry is limited to 900 people per day on a first-come, first served basis, except for Thursdays which is reserved for groups. For group reservations call 212-206-5549.

HOURS: Tues., Wed., Fri., Sat.: 10-4.
LOCATION: 62 Fifth Ave. at 12th St., N.Y.C.
TELEPHONE: 212-206-5548

Pennsylvania Museums

THE FRANKLIN INSTITUTE

The venerable Franklin Institute was always a pioneer in hands-on exhibits. Now it has leapt into the future with a soaring modern hi-tech addition to the original classically designed building. Architecturally it's like going from the 18th to the 21st century. As for exhibits - they range from the old hands-on favorites to new Disney World style contraptions. The museum now has four main sections: The Science Center, Futures Center, the Fels Planetarium and the Omniverse Theater. In addition there are 42 computer terminals that can answer your questions about what is where and how you can find it. What you will find is:

The Science Center: This is the original museum which still has most of its popular exhibits. There's the 36 times life-size heart you (or at least a child) can walk through. And the steam locomotive in the basement that chugs along for ten feet every hour. And the giant lever you can pull down and swing on. And the T-33 Air Force jet trainer you can "fly" plus lots of other exhibits on physics, printing, and such.

The Fels Planetarium: The 340 seat planetarium remains from the old days, but it is now outfitted with a state-of-the-art Digistar projection system which gives viewers a three-dimensional feel to their star-gazing.

The Future Center: This brave new world is divided into eight permanent exhibits with names like FutureSpace, FutureEarth, and FutureComputers. Here you will find such things as a fiberglass model of a human cell one million times its actual size; a computer that let's you "age" yourself so you know what you'll look like twenty years from now (aaaargh!— but it's great for kids); a model of a NASA space station; a ten foot globe with fibre-optic lights to show population growth shifts; a man-made forest and a host of other futuristic displays.

The Omniverse Theater: There are 350 large reclining seats arranged in steeply angled rows. Above and around you is the movie screen, 79 feet across and four stories high — a hemispheric dome. Lots of loudspeakers to project the sound all over.

This is the place for nature films that roar, soar, and surround the audience. Since seating is limited it's hard to get in to see this one unless you reserve a seat.

The museum now has underground parking and three restaurants (two of them kid-oriented), a huge atrium for resting and an outdoor science park is in the offing. Expect to spend at least four hours here.

> **HOURS:** Daily. Science Center: 9:30-5. Futures Center: Same except open to 9 pm Wed. - Sun.
>
> **ADMISSION:** Science & Future Centers: Adults: $8.50; Children, Seniors: $7.00. Separate prices for Omniverse, planetarium or combination tickets.
>
> **LOCATION:** 20th St. and Benjamin Franklin Parkway, Philadelphia
>
> **TELEPHONE:** 215-448-1200

PHILADELPHIA MUSEUM OF ART

It is a Greek temple that surveys the town and the river from an imposing height, with a magnificent flight of steps leading up to its classical columns. The steps, in fact, are as famous as the museum ever since Sylvester Stallone ran up them in the movie, "Rocky".

But inside the pillared entrance (you can avoid most of the steps by parking in the back parking lot), one of the best collections of art in North America awaits. Galleries of European art include the Johnson Collection on the first floor, which is heavy in Renaissance paintings. Twentieth Century art comes next and includes Marcel DuChamps' famous "Nude Descending A Staircase." The variety of the museum is evidenced by the fact that there is a medieval cloister, an Indian temple, a Chinese palace hall and a Japanese teahouse all within these portals.

The kids will find the collection of armor, which includes swords, lances, maces, chain-mail and breastplates, to be fascinating. And one whole section, devoted to Americana, includes period rooms filled with Philadelphia style bonnet-and-scroll top bureaus, secretaries and chests. There is plenty of early silverware, also.

Tours are offered by volunteer guides at no extra cost. They leave on the hour, from 10 AM to 3 PM and originate in the West Entrance Hall. Downstairs, there is a pleasant restaurant and gift shop.

HOURS: Tues. - Sun.: 10-5. Closed legal holidays.
ADMISSION: Adults: $5.00; Children: $3.00. Under 5 free. Free on
Sunday until 1 PM.
LOCATION: Benjamin Franklin Parkway & 26th St., Philadelphia
TELEPHONE: 215-763-8100

PENNSYLVANIA ACADEMY
OF FINE ARTS

An ornate Victorian building created by architect Frank
Furness, it is as striking an edifice as you will find anywhere.
Inside, a domed ceiling of deep blue with twinkling stars, orna-
mental bronze railings and marble floors recreate the atmosphere
of 1876 when this structure went up in time for the Philadelphia
Centennial. A teaching institute as well as a museum, the Academy was originally founded by Charles Willson Peale and was
home to Thomas Eakins and Mary Cassatt.

The permanent collection is dominated by American artists —
Peale and Gilbert Stuart and others. Benjamin West's well-known
"William Penn's Treaty with the Indians" hangs in the rotunda. A
number of portraits of George Washington (it was not unusual
for an artist to copy the same work over and over again in those
days) hang in the rotunda also. However the collection also
emphasizes more recent artists on the American scene.

The Academy is situated in Philadelphia's Center City, close to
the grandiose City Hall. From September to July, an hour tour
leaves the Grand Stairhall on weekdays at 11 & 2. Special tours
can be arranged for groups, of course.

HOURS: Tues. - Sat.: 10-5; Sun.: 11-5. Closed major holidays.
ADMISSION: Adults: $5.00; Seniors: $3.00; Students: $2.00. Free
on Sat. 10-1.
LOCATION: Broad and Cherry Streets, Philadelphia
TELEPHONE: 215-972-7600, 972-7633

ROSENBACH MUSEUM
AND LIBRARY

Located two blocks south of Rittenhouse Square in a lovely
section of Philadelphia, this townhouse was once the home of
rare book collectors. The books and furnishings of the Rosenbach
brothers are at once a paean to the good life and a paradise for

collectors. Since one brother searched for antiques while the other concentrated on books, the home is a treasure trove of decorative arts. At the same time it is an important research library.

There are 130,000 manuscripts and 30,000 rare books which range from medieval illuminated manuscripts to letters written by George Washington and Abraham Lincoln stored here. Lewis Carroll's own edition of Alice in Wonderland and the manuscript of James Joyce's Ulysses together with hundreds of first editions are shelved in what is essentially still a home with beautiful and delicate furniture.

The dining room where the brothers entertained wealthy guests features an Empire style table, Venetian Grand Canal scenes, Chippendale chairs and a delicate glass chandelier. A painting of Fanny Kemble by Thomas Sully and a scrolled fireplace adorn the cozy parlor. Some of the upstairs rooms are more museum-like with displays of special exhibits in glass cases and there is a room devoted to the illustrations of Maurice Sendak. Up here you will also find the personal library of Dr. Rosenbach. The Doctor made a career of finding rare books for wealthy clients, but when he made a particularly good discovery he often kept it for himself. Hence this collection of thousands of first editions and gold-bound tomes.

Admission includes a guided tour (unless you are coming to see the special exhibit only, in which case the price is less). The guide sprinkles many personal anecdotes in with the recital of facts. Loves, hates, mistresses, fallings out — you learn it all.

Although the Rosenbach brothers lived in this house only from 1950 to 1952, when they were both old, the house and collection seem to come out of some turn-of-the-century novel by Henry James. It seems incredible that this cultured, even dandified atmosphere existed in the post-World War II period. Yet it's all here — oriental carpets and Herman Melville's bookcase (stacked with first editions of "The White Whale"), 17th Century gold chests and delicate French parlors. The museum is a must for collectors, librarians, art historians and anyone who wants pointers on how to live with class. Not for children, but senior high school and college students are welcome. Since the tour takes over an hour, allow sufficient time.

HOURS: Tues. - Sun.: 11-4. Closed holidays. Closed August.
ADMISSION: Adults: $2.50. Students, Seniors: $1.50
LOCATION: 2010 Delancey Place, Philadelphia
TELEPHONE: 215-732-1600

117

UNIVERSITY OF PENNSYLVANIA ARCHAEOLOGY MUSEUM

A full-blown museum, three stories high and a must for lovers of archaeology, antiquities and mummies, the University Museum is set amidst the congestion of the U of P campus in Philadelphia. But once inside, the halls echo of timeless antiquities even though modern pollution is slowly leeching the limestone from an ancient temple.

The Egyptian section is particularly good. A towering lotus-leaf pillar and one of the world's twelve remaining sphinxes (a small one but complete except for the eroded nose) are some of the many artifacts here. And upstairs one room is devoted to the art and science of mummy making. Statues of pharoahs, cats and gods are all part of the first-rate Egyptian room.

Another gallery is devoted to Chinese statues and miniatures, many of them acquired in the 1920s from money hungry Warlords. Some excellent pieces, including Buddhas, horses and ancient vases are to be found here. A full tour of the museum also brings to light rooms devoted to the Near East, Polynesian and African cultures.

Since this is a working museum, don't be surprised if you stumble over art students doing sketches of masks and statues. The archaeology students are dispersed around the world, digging up even more treasures. Volunteer guides conduct gallery tours on Wednesday and Sunday at 1 P.M. and a small cafeteria offers small lunches and hamburgers.

HOURS: Tues. - Sat.: 10-4:30; Sun.: 1-5. Closed Holidays. Closed Sun. from Mem. Day to Labor Day.
ADMISSION: Adults: $3.00; Children, Seniors: $1.50
LOCATION: Univ. of Pennsylvania, 33rd & Spruce Sts., Philadelphia
TELEPHONE: 215-898-4000

THE BARNES FOUNDATION

Eccentric millionaires may be lovable from a distance but just let one leave a museum behind and you realize all the problems inherent in eccentricity. Actually, the Barnes Foundation is a museum by accident. Its true function is to serve as an art school and research center. It is open to the public on a limited basis and probably only for tax reasons.

The handsome Renaissance building is located in the lovely Philadelphia Main Line suburb of Merion, next to St. Joseph's College. The landscaped grounds seem to invite inspection. But wait! You can't put a foot on the grass without writing ahead for permission. In fact, you need permission for just about everything in this place. The rules and regulations are formidable. Only a limited number of people are allowed in at one time. All pocketbooks, by the way, must be checked downstairs before people enter the museum. No spike heels for ladies, no photographs inside or out. One gets the feeling that the ghost of Mr. Barnes (who invented Argyrol and collected this outstanding collection) does not want strangers staring at his paintings.

Is all this worth it? If you like Impressionist painters, the answer is "yes". The largest collection of Impressionists in the United States resides here along with Cubists, and 17th century masters. El Greco's "St. Jerome and the Angel" is here along with Cezanne's "The Card Players". At least I think that's what the paintings are called — another peculiarity of the Barnes Foundation is that there are no titles, no dates, and no information about any of the paintings except for the artist's name at the bottom of the frame. No brochures, no floor plans, no nothing. So you may see dozens of Renoirs — dozens of plump, rosy nudes and children holding flowers — but you have no idea when each was painted.

This can cause considerable consternation among people who are used to having it all spelled out for them. I passed a couple from my bus tour who were puzzling about the creator of an African wood sculpture housed on the second floor balcony.

"I think his name is Cote d'Ivoire," the husband said.

Helpfully, I summoned up my high school foreign language skills. "That's French for The Ivory Coast," I said. "It's undoubtedly a carving from West Africa's Ivory Coast, circa 1800."

The couple smiled and slunk away. It made my day.

If you go to the Barnes Foundation, for Heaven's sake make reservations first. And be prepared for bad lighting, eccentric hanging of pictures (you can miss a Picasso because it's up there over the transom) and a host of rules and regulations. But in spite of all the obstacles, this is a first-rate collection which every art lover should see.

HOURS: Fri., Sat.: 9:30-4:30. Sun.: 1-4:30. Closed July & Aug.

119

ADMISSION: $1.00. No children under 12.
LOCATION: 300 N. Latches Lane, Merion, Pennsylvania
TELEPHONE: 215-667-0290

THE MERCER MILE

Three unusual museums in Doylestown are the legacy of Henry Chapman Mercer (1856-1930) a businessman, ceramicist, archaeologist, and according to many, an eccentric. The highly individual creations are known collectively as the Mercer Mile since they are within close distance of one another. They consist of:

THE MERCER MUSEUM: A sprawling, turreted structure of reinforced concrete, the museum houses a vast collection of America's pre-Industrial tools and crafts. Mercer was one of the first to collect early Americana (although everyone seems to be doing it now). He collected with the eye of an archaeologist, and all the minutae of everday life — from kitchen utensils to hatmaking machines — are revealed here. Small objects are exhibited in rooms by craft (e.g., the evolution of buttermaking) while larger objects are left free-standing or are suspended. Visitors often gasp when they step into the main section of the museum and find Conestoga wagons, harpoons and whaling skiffs suspended from the ceiling. Six floors of exhibits surround the central hall. Gallows, hearses, prisoners docks and the kitchen sink — it's all here. A library of early Americana is also on the premises.

HOURS: Mon. - Sat., 10-5; Sun.: 12-5. May be closed in winter.
ADMISSION: Adults: $4.00; Seniors: $3.50; Students: $1.50
LOCATION: Green & Ashland Sts., Doylestown (Take Rte. 202 or Rte. 611 to Ashland St.)
TELEPHONE: 215-345-0210

FONTHILL MUSEUM: The home of Mercer, it looks like a Spanish fantasy set on the quiet Pennsylvania landscape. Filled with the colorful Moravian tiles from his factory, the home has arches and winding stairways and uneven rooms and beautiful views. Guided tours only. Reservations required. *Hours:* Daily 12-5. *Admission:* Adults: $4.00, Seniors: $3.50, Students: $1.50 *Location:* E. Court St. off Rte. 313, Doylestown. *Telephone:* 215-348-9461

MORAVIAN POTTERY AND TILE WORKS: A short walk from Fonthill, the Tile Works shows the machinery and raw materials of the tile making process (workers are not always present) and also houses a gift shop where these unusual tiles may be bought. *Hours:* Daily 10-4:45. *Admission:* Adults: $2.50, Seniors: $2.00, Students: $1.00. *Location:* E. Court St. off Rte. 313. *Telephone:* 215-345-6722.

THE BRANDYWINE RIVER MUSEUM

From the front it's a century old grist mill; from the back it's a strikingly modern glass tower overlooking the Brandywine River, and altogether it is a most pleasant museum where the setting and structure are almost as interesting as the paintings within.

Inside the stone and glass structure, the atmosphere belongs to the Brandywine River artists (a group that formed around Howard Pyle and N.C. Wyeth) and to Wyeth's talented progeny, particularly Andrew and his son Jamie. Both Pyle and N.C. Wyeth were famous illustrators and many an older edition of "Treasure Island" or "King Arthur" contain their realistic action pictures. Although storybook illustrators have never reached the heights of adulation that "purer" artists enjoy, nevertheless they are among the most respected painters in America.

Howard Pyle began a summer teaching center in the Brandywine Valley in 1898. The artists from this regional center include Maxfield Parrish, Peter Hurd, Frank Schoonover, George Weymouth, and, of course, N.C. Wyeth. But it is Andrew Wyeth, whose painting "Christina's World" is world famous, who holds the compelling interests for viewers in this museum. The strong emotional impact of his many canvasses dominates the collection here. And the recent "Helga" series has made Andrew even more notorious. You can also find a small number of Jamie's paintings in the permanent collection and of course there are always special exhibits which emphasize one or the other of the Brandywine artists.

After viewing the exhibits, you can lunch at the newly expanded cafeteria. Here you can look down on the leafy trails, the meandering river and the wildflower garden below. This lovely preserve is part of the Brandywine Conservancy, which keeps 5,000 acres in a state of nature — a most poetic place that seems to attract strollers, readers and young romantics.

As for children, there is a special Christmas display intended for them which runs throughout the month of December. It includes model trains, porcelain dolls and decorated Christmas trees.

HOURS: Daily except major holidays, 9:30-4:30
ADMISSION: Adults: $4.00; Seniors: $2.50; Children: $2.00; under 6 free.
LOCATION: On Route U.S. 1, Chadds Ford, Pa.
TELEPHONE: 215-388-7601
610-388-2700

See Also: Museums that are part of a larger entity are mentioned under the title of the larger attraction — e.g., *The Glass Museum* (Wheaton Village), *West Point Museum* (West Point). New Jersey planetariums that are not part of a museum are listed in a separate chapter entitled, "Other Outings."

THE CLASSICS

Photo: Courtesy N.Y. Convention & Visitors Bureau

In This Chapter You Will Find:

United Nations Headquarters, N.Y.
The Statue of Liberty
Ellis Island
World Trade Center, N.Y.
Empire State Building, N.Y.
Circle Line Tour, N.Y.
West Point, N.Y.
Independence Mall, Philadelphia, PA

UNITED NATIONS HEADQUARTERS

The first thing you notice as you approach the United Nations complex is the line of colorful flags half-circling the entrance. All member nation flags are flown at the same height —only the UN flag is unfurled higher. The next thing you notice as you step through the iron gates is that this place is clean! No old newspapers, candy wrappers or soda cans litter the area. The United Nations may not police the world, but they sure know how to police the grounds!

Outside sculpture includes a gigantic abstract object next to the circular fountain, a Japanese Peace Bell ensconced in a pagoda, and a Soviet "heroic" style sculpture of a man beating his sword into a plowshare. If you visit in the spring be sure to check out the gardens which are in back of the buildings. Daffodils and cherry trees bloom in early spring while the rose garden with its twenty varieties of tea roses blossoms later.

Tours of the UN are still popular although nowadays you must enter the building through an airport-type security system. The tours combine a short history of the aims, structure and activities of the United Nations itself with a description of the art and architecture you pass along the tour route. Here you will find out about the behind the scenes work of UNESCO, WHO and other specialized agencies. Many photographs of their work decorate the walls. Unfortunately, there are also many propaganda displays in the halls, and a tone of beligerence seems to dominate.

The number of chambers you enter during the tour depends on whether the various Councils are meeting or not. The General Assembly, which is usually open, is a huge hall with high domed ceiling and more than 2,000 seats. The slatted back walls are interspersed with banks of windowed booths where translators, photographers and TV people sit. This is the hall most often seen on television when a world-shaking meeting takes place.

The other chambers were designed by Norwegian, Swedish and Danish architects and their furnishings were donated by those countries. They all display the vertical and horizontal lines and rich wood grains we associate with "Danish Modern." In fact the whole complex has a definite Scandinavian look. A human thirst for color and representational art is seen in the gifts of other countries: a colorful tapestry from Senegal, the blue stained glass windows of Chagall, the stark reds of Rouault's "Christ Crucified," and a crimson Peruvian cermonial mantle.

The tour ends in the Public Concourse where you can proceed to the bookstore, gift shops and postal counter (a mecca for stamp collectors). Handicraft items from around the world, flags, dolls of all nations are priced reasonably, but no better than anywhere else. The bargain is the fact that there is no sales tax anywhere in the UN complex! For hamburgers and french fries there's a good coffee shop here. It is also possible to eat in the reasonably priced Delegates Dining Room.

HOURS: Daily: 9:15-4:45 Jan., Feb.: weekdays only.
ADMISSION: Free. For tours — Adults: $5.50, Students & children: $3.50. Seniors: $4.50 Children under 5 not admitted on tours.
LOCATION: 1st Ave. between 45th & 46th St., N.Y.C.
TELEPHONE: 212-963-7713

STATUE OF LIBERTY

The 1986 Birthday party for The Statue of Liberty was so spectacular, the hoopla and fireworks so memorable, that crowds have been overwhelming ever since at the newly refurbished monument. Be prepared to wait in line, both for the ferry that takes you over to Liberty Island and at the Statue itself.

New Jersey residents can embark from Liberty State Park for the short ride over. Once aboard the Circle Line Ferry, (which is a pleasure in itself on a nice, breezy day) you get a view from all angles of the newly glistening Lady as the boat turns to make port. As you disembark, the first building you see is the gift and souvenir shop (which has been transferred over here to ease congestion at the Statue itself.) Here you can stock up on mugs, pennants and postcards.

Liberty lsland is larger than you might expect. On its 12 1/2 acres, there are administration buildings, a snack shop, a pleasant tree-shaded picnic area and esplanades rimming the island. Here you can savor the view of Manhattan's towers plus the wide expanse of the harbor with its bustling boats.

But first, the Statue. There are lines for everything now (unless you luck into a rainy day in October) . There are lines for the pedastal, for those who want to walk to the crown, and even for the museum. The museum, just a short walk up a flight of stairs within the main lobby, is devoted to the building and restoration of the statue itself. It includes an incredible amount of displays and information. There are architectural mock-ups, and an audio-visual section where you hear the voices of immigrants who first saw the statue. The museum that was devoted to American immigration has been transferred to Ellis Island, however, and that space will be developed in the future.

As for those who actually walk the 22 stories up to the crown — expect your calves to hurt for the next week. This is not for the frail or short- of-breath. You must walk all the way up since the elevator now goes only to the pedestal (where there is no access to the crown). Kids enjoy the hike just to prove they can do it.

Both as a visit to a national shrine and as a pleasant day's outing on the water between two great ports, a trip to the Statue of Liberty is a must —a least once in a lifetime.

HOURS:	9-5 Daily.
FERRY SCHEDULE:	(Liberty State Park) Daily 9:30-3:45 schedule may be expanded in summer, shortened in winter. (Battery Park, N.Y.) Daily every half hour.
ADMISSION:	Free for statue. Ferry fee is: Adults: $6.00; Under 17: $3.00.
LOCATION:	To reach Liberty State Park take the N.J. Turnpike to exit 14B. The ferry is a short distance from the park. Follow signs. Parking fee.
TELEPHONE:	(Circle Line) 201-435-9499. (Liberty State Park) 201-915- 3400. (Liberty Island) 212-363-3267.

ELLIS ISLAND

The hoopla surrounding the re-opening of Ellis Island was almost greater than the Statue of Liberty bash. So many people came, and stayed for so many hours, that the halls were awash once again with teeming humanity. If it weren't that entrance is restricted to those who come by ferry the whole island would probably sink under the weight of all those descendents of the original immigrants.

For this is the basic museum which commemorates the peopling of America, not only those who set foot on this particular island (for that is only one section) but the story from the beginning, with emphasis on the late 19th and early 20th century. A movie, shown in two theaters, recounts the experience of those who left troubled homelands to take the sea voyage to the new land. First it was in wooden ships that took six weeks to make the voyage and left everyone sick. Later it was the steamship lines who filled up their steerage section with poor immigrants. If the immigrants were turned back because of sickness or other reasons, the steamship company had to pay for the return passage.

Earlier immigration sites, greed, corruption, and the one-day processing of thousands of people are all covered in the movie as well as the displays. But there is also an amassing of hundreds of trunks, shawls, tickets, flyers and other mementos of the immigrant experience. Newspaper cartoons depict the rising tide of intolerance against the newcomers which finally culminated in a restrictive law in 1924 which ended the mass migration. Ellis Island was closed in 1954. In its newly refurbished state it is a wonderful learning experience, and an emotional one as well for anyone who descended from all those Germans, Greeks, Italians, Jews, Irish, Turks, Jamaicans and others who first came to these shores.

HOURS, ETC.: Check Statue of Liberty entry.
TELEPHONE: (Circle Line) 201-435-9499; (Ellis Island) 212-363-3204

WORLD TRADE CENTER

The highest skyscraper in New York offers the best view of the metropolis, the river, New Jersey and Brooklyn. On a clear day the 360 degree view is terrific. You buy tickets on the mezzanine floor and then take a special elevator that whisks you up to the 100th floor in a few seconds. Once there, you can sit at the various windows and drink in the panorama of the bay, the city and the provinces beyond. Conveniently, the outlines and names of landmarks are traced on the glass at every viewpoint, so you know what you are looking at.

There are also exhibits on the inner walls, a souvenir shop and a snack bar (featuring the world's most indifferent employees). For those who like to go outside, there's a rooftop promenade several flights up which is open when the wind is not too strong.

The Center also offers the popular Windows on The World restaurant and in summer there are often special events going on downstairs. A brochure of a self-guided tour of the area is available here. Call 212-466-4170 for a copy.

HOURS: 9:30 AM - 9:30 PM
ADMISSION: Adults: $3.50; Children & Senior Citizens: $1.75; Under 6 free.
LOCATION: 2 World Trade Center Plaza, N.Y.C. Take PATH direct from Hoboken or Jersey City.
TELEPHONE: 212-466-7377

THE EMPIRE STATE BUILDING

The 86th floor observatory has both an enclosed area and an open promenade. High powered binoculars are available for a fee. Here you will also find the snack bars, vending machine and souvenir counter. The view to the west offers New Jersey and the Hudson, to the north you get Central Park and beyond, while the east gives you the UN building and Queens. While the observation windows here may not be as wide as the World Trade Center, nor the tower as spiffy as it once was, you are closer to the heart of Manhattan from this vantage point. There's an observatory on the 102nd floor included in the same ticket. This one is enclosed. And you can find the *"Guinness World Book of Records"* Museum in the basement of the Empire State Building where, for a separate fee, you can see all sort of oddities.

HOURS: 9:30 AM —Midnight daily
ADMISSION: Adults: $3.50; Seniors, Children: $1.75
LOCATION: 34th Street & 5th Avenue, N.Y.C.
TELEPHONE: 212-736-3100

THE CIRCLE LINE TOUR

A standard tourist attraction since it started in the post World War II era, this boat ride takes three hours and covers 35 miles. Basically, you circle Manhattan island in a three-floor "yacht" (which doesn't look much different than a three-floor ferry) which has both open and closed areas and long benches for seating. From the 42nd Street pier the boat heads southward on the Hudson, gaining views of both New York and New Jersey. Passing the Statue of Liberty, the ride continues around the tip of Manhattan then up the East River, around the Harlem River as far as Spuyten Duyvil and then back to home base. An announcer points out the monuments, skyscrapers, bridges and churches, offering anecdotes on the more interesting ones and lots of facts and figures. High point for the kids is the Little Red Lighthouse underneath the George Washington Bridge.

You can get a nice river breeze on this one and Manhattan never looks better than from a distance. But the price has really jumped in recent years.

HOURS: Mid-March to Mid-November. From two to seven sailings a day depending on season.
ADMISSION: Adults: $16.00; Children under 12: $8.00.
LOCATION: Pier 83, Foot of West 42nd St., N.Y.C.
TELEPHONE: 212-563-3200

WEST POINT

West Point has a beautiful view of the Hudson, grey Collegiate Gothic buildings that rise from rocky inclines, parades of cadets on Saturday mornings and football games in the fall. Many people begin their tour at the Visitor's Center, which is two blocks outside of the actual gates of the Point.

The center has displays, a movie about army life, and a busy gift shop. It is also the point of departure for bus tours which leave regularly during the warm weather for a 50 minute tour of the campus. The narrated tour stops at the magnificent Gothic chapel where all those spiffy weddings take place, the old chapel, at various monuments and at scenic views. If you don't want to wait for a bus tour, you can park within the campus and walk around yourself. There are benches where you can picnic, and the Thayer Hotel, which is on campus, has restaurants open to the public.

Behind the Visitor's Center in Olmstead Hall is the new **West Point Museum**, with three floors of exhibits, models, mock-ups and memorabilia. The decisive battles of the world are recreated here by tiny toy figures set in fighting position behind glass. A full explanation of each battle and its significance is printed below the display. The Dark Ages began because the Roman infantry could not hold out against the Gothic cavalry. The Modern Age began when guns replaced swords, and technology replaced prowess. An interesting place with a particular point of view. Lots of armor and costumes around. The West Point trivia was fascinating also. Did you know James Whistler dropped out because he couldn't pass chemistry? His watercolors are great, though, and those of Ulysses S. Grant aren't bad either.

If you're visiting with your family you may find the kids are most fascinated by the clean-cut cadets who are unerringly polite and meticulously dressed. Hikers will like the hilly terrain and outstanding view.

HOURS: Visitor Center: Daily 9-4:45; Museum: 10:30-4:45.
LOCATION: Route 218, West point, N.Y.
TELEPHONE: 914-938-2638

INDEPENDENCE MALL, PHILADEPHIA

If the Bicentennial did nothing else, at least it got the city of Philadelphia to spruce up its historic area, to revamp or rebuild everything and turn Independence Mall into a first-class tourist attraction. The National Park Service administers many of the historic buildings, although the city and private organizations operate quite a few also.

First stop should be the great big, brick **Visitor Center** at Chestnut and 3rd Street. Here you can pick up a clearly marked map of the historic areas. A thirty-minute film is shown here about once an hour, which will give you the necessary background for your tour. Special exhibits are also on view here.

If you have children with you, certainly stop to see **Franklin Court** (at Chestnut and 4th Street). This complex includes a very interesting underground museum. As you descend a winding ramp you pass many displays of Benjamin Franklin's inventions, furniture, etc. At the bottom area there is an unusual show. A miniature model of the 1776 Continental Congress rises up, and taped voices discuss the adoption of the Declaration of Independence. Then the model sinks down again. Over to one side a bank of telephone receivers stands. Here you dial a particular number to hear what various famous people such as Mark Twain or John Adams had to say about Franklin — a lively way to impart history.

Next, it's on to the grassy mall (bounded by Chestnut, Walnut, 5th and 6th Streets) where **Independence Hall** and the **Liberty Bell** await. The bell is in its own glass pavilion. The line is usually not too long since it doesn't take that long to get a look and take a picture. The bell is huge, of course, and looks just like you would expect it to.

Independence Hall is shown by a Department of Interior guide, so there may be a wait, but there's a separate room where you can sit down and hear a preliminary talk. The Hall is most impressive, although not very large by today's standards. You can see the inkstand used by the signers of the Declaration of Independence, benches, etc. The guide gives a very full explanation of the events surrounding the adoption of the Declaration.

Since it's only a few blocks away, most tourists walk over to the **Betsy Ross House** at 239 Arch Street, which is open daily. This small building with its narrow staircase is always so crowded that you only have time to glimpse the mannequins who represent Betsy and other Colonials. In fact, the small house is almost overpowered by the adjacent gift shop. Here you can stock up on Liberty Bells, facsimiles of the Declaration of Independence, and of course the 13-star flag which Betsy is reputed to have sewn. (*Telephone:* 215-627- 5343).

> **HOURS:** Some buildings may be closed in winter. 9-5 Daily.
> **ADMISSION:** Free
> **TELEPHONE:** (Visitor Center) 215-597-8975.

THEME PARKS, AMUSEMENT PARKS, BOARDWALK AMUSEMENTS

Photo: Courtesy Great Adventure

In This Chapter You Will Find:

Great Adventure, NJ
Hersheypark, PA
Action Park, NJ
Dorney Park- Wildwater Kingdom, PA
Sesame Place, PA
Shawnee Place, PA
Land of Make Believe, NJ
Gingerbread Castle, NJ
Boardwalk Amusements, NJ
    Keansburg
    Asbury Park
    Point Pleasant
    Seaside Heights
    Atlantic City Area
    Wildwood

Other Amusement Parks
    Bowcraft
    Clementon Lake Park
    Fairy Tale Forest
    Storybook Land

GREAT ADVENTURE

Great Adventure is a theme park without any discernable theme. It is more like a giant amusement park with a drive-through Safari tacked on. However, it is colorful and popular, although its huge acreage often tires young visitors. Like many other parks, its emphasis had been on teenage attractions. Recently, however, the park has tried to broaden its appeal. The new rides have less emphasis on teenage screaming and are geared more for family participation. "Roaring Rapids," for instance, is a rather mild ride down a man-made river. The idea is to get you wet rather than get you scared.

When you enter the main plaza, with its water fountain and shops, over 1100 acres lie before you. If you turn to the right from the entrance, you will find the largest concentration of rides, especially those designed to test the stomachs of the brave. The big roller coaster that turns you upside down is in this area, as is a number of Trabants, Himalayas and other whirling devices.

In the center of the park is the giant Ferris Wheel, the old-fashioned carousel, a lakeside bandstand, and a pretty Yum-Yum palace all designed to echo the look of a turn-of-the century amusement park. Unfortunately, the crowds, the noise and the litter tend to defeat that charming ambience. Further on, there are numerous arcades and small rides.

The expanded children's area, called Looney Tune Land, offers more than ding-dong boats and Red Baron airplanes. The Sesame Place look — active play elements such as plastic mazes and climbing ropes — has invaded here too. There are also costumed characters, such as Bugs Bunny and Daffy Duck walking around.

On the extreme side of the park you find a western motif. The Great Teepee offers gifts, and the Western Fort houses both the Runaway Train and the Sky Ride. The biggest log flume is here too, with extra added water sprays, just in case you don't get properly soaked in the splashdown. Across the river a double track roller coaster called Rolling Thunder appeases the mounting coaster mania among teenagers. To create even greater thrills, stand-up style cars have been added to the roller-coaster tracks.

For those who want to rest from the rides, there are a number of family shows. One of the best is "High Divers" a combination of skilled diving and buffoonery which alternates with the trained dolphin show at the Aqua stadium. Over at the Great Arena, circuses and other family entertainments are featured. Popular singers, and "soft" rock groups have been recent headliners.

If Great Adventure has improved in the range of its rides and shows, it varies from year to year in such areas as crowd control, litter and accidents. There are plenty of Security guards around recently though. As for food — don't expect gourmet fare. There are burgers, fried chicken, roast beef sandwiches, etc. - usually tough. Many people subsist on ice cream and Coke. Veteran visitors bring picnics in their coolers and just tailgate it in the parking lot. (You are not allowed to bring food inside the park except to the designated picnic area near the Safari section). And of course, you should not eat too much if you are going on any of the fast rides. It's also a good idea to bring along towels and some dry clothes for the long drive home. Those water rides can really drench you.

> **HOURS:** Early Apr.-mid June: call first. Last week of June-Labor Day: 10-10. Safari opens 9 AM. Open weekends, Sept., Oct.
> **ADMISSION:** Adult: $26.00 (Combination Park-Safari ticket). Under 54": $17.00. Seniors: $13.00. Under 3 free. Parking and tax extra.
> **LOCATION:** Jackson Twp., Ocean County. Take NJ Tpke to Exit 7A, then 195 to Exit 16.
> **TELEPHONE:** 201-928-3500

HERSHEY PARK

When the urge to get away for a two or three-day vacation (complete with amusement park for the kiddies) combines with an urge to avoid the crowds at the seashore and the snailpace on the Garden State Parkway, one place to consider is Hershey, Pennsylvania. Set in the green and rolling hills of the Pennsylvania Dutch dairy country, the town that gave birth to the great American chocolate bar offers a theme park, a zoo and several resorts for an overnight stay. Since it is situated a bit of a drive over the New Jersey border, many travelers find it more convenient to sleep over and spend one day at Hersheypark, one day exploring the countryside.

As for Hersheypark, itself. It's a theme park very much like Great Adventure, but smaller. There are several open theaters where parents can rest their feet and enjoy Broadway-style entertainment while the kids try the Fender Bender for the fourth time. A single admission price pays for all the rides and shows although of course they get you for the extras. The crowds here are well behaved and there is little problem of anyone ducking ahead in line. Of course the number of people in the park varies from time to time, but since Hersheypark is a little out of the way, it does not seem to get flooded with humanity. It is green and clean, as they advertise. You enter Hersheypark through *Tudor Square*, a small Elizabethan enclave of shops and restaurants. Then it's on to the *Rhineland* with its many rides. Here you will find the kiddie rides, a giant carousel, a two-armed Ferris Wheel and some inbetweeners. The next area, *Der Deutschplatz*, is dedicated to Hershey's Pennsylvania Dutch milieu and includes a crafts barn featuring local talent.

An aquatheater featuring dolphin and human diving acts, an amphitheater for the song-and-dance shows and two small theaters for puppet shows and children's comic shows all offer alternatives to rides. For the strong stomachs there are three roller coasters including the new Sidewinder, which goes upside down and backwards. The Coal Cracker is an extended flume ride for those who like to make a big splash.

There is a good, medium-sized zoo covering ten acres off to one side of the park, which does give something to those who hate rides. The Kissing Tower, a gentle space needle, offers a nice view and is something different for mothers with young children. Monorails, skyrides, and antique auto rides make this park well suited to families with kids under ten, although there are enough scary rides to please the teenagers and young adults. And in response to competition from Sesame Place, the park has expanded its children's area to include such features as a "ball crawl" and a cargo net climb.

Outside the park, and absolutely free, is Hershey's **"Chocolate World,"** a simulated factory tour in the Disney style. There you ride in automated cars past scenes of dairy farms, African cocoa tree plantations, and assembly belts full of kisses and chocolate bars. The whole time you are wafted past rivers of milk and glowing red roasters the smell of chocolate assails your nostrils.

For those who have time, a visit to the town itself, the nearby rose gardens (separate listing in this book) and **The Hershey Museum** are all pleasant excursions.

HOURS: Late May - Labor Day: 10:30 - 10:00. Weekends and shortened hours, May & Sept.

ADMISSION: Adults: $20.95; Children 3-8: $17.95; Seniors: $13.75; 3 and under free.

LOCATION: Route 322, Pennsylvania, approachable from either 283 off The Pennsylvania Turnpike or Route 83 off 81.

TELEPHONE: HersheyPark: 717-534-3900; Visitor Center: 717-534-3005

ACTION PARK

Over the years, Vernon Valley has burgeoned from a summer stop that offered go-kart rides into a multi-million dollar action park. They have an Alpine Slide (that's a low, wheeled cart you maneuver down a fiberglass chute), speed boats, paddle boats, swimming pool, tidal wave pool, scenic sky ride (that's the ski lift left over from winter), bumper boats and a complete children's section. But it is the large variety of water slides and rides that brings the teenagers and young adults out here in droves. The terrain is steep and craggy and the water slides are for the most part built up against the mountain. There are rubber tube rides that twist and turn, straight slides that jackknife you into the water, closed chute rides and the Tarzan water hole where you just jump in from a swinging rope. Scrapes and bruises are not unusual from some of these rides.

The tidal wave pool is a Japanese attraction. It was terribly overcrowded the day I was there, and Americans, unlike the sedate Japanese, jump in the waves, float on rafts and generally create a dangerous situation.

As for the race cars and speedboats — driver's licenses are required for these. Because each person takes a long time the waiting lines move at the pace of a turtle. Those who use the race cars must sign a waiver absolving the park of responsibility in case of accident.

There are also, surprisingly, some tame areas, such as miniature golf, a sky ride and shops. However, the major thrust of the park is thrills and ever more thrills. The latest addition is a Bungee jump. Obviously for those who like a little risk with their pleasure.

The park appeals primarily to teenagers and young adults. Obviously, the time to visit here is during the week when access to the rides is easier. The rides themselves, by the way, seem to be in perfectly good condition and there are plenty of lifeguards around. However, this is an action park where people operate the rides themselves, so accidents do happen.

138

Lockers and changing rooms are available for those who bring swimming gear. Liquor is served, and there are concerts and live shows (although some of the special Festivals are held in the fall, after the regular park closes down).

HOURS: July 1st to Labor Day — Daily. Call for Spring & Fall hours.
ADMISSION: All day ticket: Adults: $19.00; Children: $15.00 ($16 weekends) Under 4 free.
DIRECTIONS: Route 80 to Route 23N to 94E for 3 miles
TELEPHONE: 201-827-2000

DORNEY PARK & WILDWATER KINGDOM

This is basically a double-personality park. On one side is Dorney Park, a standard old-fashioned amusement center (it's been around since 1884) which features carousels, cyclones, glass houses, train rides and a large, new rollercoaster. (It also includes a new "kidcenter" for young children's activities — such as climb-through netting and a plastic ball jump). The park also features an outdoor stage devoted primarily to rock shows at the moment. All the rides and shows come under Dorney's single-price admission — except for the speed car and water boat racing which cost a hefty extra fee — and was my family's choice activity.

On the other side of Dorney Park — and separated from it by a large parking lot — is Wildwater Kingdom. This is a highly popular waterpark which offers water slides in all sorts of variations. You will find looping, speeding, inner tube and kiddie water slides here. The giant wave pool (which manufactures artificial waves every ten minutes) has two sections: one for those who ride plastic surfboards and mattresses and one for those who stand and jump. Don't expect to be able to swim in all this mass of bodies. But the park does provide plastic sun chairs and lounges so that parents can sit and sun while their offspring surf and slide. Locker rooms and showers are available, as are surfboard rentals.

Both parks allow picnicking in designated areas and of course there are plenty of hot dog, soda and ice cream stands around. One advantage of this park is that you do not need to buy the combination ticket. You can go to either Dorney or Wildwater or

139

both depending on the weather and your inclination. The park is located just beyond Allentown. Parking is extra.

HOURS: Daily 11-10 Full Season. Shorter hours April-mid-June & Sept.
ADMISSION: Combination ticket: Adults: $20.95; Children 3-6 & Seniors: $12.00.
LOCATION: 3830 Dorney Park Road, Allentown, PA. Take Route 78 past Allentown, look for signs.
TELEPHONE: 215-395-3724

SESAME PLACE PLAYPARK

When Sesame Place first opened over ten years ago it was the first activity park devoted directly to the younger set. Children from three to thirteen were supposed to stretch their minds and muscles in a series of innovative "play concepts" like swimming in thousands of plastic balls and climbing up cargo netting. While these activities still exist, the park is now more commercially oriented with enough grown-up water rides to interest Dad, Mom and older siblings in the day's entertainment. In fact, here, as in many other amusement parks, the water rides have swept away the competition.

For those who like it slow, there is Big Bird's Rambling River, a level waterway for rubber tubing (both parents and children can enjoy this). The Rubber Duckey ride is for small fry who want to take a tube ride down an incline with a little roll to it. The larger water rides are exactly like the ones at the Jersey shore or Action Park - metal structures where you chute down on a cushion of water - using either your backside or a mat. Some twist and turn, some are partially enclosed and some are straight down - you end up in a small pool of water all the same. The lines are long but they move in an orderly fashion and the park personnel make sure you don't bump into your neighbor. For those who are scared of water rides (and many young children are), there is a simple fountain in the center of the park where everybody can just jump around and get wet.

There are lockers available for a fee (you have to get on line immediately if you want to grab one) and changing rooms (which can get pretty messy, so wear your bathing suit when you come).

What if you hate water? Well, there's still the Cookie Bounce (a sort of open moonwalk), a slippery mountain climb, the plastic

Sesame Place has Bert and Ernie — so now Great Adventure has added Bugs Bunny to its expanded kiddie section.

141

ballroom, the giant punching bags and of course, the shows. There are three theaters. One is a small outdoor arena which features bird and animal acts. Another large stage offers a song-and dance revue starring Bert and Ernie. The most innovative show is called "make-your-own movie" and it takes place in a small auditorium in the Science Building. Selected audience members coordinate their movements to a blue screen above. Later you see them and the whole audience in a rollicking adventure movie.

The Science Building also hosts several do-it-yourself gadgets and the Computer Gallery (a separate building) offers simple games at three for a dollar. On a rainy day these two buildings get heavy patronage but otherwise you should be able to get in easily. Outside, there are occasional bands playing, a number of Sesame Street characters who stroll by and numerous picture taking opportunities. There are now two eateries, but since plenty of picnic tables are available, why bother standing in line for food?

When is the best time to visit Sesame Place? Weekdays when the Daycare and camp busses come in droves, or weekends, when families arrive en masse? When its cold and rainy and you miss half the water rides, or twilight, when the admission is less? Depends on the age of your children and your stamina. Bring food, towels, strollers (no rentals), and sun-tan lotion.

HOURS: 9:30-8 July & August; Shorter hours May, June, Sept. Weekends only Mid-Sept.-mid-Oct.
ADMISSION: Adults: $15.95; Children: $17.95; Seniors: $10.00; 2 and under, free. Parking $3.00.
DIRECTIONS: Route 1 South through Trenton to Oxford Valley Mall, Langhorne, PA. Turn right at New Oxford Valley Road just before Mall.
TELEPHONE: 215-757-1100

SHAWNEE PLACE

Here is another children's "active play" park, this one set in a green, leafy area of Pennsylvania's Pocono Mountains. It offers two waterslides, a heated wading pool, a cable glide, those large cargo nets that kids climb on, and the inevitable trough filled with thousands of colored plastic balls. Magic shows are put on regularly. There is also a snack bar and cocktail lounge at the

Base Lodge (in winter the park becomes the Shawnee Ski Area) and a picnic area. The ski-lift becomes a ride with a view in the summer. Pony rides and video games are also available.

Although this place is much smaller than Sesame Place, and the waterslide is the simple, old fashioned straight kind, it does not get as crowded. Because most of the activities here are geared strictly for kids, adults can pay a "spectator" fee if they choose not to participate.

HOURS: Mem. Day-Labor Day: Daily, 10-5. Weekends, Sept. & early Oct.
ADMISSION: $9.50. 40" & under, free. Non-participant: $3.50.
LOCATION: Rte. 209 to Shawnee Mtn. Ski Area, Poconos, PA.
TELEPHONE: 717-421-7231.

LAND OF MAKE BELIEVE

Compared to the super-slick, multi-million dollar theme parks, Land of Make Believe looks amateurish — yet there is something relaxing about the place. It is definitely designed for younger children (3 to 9 approximately) and has less of that nervous-making razzmatazz usually associated with amusement areas.

A simple maze, a candy cane "forest" (which kids try to climb), a high balance beam, a talking scarecrow (my eight-year-old never figured out how this was done) are a few of the staples here. *Santa's Barn* is where you creep through a magic chimney to the darkened room where Santa sits. (Some young children might find this frightening, so parents must accompany them).

The mechanical rides include a miniature 1863 train, a small roller coaster and several standard little kiddies rides. The hayride is the best bet, if you have no allergies. There is also a canoe ride and some active play elements in the *Sesame Place* tradition, such as a rope climb and bouncing balls. And the recent addition of games of chance brings a boardwalk feel to the place. No water rides, though.

The scenery, the wide-open blue sky, the picnic area in a country field and the closeness to Jenny Jump Mountain all add up to a pleasant excursion. It's way out in the country and everything about it — including the gravel and grass parking lot is bucolic. As for food, you can picnic or buy hamburgers, pizza, ice cream and snacks at a number of locations.

HOURS: Weekends from Memorial Day. Mid-June to Labor Day: 10-5; Sundays: 10-6. Sundays only after Labor Day.
ADMISSION: Adults: $8.50; Children: $10.50.
LOCATION: Route 80 to Exit 12. Two mi. to Hope, N.J. Follow signs.
TELEPHONE: 201-459-5100.

GINGERBREAD CASTLE

This fanciful castle, with its stone turret and colorfully painted ornamentation was probably quite an attraction when it first opened in 1928. There were statues of giant spiders and witches and a humpty-dumpty who sat on a wall. All this was created by a stage designer. With a proper tour guide and a little imagination it probably made a nice family outing. Years later, generations brought up on television and electronically controlled rides found the Castle pale stuff and so the place eventually closed.

Recently re-opened, the main castle remains the same, but there is now more going on outside the castle walls. As part of the ticket price you get a small show featuring the guides dressed as Goldilocks and the Three Bears (or whatever story is on for the day). This takes place on a small outdoor platform and children are asked to be part of the play. Afterwards there are picture taking opportunities and of course the tour of the spooky castle itself.

The main visitor center is now used as a dinner theater from spring to December. However, families will still find hot dogs, soda, gingerbread cookies and souvenirs available to castle visitors. There is also a small zoo featuring farm animals out near the parking lot. The resurrected Gingerbread Castle is geared to young children and adults who remember it from their own childhood visits.

HOURS: Late June-Labor Day 10:30-6.
ADMISSION: $6.00 Under 2 free.
LOCATION: Rte. 80 to Rte. 23N to Hamburg, Sussex County.
TELEPHONE: 201-827-1617

BOARDWALK AMUSEMENTS

There are small arcades, video game rooms and miniature golf places at any number of Jersey shore resorts. However, you can find the larger amusement centers at the following towns. They are located on the beach so just keep driving until you hit the ocean. Don't expect cleanliness or good restroom facilities at these places — they are often dirty, sweaty, greasy and carny. However, they are a tradition associated with summer (the season lasts from Memorial Day to Labor Day) and they are cheaper than theme parks. They also offer certain advantages which theme parks do not: rainchecks on tickets, easy availability from any shore point, no waiting lines and no need for parents to pay for tickets if they don't like the rides.

However, the larger amusement piers have become more sophisticated over the years. They have increased the size of their rides so there are now huge roller-coasters, full pirate ships and taller rides than ever. And on certain days they offer a set price for all rides if you buy for six hours.

For years there have been individual waterslides up and down the Jersey shore but now some boardwalks offer waterparks that are as big as anything you'd find at a theme park (although they may be more compacted to save space.) What's more they have plenty of lifeguards about. You'll find the lazy river ride for kids (and timid adults), slides that are partially enclosed (to give you a scarier feeling) slides with mats and slides where the only cusion on the water is your backside.

I guess the entrepreneurs at the shore have decided that whether or not the ocean is closed for pollution (as it was several summers ago) any beach-going tourist is going to find some way to get wet. With the prices they charge (generally about $9.50 for two hours) I could also say that you have a chance to get soaked, except these new waterparks seem to be clean and well-tended and the price is probably worth it.

KEANSBURG: An older area that had its heyday back in the 1940s. This is where Ralph Kramden was always going to take Alice in "The Honeymooners." The boardwalk runs about 4 or 5 blocks long and includes 30 kiddie rides, 15 adult rides, a pool, and a water slide. Concessions and arcade. *Directions:* G.S.P. to Exit 117, then Route 36E.

ASBURY PARK: The long boardwalk on Ocean Avenue is dotted with a few miniature golf games, and rides and indoor arcades, but the Palace Amusements casino and the carousels are gone. A new amusement center is planned for the future, but right now everything looks forlorn. *Directions:* G.S.P. Exit 100A-N or 102S.

POINT PLEASANT: A smaller amusement center with rides geared more for children although there are a number of adult rides present. Indoor arcade and miniature golf. Less variety than some of the larger amusement areas and the prices are slightly higher, but the atmosphere is not as honky-tonk and I found it rather pleasant. *Directions:* G.S.P. Exit 98-S or 90N.

SEASIDE HEIGHTS: New Jersey's version of Coney Island. One of the largest of the boardwalk amusement centers, with solid amusements and concessions along the boardwalk and on the piers. Some larger rides are here such as a big Ferris Wheel and the Pirate Ship besides the usual assortment of Trabants and Red Barons. **Water Works** is a complete condensed version of a waterpark on the square block opposite **Casino Pier**. Everything from easy tube rides to the "adult" twisting waterslides.The indoor arcade includes a carousel, air hockey games and food stands along with the usual Skeeball and machine games. Rides active even during the day. A popular teenage hangout. *Directions:* G.S.P. Exit 82 to Highway 37E. Go through Toms River to bridge, follow signs.

ATLANTIC CITY/OCEAN CITY: As of now, only the **Central Pier** and the **Tivoli Pier**, a six-story amusement center built inside of the TropWorld hotel, offer boardwalk style amusements in Atlantic City. Over at Ocean City, the boardwalk has a long stretch of stores, eateries and arcades. **Gillian's Wonderland Pier** is a medium sized amusement area with a large Ferris Wheel. **Gillian's Water Wonderland** offers a smaller version of the ever-popular water park with plenty of kiddie-sized rides.

WILDWOOD: The amusement section of the boardwalk goes on for miles and there are several separate fun piers. The piers vary in solidity of their wood planking (one is actually concrete) and their prices, but the rides are very similar. The usual lineup is a haunted house, a crazy house, a few kiddie rides and the popular adult rides such as Flying Bobsleds, Tilt-A-Whirl, Trabant, etc. Roller coasters, and sack slides are specials at several piers.

And both the boardwalk and the piers boast an endless number of concessions, games and food stands. Here again, the waterslide craze has taken over. Both **Morey's Pier** and **Mariner's Landing** offer a complete waterpark which is tacked on to the end of the pier. All manner of straight and looping slides and tube rides for a set price (either full day or 2-hours). *Directions:* G.S.P. Exit 4.

OTHER AMUSEMENT PARKS

BOWCRAFT AMUSEMENT PARK: A small park set down plunk amidst the hurly-burly of Route 22, it is open all year round although many rides are not available in winter. Paddle boats, a train ride, miniature golf and several kiddie rides make this a popular place for the under-ten set. Go-karts, baseball batting, Tilt-A-Whirl, Scrambler and auto-cars bring out the teenagers and the dating groups. And the arcade area keeps video game buffs busy all year round. The usual dirty, carny atmosphere here at the rides and the tent arcade, but it's very convenient for people in the area and you don't have to battle the beach traffic to get there. *Season:* Winter: Arcade only. Warm weather: full park. *Location:* Route 22, Scotch Plains, Union County. *Telephone:* 201-233-675.

CLEMENTON LAKE PARK: Set on 40 acres about eight miles east of Camden, this amusement park has been operating for many years now. Rides include an old- fashioned carousel and roller-coaster called the Jackrabbit. A small size showboat offers rides around the lake. Newer rides include a log flume and a pirate ship. Playport area for kids, plus traditional kiddie rides. *Hours:* Mid- May -Late June: Weekends only, 12-8. July — Labor Day: Daily, except Monday, 12-10 PM. *Location:* Route 534 off Routes 30 or 42, Clementon, Camden County *Telephone:* 609-783-0263.

FAIRY TALE FOREST: Old-fashioned style kiddie park set in a wooded area in northern Jersey reminiscent of the Black Forest. Molded storybook characters, such as Goldilocks and the Three Bears, inhabit little houses where the children can look in. The animated toy circus is for viewing but kids can use the carousel and miniature train ride (extra fee). Picnic facilities.

Hours: Mid-June- Labor Day: Mon.-Sat.: 10-5; Sun.: 10-6. Weekends only, spring and fall. Admission: Adults: $6.50; Children: $5.25. *Location:* Route 23, Oak Ridge, Passaic County. *Telephone:* 201-697-5656.

STORYBOOK LAND: Another children's park with small structures in the shape of The Gingerbread House, The Old Woman's Shoe, Noah's Ark, etc. The petting zoo, miniature train ride, antique car ride, and other attractions are included in the price. Christmas light display in December. Picnic area, snack bar. Ten miles west of Atlantic City. *Hours:* Mid-June-early Sept.: 10-5:30. Shorter hours spring & fall. *Admission:* $7.95 (under 1, free). *Location:* Routes 40 & 322, Black Horse Pike, Cardiff, Atlantic County. *Telephone:* 609-641-7847.

ZOOS, AQUARIUMS,
NATURE CENTERS
WILDLIFE REFUGES

In This Chapter You Will Find:

THE BRONX ZOO

While the smaller zoos of New Jersey are fine for younger children, once the kids have reached third grade it's time to take them to the largest urban zoo in America. Not necessarily the best (that honor belongs to the San Diego Zoo according to most experts) but the largest. Actually, the Bronx Zoo is in a period of transition. One section is devoted to the older concept of caging animals for inspection in structures built like Greek temples. Victorian-style esplanades allow room for throngs of visitors, while the animals are cramped into small, concrete spaces. On the other hand, the open sections allow the animals to roam free while visitors watch them from across moats, from skyrides, and in summer, from the monorail. And the newly opened **"Jungle World,"** an indoor home for tropical Asian wildlife, combines a natural habitat with controlled climate for the best of both worlds.

Since there are over 5 miles of terrain to cover and over 3,600 animals to see, it's a lot easier to take either the skyride or the monorail (or both) when they are in season. These may cost extra depending on the day you visit (Donation day or full admission day). The open sections are divided geographically as follows: **Wild Asia**: Open only in summer. A 40 acre habitat where elephants, rhinos, deer and antelope roam free. Visitors view them from the glassed-in monorail, "The Bengali Express." **Africa**: Lions, gazelles, antelopes, zebras and gnus roam the grassy slopes. You can view them from surrounding walkways and bridges or from the slow-moving Skyfari ride. **South America**: A smaller section devoted to anteaters and such. There is a wildfowl pond nearby where you can enjoy the aquatic birds at their colorful best. **North America**: An extensive section that includes a walk-in Wolf Wood (no, they don't bite you), polar bears (how do they take the New York summers?), and lots of bison and bull elk.

Certain special houses, open all year round, offer the best this zoo or any other can come up with. First is *"The World of Darkness."* A top-notch display of bats, owls, and other nocturnal animals, it costs extra and is worth every penny. Special lights allow you to watch the racoons, porcupines and bush babies cavort on the forest floor. They think it's night because the zoo has reversed the light cycles. It's a world of strange creatures with glittering eyes, unique and thrilling; and to top it all, there are special bat-flying demonstrations twice a day.

The *"World of Birds"* is free and is housed in an ultra-modern concrete cylindrical building. Here you will find three floors of birds in a unique setting. Trees vault up the three stories while a variety of birds perch on the first, second and third story branches. Other special houses include the Penguin, Aquatic Bird, the extensive Reptile House and a new Zoo Center.

The *Children's Zoo* offers a host of fun things especially for kids under ten. Giant rope "spider webs" to climb, snail "shells" to ride in, and prairie dog burrows to explore practically turn this into an educational amusement park. The cost is extra but well worth it. You could spend almost an hour here alone. Another kids' favorite is the elephant and camel ride section (open warm weather only), and of course the *Bengali Express* with its narrated safari ride is always popular.

If you don't bring a sandwich (and there are plenty of tables if you do), there is a cafeteria open all year round. Warm weather opens the snack stands, the Pub and the zoobar.

HOURS: Daily, 10-5, Sun.: 10-5:30 PM. (Winter: 10 AM - 4:30 PM.)

ADMISSION: Donation Tues.-Thurs. Friday-Monday: Adults: $3.75; Children 2-12: $1.50; Seniors free. Parking fee.

LOCATION: George Washington Bridge to Cross Country Expressway east to exit 4B, Bronx River Parkway North. Take exit marked "Bronx Zoo" then left to Bronxdale parking field.

TELEPHONE: 212-367-1010.

THE SAFARI AT GREAT ADVENTURE

The largest safari outside of Africa takes about an hour to drive through and covers six miles and six continents. And although you do not get to see certain animals (such as tigers, panthers and lions) close up, you do get to see scads of them. Other animals, such as camels, elk in heat, jealous giraffes and short-tempered rhinos get almost too close for comfort. The brochure warns that you should keep car windows closed at all times so take an airconditioned car if you're visiting on a 90-degree day.

The road through the Safari is three lanes wide and you may travel at your own speed. Each area is separated from the other by wire fences so you must wait for the guards to open the gates between one habitat and another. Surprisingly, the warning signs to keep windows closed are apparent only in the dangerous cat sections. I noticed a number of cars with open windows and people who nuzzled deer and fed popcorn to camels. Camels, in fact, seem like the beggars of Great Adventure — they sidle up to the cars in the motheaten rags of their summer skin and seem to be looking for handouts.

In the African Plains section you can watch herds of elephants eat and socialize. And nothing can make you feel smaller than to sit knee-high to a giraffe as he nudges up against your car — unless it's sitting between two giraffes who are having a love-triangle spat and using your car as a barrier zone. The animals have right- of-way here, and if you get in real trouble honk for a Safari guard. One rhino did take particular exception to our baby blue station wagon. He looked suspiciously as if he were going to charge and sure enough a guard did wave us on quickly. I don't know what statistics there are on car bumping at Great Adventure, but the modern light-weight compact car is no match for a two-ton rhino.

The Australian section is unique. No other safari has animals from this side of the world. Great Adventure has gone to some pains to re-create a familiar habitat for these shy creatures. Kangaroos, wallabies, wallaroos and the flightless emu strut, waddle and bound on the hilly terrain. The kangaroos are much smaller than I had imagined and do not spend their time standing up, ready to punch. They move about on all fours and since their front legs are so much shorter than those powerful hind-quarters, they look for all the world like lopsided dogs with giant tails.

For those with metal-topped cars the ride through monkey territory is always of interest. These curious simians will scamper all over your car, check on the occupants, pull on the hood ornament, knock your grillwork and then pass on to the next car.

An air-conditioned bus ride through the whole park is an alternative to driving your own car, but it costs extra for each rider.

HOURS: 9-6 Daily, late June - mid-Sept. Weekends
            April, May, Oct.
ADMISSION ETC.:   See Great Adventure entry.

THE PHILADELPHIA ZOO

This is America's oldest zoo and like the Bronx Zoo, it offers a combination of old fashioned zoo houses filled with caged animals and modern landscaped animal "habitats". The most interesting of the latter is *The World of Primates.* Orangutans, gibbons and gorillas live here and you can actually see a gorilla family sitting on the grass outside the building.

The Treehouse - a special exhibit for children - allows kids to climb into a ficus tree, ride on a caterpillar and explore a river, a marsh, a meadow and other environmental features. One can smell the rainforest, hear the birds chirping, feel the skin of various animals and generally have a good time at this popular hands-on exhibit. It is housed in a separate building and costs $1.00 extra.

Besides the lions, tigers, bears and hooved animals one would expect at a major zoo, you can also find Australia's gift to the world - kangaroos and wallabies, - plus a Rare Animal House filled with some unusual varieties of monkeys and other species.

During summer a "Birds of Prey" show on an open stage has hawks, eagles and such demonstrate their prowess during free flight. Camel rides and elephant pictures are available April through September. Other features are a monorail ride around the premises and a baby animal nursery where you can watch the newborns frolic. The zoo covers 42 acres, which makes it large, but not impossible to cover in one day. There are several nice picnic areas, plus two major eateries. It is inside the huge Fairmount Park which also includes many of Philadelphia's museums and historic houses.

HOURS: Weekdays: 9:30-5; Weekends: 9:30-6.
ADMISSION: 12 & up: $5.75; Seniors, children 2-11: $4.75
LOCATION: 34th & Girard (Use Girard Ave. Exit of Route 76).
TELEPHONE: 215-243-1100

THE TURTLE BACK ZOO

Fifteen years ago, Turtle Back was probably the best zoo in northern New Jersey. There were seven hundred animals, and fanciful settings such as a large wedge of cheese to house rodents and a large piggy bank for the pigs. Well, a loss of funds plus a change in direction has left this zoo in limbo. Most of the cute settings are gone, the number of animals is down, and the place looks dirty and disheveled.

There are still many of the hooved animals, especially various types of deer, camel and bison. A few of the large cats, such as a cougar and a bobcat, remain. The seals still romp in the seal pond, and the bat cave (a dark tunnel where you can see a few of the winged animals) is still of interest. A small petting zoo with goats and sheep still exists and best of all, the miniature train ride, which takes you on a nice long trip through the woods, is now included in the admission price. The zoo is built on hilly terrain, so you do get a good hike, but most of the exhibits are rather sad looking.

The only new and worthwhile exhibit, and one that reflects the "naturalistic" philosophy, is the wolf woods. Here you can look through a plastic shield and see a pack of wolves at work and play. There are other new exhibits planned and there is some construction going on, but at the rate they are moving it will be a long time before this zoo is considered first rate again.

The educational center presents lectures on animals to individuals and classes, and this seems to be the emphasis here now. A fast food eatery and a picnic area afford plenty of seating space for those who lunch. The facility is run by Essex County, by the way; they ought to figure out some way to upgrade this place.

HOURS: Mon.-Sat.: 10-5; Sunday: 10:30-6. Winter: 10-4 Daily.
ADMISSION: Adults: $4.50; Children, Seniors $1.75. Under 3 free.
LOCATION: 560 Northfield Rd., West Orange (behind South Mountain Arena), Essex County.
TELEPHONE: 201-731-5800

CAPE MAY COUNTY ZOO

Cape May County has poured a lot of money into this park which once offered just a few scrawny cages. Now the landscape artists have been out in force, and the various animal enclosures are arranged along meandering paths with pleasant foliage all about. Some of the enclosures simulate the natural terrain of the animals. Others, particularly those for the big cats, are the traditional cement floor cages. But the zoo is within a park filled with the tall scrub pine and sandy soil of the region, so the general effect is of seeing animals within a natural environment. The giraffe, for instance, actually eats the leaves from a real tree.

Among the 120 species of animals here, you will find zebras, llamas, tigers, jaguars, bears, spider monkeys and a lion. The white-maned tamarin was the most unusual specie I saw there. Quite a variety of birds are on hand also, including cockatoos, toucans, a myna bird, peacocks, eagles and barnyard fowl.

155

Outside the zoo, there is a childrens playground, a picnic area and a number of concession carts for those who didn't bring lunch. All in all, a very pleasant outing. Free.

HOURS: Daily, 9-4:30 weather permitting
LOCATION: Route 9 & Crest Haven Road, Cape May Court House.
TELEPHONE: 609-465-5271 or 465-9210

STATEN ISLAND ZOO

This square-block, city zoo is of interest for three reasons: 1) it is convenient to those within easy driving distance of the Goethals Bridge, 2) it is primarily an indoor zoo, so it is available during the winter, 3) it is cheap.

The big collection here is the snakes. Since snakes take up little room (experts assure us that snakes like those little glass cubicles where zoo-keepers put them), it is possible to crowd an amazing variety of them into one large zoo-house. The biggest rattlesnake collection in the world resides here, along with cobras, pythons, cottonmouths, a krait, an asp — you ask for it, they got it. Since reptiles are not very active you may find two — or is it three, or one? — pythons curled around one another with head and tail indistinguishable. At the end of the room a family of alligators remind you there's more to the reptile class than just snakes.

In the *Mammal House,* there resides one panther, one lion, one leopard and one Siberian tiger, but these animals pace the traditional city zoo cage and seem unhappy at the prospect of a lifelong jail sentence. The monkeys, on the other hand, seem to have a fine time.

The zoo is unusual in that it also sports a small aquarium. Coral fish, sea anemones, and piranhas are among the colorful and dangerous fish floating behind glass. Invertabrates, including spiders, scorpions and centipedes, are also displayed in lighted niches.

Outside, in warm weather, there are flamingoes and Galapagos tortoises on display. A pleasant children's center includes a farm and petting zoo. Altogether, a pretty place with trees, benches, picnic tables and snack bar, the Staten Island Zoo is marred only by those old-fashioned cages for the big cats. There are no hooved animals here, by the way — there is no space.

Whenever my son watches one of those disaster movies on TV wherein the local population is being devoured by overactive tarantulas or man-eating fish, he turns to me and says: "Where was that zoo where we saw the piranhas and the spiders and the poisonous lizards?" It was the Staten Island Zoo.

HOURS: 10-4:45 Daily. Closed Holidays.
ADMISSION: $1.00; Under 3 and seniors free. Wed. donation.
LOCATION: 614 Broadway, Staten Island. Take 278 E to Clausen Ave., Exit.
TELEPHONE: 718-442-3100

TERRY LOU ZOO

A privately owned zoo therefore more expensive to enter than a tax-subsidized one, Terry-Lou has been a New Jersey fixture for many years. It doesn't look like much from the outside — a small barn-like structure across from a corner of the Ash Brook Golf Course serves as the main entrance. It does, however, contain an interesting variety of animals in its collection.

For instance, a pygmy hippo, lions and tigers, giraffes, bison and llamas all reside here. Some of them are stars. The tiger has appeared in Exxon commercials and the two giraffes have had a stint in show business also. As for the monkeys, well, they're always the stars of a zoo anyway. They are housed indoors where you will find several chimpanzees, two mandrills, some ringtail lemurs and a few frisky types. Orangutans are the proud new additions here.

Because cages at the Terry-Lou are mesh (a heavy Cyclone fence type) you can get a closer look at these animals than at many other zoos. In fact, if it weren't for the smell that is an inherent part of a monkey house, I would have continued an eyeball-to-eyeball confrontation with an intelligent chimpanzee for an hour.

The main outside area features mammals with an adjacent section for birds and alligators. Large animal crackers are available, and the mesh cages allow you to feed llamas, deer, etc. without fear of fingerbite.

The complete area of the Terry-Lou Zoo runs about one square city block. The area is flat and easy for young children and older folk to navigate. It should take about one hour to see it all, depending on the attention span of your children. A few animals may be petted, but by no means all. Pony rides are often available.

HOURS: Weekdays: 10-4; Weekends: 10-6. Closed winter.
ADMISSION: Adults: $6.00; Children 1-12: $3.00; Under one year free.
LOCATION: 1451 Raritan Road (corner of Terrill) Scotch Plains, Union County
TELEPHONE: 201-322-7180

SPACE FARMS ZOO

Another private zoo, this one in a completely rural area that closely approximates the natural surroundings of many of the animals housed there. The trip takes you well into the mountains of northern Sussex County, past farms of Herefords and horses grazing peacefully among the green hills.

The zoo is set up for family outings with many picnic tables, swing sets and slides for the youngsters. There is plenty of space at Space Farms (although the name derives from the family that runs it.) One hundred acres are devoted to rather simple cages of grizzly bears, lions, tigers, hyenas, monkeys, etc. plus several buildings filled with antique cars, sleighs and other collections. A large pond at the center of the acreage allows ducks and geese to paddle about, while pens of yak, llamas, buffalo and goats dot the surrounding hill.

Bears include Goliath, the largest brown bear in captivity, grizzlies, polar bears and the rare Hokkaido bear from Japan. Although the bear cages seemed smaller than those at public zoos, Mr. Space assured me the bears inside were happy. At any rate, Space Farms has the highest reproduction rate for animals in captivity of any zoo in America, according to Mr. Space. Maybe it's the fresh air, or the diet of fresh meat, or the natural smell that emanates from the bear cages — but there were plenty of cubs rollicking around on the day I visited.

The entrance building to the property includes a *Museum of Americana* (everything from Indian arrowheads to old clocks), a snack shop and a gift shop. And on the hills to the left of the zoo there are more museums with collections of old buggies, cars and everything but the kitchen sink. Although the entrance fee is relatively high here, between the animals, the museums, the swings and the slides you can make a day of it. Picnic lunches allowed.

HOURS: Daily 9-5, May 1 - Oct. 31.
ADMISSION: Adults: $7.50; Children 3-12: $3.50
LOCATION: Beemerville Road, Sussex, Sussex County. Take Rte. 80 to Rte. 206N to Route 519. Follow signs.
TELEPHONE: 201-875-5800

OTHER SMALL ZOOS (NEW JERSEY)

There are a number of small zoos tucked away in local city and county parks that are pleasant to visit when you are in the vicinity. Among them are:

VAN SAUN PARK ZOO: A charming children's zoo with a birdhouse, a small collection of animals, an adjacent 1860s farm and a miniature train ride. Recent additions have expanded the quality and quantity of the animals. All this is set in a large country park with lots of picnic tables and a duck pond. *Location:* Forest Ave. (off Route 4), River Edge, Bergen County. *Telephone:* 201-262-2627.

COHANSIC PARK: Good sized city zoo set inside an 1100 acre park that borders the river in Bridgeton. Over 200 animals including lion, bears, wolves and zebras. The park also includes picnic areas, nature trails, lots more. Location: City Park, Bridgeton (Routes 49 and 77) Cumberland County. *Telephone:* 609-455-3230.

POPCORN PARK: A 7-acre licensed zoo that caters strictly to injured, abandoned and unwanted wildlife. One section houses rescued animals such as Lacey the Lion, another includes the kennels of abandoned pets waiting for adoption. The facility is run by the Associated Humane Society. *Admission:* Adults: $2.25; Children, Seniors: $1.25. *Hours:* Daily 1-5. *Location:* Humane Way and Lacey Road, Forked River, Ocean County. *Telephone:* 609-693-1900.

THE NEW YORK AQUARIUM

It's in Brooklyn, of course, and you can get there easily (since getting lost in Brooklyn is an even more traumatic event to New Jerseyans than getting lost in Manhattan). Since the aquarium is right smack in the middle of Coney Island, many people prefer visiting in the spring or fall to avoid getting caught up in the hurly burly of boardwalk amusements.

This concrete aquarium is home to whales, sharks, seals, penguins and a variety of tropical fish. One star attraction is the electric eel which lights up every once in a while. The whales swim around lazily in the big tank — what you see is mostly their underbellies, and the sharks, most of which are rather small, have a building all to themselves. For many, it's the yellow tangs and sturgeon fish and other strange and beautiful denizens of the deep that make a trip to the aquarium worthwhile.

In good weather a training show takes place in an outside arena. A dolphin or whale jumps up and learns to take a fish from the trainer. Since they are just learning this can sometimes look more like amateur night than Broadway. In fact, many people are disappointed in the New York Aquarium, partly because of this and partly because it is not large. It certainly does not compare to Marineland or Sea World with their lush foliage and super trained sea animals — but of course, those places are profit-making entertainment centers.

This is the only decent-sized aquarium within easy driving distance. And it does have real whales and real sharks and penguins and an area where children can handle starfish and other creatures of the sea. So if your children have never been to an aquarium, if they have never seen fish that look like rocks and fish that look like dragons, or sharks at feeding time, it is certainly worth a visit. There is a nice souvenir stand by the way and a nice view of the beach and ocean.

HOURS: 10-4:45 daily. 10-6 weekends. Shorter winter hours.
ADMISSION: Adults: $3.75; Children: $1.50; Seniors free 2-5, M-F.
LOCATION: 8th Street and Surf Ave., Brooklyn. Take the Verrazano Bridge to the Belt Parkway (direction of JFK Airport) and stay on until 8th Street exit. There is a sign for the Aquarium.
TELEPHONE: 718-265-3474
PARKING: $4.00. Weekends $7.75 (includes one adult admission).

PEQUEST TROUT HATCHERY

This sparkling new concrete building complex has three purposes. One is to raise the fingerlings that grow into the trout that are later thrown into the state park lakes to become some lucky fisherman's catch. The second is to introduce youngsters to proper fishing techniques and to educate them in wildlife conservation. The third is to manage the huge acreage that surrounds the modern concrete and wood buildings and the wildlife that lives therein (including the birds whose chirping is amplified in the main building).

The Visitor Center includes a large room with many hands-on exhibits. There are also charts, displays, and a tankful of adult trout so that even those among us who do not fish can get a look at these ugly fellows. In another room a continuous movie shows the work that goes on here: how the fish are bred, fed and finally transported by truck to be unceremoniously dumped in fresh water streams. Finally you can go outside to see the ponds where the young fish are. A look into a glass sided building will allow you to see the tiny fingerlings.

This a popular place for school and scout groups, because during a group tour the kids often get to wield a fishing rod. There are also special Saturday classes on fishing techniques during certain months. You can buy fishing and hunting permits here plus the special trout stamps which help to fund this state center. Free.

HOURS: (General public) Fri.-Sun. 10-4.
LOCATION: Pequest Road, Oxford, Warren County (off Rte 46).
TELEPHONE: 908-637-4125

Wildlife Refuges

THE GREAT SWAMP

The remains of a glacial pocket, the Swamp serves as both a refuge for animals and a 5,800-acre barrier to suburban development. It was saved some years ago from the fate of airport development by a group of conservationists and donated to the Federal Government which now administers it. The area is a combination of marshes, grassland, swamp woodland and hardwood ridges. There are some stands of mountain laurel and rhododendron but a botanical wonderland it's not.

Actually, there are sections that look like a great locale for a movie called "The Creature From the Black Lagoon." Tall, leafless trees, crackling twigs, swampy underbrush — well, it's a swamp after all. Not smelly like the Okefenokee, and not deep, but still a swamp. Wooden boardwalks have been built in several observation areas so that families can traverse the wetlands and observe whatever wildlife is around. Mostly it's small — woodchucks, muskrats, frogs — and there are deer and fox, too, though they tend to stay in the interior away from humans. There are blinds for picture taking which most often will turn out to be of birds and insects. Swamp officials recommend visits in the early morning or late afternoon. Sunday afternoon the wildlife won't come out because there are too many people around.

The Swamp consists of two-thirds wilderness and one-third management area. There are several hiking trails in dry areas but picnicking is verboten. Observation centers are at Long Hill Road in New Vernon and at 247 Southern Boulevard in Chatham Township (this one run by Morris County). Old sneakers or waterproof shoes are recommended. Insect repellent in the evening. Free.

HOURS: Dawn until dusk. So. Blvd. closed summers.
LOCATION: Morris and Somerset Counties. Headquarters at Point Pleasant Road, Basking Ridge. Also Nature Centers run by Morris and Somerset Counties have interpretive centers. Read Nature Center section.
TELEPHONE: 201-647-1222; 635-6629

BRIGANTINE NATIONAL WILDLIFE REFUGE

Only eleven miles from Atlantic City but a world of immense quiet and peace. There are over 20,000 acres of grassy tidal marsh interspersed with tidal bays and channels with some brush upland area that support deer, fox and other small animals here. But the main area of the refuge is for the protection of waterfowl that use the Atlantic Flyway in their travels from Canada to Florida. Many birds (up to 150,000) winter completely in New Jersey now.

The snow goose, Canada goose, brant and black duck are among the many birds who stop here. The refuge offers a calendar of wildlife events — e.g., November 1-10: concentration of 100,000 ducks, geese and brant; June 20th: Canada goose round-up.

A self-guided tour of eight miles by car or foot circuits the waterfowl impoundments. Hundreds of birds are here no matter what time of year you visit. The vistas are flat and beyond the muddy marshes where the birds feed you can see the towers of Atlantic City. There are places where you can stop your car to take pictures (and even eat lunch, they say) but the insect population is heavy here also. Free.

HOURS: Daylight except during hazardous conditions.
LOCATION: U.S. 9, one mile east of Oceanville, Atlantic County.
TELEPHONE: 609-652-1665

WETLANDS INSTITUTE

Set in the middle of a 6,000 acre publicly owned tract of salt marsh, this attractive cedar shake building includes classrooms, an exhibit and lecture hall and six research laboratories. The casual visitor will find a recently expanded "touch" museum for children, saltwater aquariums, and a nice gift shop. There is also an observation tower which provides a view of the surrounding wetlands (and an occasional osprey nest). Periodic guided tours of the marsh, plus a number of lectures and ecology classes are available. Once a year the Institute operates the *"Wings 'N Water Festival"* a popular weekend fest in September that includes special events in all the local towns. Wooden duck carving, seafood dinners, and open houses are included.

HOURS: Tues.-Sat.; 9-4:30; Sun.: 1-4. Closed Sun. in Winter and 2 wks. Christmas.
ADMISSION: Free. Charge for classes and Festival.
LOCATION: Stone Harbor Blvd., Middle Twp., Cape May County.
TELEPHONE: 609-368-1211.

STONE HARBOR BIRD SANCTUARY

Strictly for the birds, this one, because the visitor only gets a glimpse of our feathered friends from the small parking area available. However, if you happen to pass by this 21-acre sanctuary around 7 p.m. on a summer's eve, you will see squadrons of stately birds come in for a landing as they return home from their feeding places. Dedicated bird-watchers also get up at dawn to watch the take-off. Among the species to be observed are snowy egrets, the brown ibis, and a variety of herons. There are some pay binoculars available for use. Free.

HOURS: Nesting time is May through October.
LOCATION: 111th to 116th Sts. on 3rd Ave., Stone Harbor, Cape May County. Take GSP Exit 10 to Stone Harbor.
TELEPHONE: 609-368-5102.

NATURE CENTERS

So what's a nature center? Not knowing, I expected to find a little log cabin in the woods where a grizzled old codger showed his bird nest collection and talked about owls. Actually the centers are a lot more sophisticated than that. What I found, at the few I visited, were modern buildings filled with classrooms, auditoriums, displays, professional staff and a host of activities, particularly on weekends. Of course the buildings are just the center of the nature area, which also has trails, wildflowers, birds, and small animals. Some Centers include cross-country ski trails. And weekend programs may cover such diverse activities as maple-sugaring, ski instruction, movies, lectures on backpacking, bird walks, trail walks, etc. Lectures for school groups and movies for families are staple fare. Courses usually cost a small fee while guided walks and rambles are free. And naturally, one may visit these centers and walk the trails without participating in the structured programs at all.

Not all the centers are big and beautiful but they all serve their communities well. In many cases, the displays are equal to what you would find in a small museum of natural history. Here are some of New Jersey's nature centers:

LORIMAR NATURE CENTER: 790 Ewing Ave., Franklin Lakes, Bergen County. *Telephone:* 201-891-1211. Run by the Audubon Society. There is a Living Museum and a demonstration farm besides the nature program and field trips. Nature trails open every day while the Visitors' Center is available.

FLAT ROCK BROOK NATURE CENTER: 443 Van Nostrand Ave., Englewood, Bergen County. *Telephone:* 201-567-1265. Solar-heated building, 150 acres of forest with trails, brook. Various weekend activities, tree identification, classes for schoolchildren, local artists' show. Run by self-supporting environmental organization. Open daily.

BERGEN COUNTY WILDLIFE CENTER: Crescent Ave., Wyckoff. *Telephone:* 201-891-5571. A little of everything here — wildlife, daffodil preserve, waterfowl pond, nature trail, garden.

At the Center, museum programs and films. Open daily except for legal holidays.

HARTSHORN ARBORETUM AND BIRD SANCTUARY: Forest Drive, Short Hills, Essex County. *Telephone:* 201-376-3587. Plant and wildlife museum. Classes in basket-weaving, plant propagation, dyeing, etc. 16 1/2 acres of oak, maple, rhododendrons. Open daily. Special hours for museum.

CENTER FOR ENVIRONMENTAL STUDIES: 621 Eagle Rock Ave., Roseland, Essex County. *Telephone:* 201-228-2210. Nature walks, slide lectures, classes for both children and adults. Center is also embarkation point for many daytrips — preregistration required. Open daily.

RIKER HILL PARK GEOLOGICAL MUSEUM: Livingston, Essex County. *Telephone:* 201-992-8806. Administered by Center for Environmental Studies. Reconverted army barracks now houses fossil museum with skeletal reproductions. Quarry with fossil digs open for tours in good weather (reservations needed for groups).

TRAILSIDE NATURE CENTER: Coles Ave. & New Providence Road, Mountainside, Union County. *Telephone:* 201- 232-5930. Part of Watchung Reservation. New building, includes auditorium and displays. Old nature museum has displays of beehives, eggshells, etc. Weekend programs, nature walks. Planetarium also.

GREAT SWAMP OUTDOOR EDUCATION CENTER: 247 Southern Blvd., Chatham Twp., Morris County. *Telephone:* 201-635-6629. On one edge of the swamp and run by the county. Wooden building contains exhibits, library, classrooms. Nature trails, guided walks, wooden walkways into the swamp, special programs such as maple-sugaring. Closed July and August, when nature center moves to Schooley's Mountain Park, Route 24, Long Valley.

SOMERSET COUNTY PARK ENVIRONMENTAL EDUCATION CENTER: 190 Lord Stirling Park, Basking Ridge. *Telephone:* 201-766-2489. At the other edge of the Great Swamp. Modern building with classrooms, displays, separate solar-heated house. 8 1/2 miles of trails and wooden walkways. Bird-watching, guided hikes, winter sleigh rides.

PORICY PARK NATURE CENTER: Oak Hill Road, Middletown Twp., Monmouth County. *Telephone:* 201-842-5966.

250 acres of land with trails. Fossil bed in park, fossil walks. Museum has art and nature displays, art programs, school programs.

SANDY HOOK VISITORS CENTER: Gateway National Recreation Area, Highlands, Monmouth County, off Route 36. *Telephone:* 201-872-0092. Summer activities include canoe trips and dune walk. Center has slide show, exhibits. Winter and spring weekend activities: holly forest walks and passes for lighthouse tours and Fort Hancock batteries. Classes by reservation.

HACKENSACK MEADOWLANDS DEVELOPMENT COMMISSION ENVIRONMENTAL CENTER: 2 De Korte Park Plaza, Lyndhurst. *Telephone:* 201-460-8300. Emphasis on the urban salt marsh and history of the meadowlands. Exhibits on recycling. *Hours:* Daily except Sun. & holidays.

MERRILL CREEK RESERVOIR ENVIRONMENTAL PRESERVE: 116G Montana Rd., Washington Twp., Warren County. *Telephone:* 908-454-1213. Primarily for hiking, wildlife observation and photography of 290 acre preserve. Visitor center, timber trail. *Hours:* Daily.

N.J. AUDUBON SOCIETY: — Besides their headquarters at Lorimar, the society operates several bird and wildlife sanctuaries and observatories and holds various programs of interest to birdwatchers and others. Among these are: **Scherman-Hoffman Sanctuaries**, Hardscrabble Road, Bernardsville (Tel. 908-766-5787); **The Cape May Bird Observatory**, 707 East Lake Drive, Cape May Point (Tel. 609-884-2736) - famous for its early May Cape May Weekend when millions of birds can be tracked; **Owl Haven**, Englishtown-Freehold Road, Tennent, (Tel. 908-780-7007); and **Rancocas Nature Center**, Rancocas Road, Mt. Holly, (Tel. 609-261-2495).

Note: Parents of young children should also check out the mini-zoos in such places as *The Newark Museum, The Morris Museum and the Bergen Community Museum.*

THE OUTDOOR LIFE

Photo: Courtesy N.J. Div. of Travel & Tourism

In This Chapter You Will Find:

SKI AREAS

New Jersey Ski Areas

GREAT GORGE — VERNON VALLEY: One ticket buys access to the whole complex. By far the largest ski area in New Jersey, this place can get awfully crowded on weekends with lines at both the lifts and the cafeteria. The most persistent complaint is that on weekends busloads of amateur hotshots take over the slopes here. Night-skiing and half-day tickets available. Altogether GG/VV has 13 double chairlifts, one triple chairlift, several tows, complete snowmaking equipment, 3 mountains, 52 trails, ski rentals, lessons, and nursery. Cafeteria and bar at both base lodges. Nighttime entertainment. Vertical drop of 1033 feet.

    LOCATION: Route 94 near McAfee in Sussex County.
TELEPHONE: 201-827-2000 - for general information. 201-827-3900 — for ski report.

HIDDEN VALLEY: Once partially private, now a public ski area with day, twilight and night time skiing. 4 slopes, 12 trails, 620 foot vertical drop. Ski lessons plus separate racing program. Cafeteria, bar, lodge entertainment.

    LOCATION: Breakneck Road, Vernon Twp., Sussex County
TELEPHONE: 201-764-4200, 764-6161

CRAIGMEUR: One chairlift, one T-bar, two rope tows. A popular family area which caters to intermediates and beginners. Four slopes, cross-country program, night lighting. It's conveniently located to the northern suburbs and can get quite crowded on weekends (actually it's the cafeteria that's crowded with mothers who sit and watch the clothing while Dad teaches the kids a few pointers). No difficult slopes here which is why it's so popular with the beginners.

    LOCATION: Route 80 to Green Pond Road (Route 513) Newfoundland, Morris County.
TELEPHONE: 201-697-4501

BELLE MOUNTAIN (Mercer County): One chairlift, three rope tows, four ski trails including one intermediate 190 ft. vertical drop. Open evenings during the week and weekends.. Lighted for nighttime skiing. Lessons, snack bar, beginner packages.

LOCATION: Valley Road (off Route 29), Hopewell
TELEPHONE: 609-397-0043

CAMPGAW MOUNTAIN (Bergen County): For beginners and intermediates. 100% snowmaking equipment. Main slope and two learning slopes, two double chair lifts, one T-bar, vertical drop of 270 feet. Lighted for night skiing, snack bar, lodge. Lessons.

    LOCATION: Campgaw Road, Mahwah
TELEPHONE: 201-327-7800

Note: Snowboarding available at all N.J. areas.

The Poconos Ski Areas

SHAWNEE MOUNTAIN: Close by. Shawnee offers eight double chairlifts, 17 slopes, snowmakers, ski school, accessory rental, cafeteria, bar and nursery. Trails include cross-country. Day, night and twilight skiing. Snowboarding.

    LOCATION: Take Route 80 to exit 52, then north on 209 for six miles.
TELEPHONE: 717-421-7231

JACK FROST/BIG BOULDER: You buy a combination ticket for these two popular mountains. Each mountain has seven lifts, two J-bars and many trails that run the gamut from "Powderpuff" to "Thunderbolt." Rentals, ski school, restaurant, cafeteria, nursery. There are 11 slopes at Big Boulder, 19 at Jack Frost.

    LOCATION: Lake Harmony and White Haven, Pennsylvania. Rte. 80 Exit 42 or 43.
TELEPHONE: 717-722-0104, 717-443-8425.

CAMELBACK: About a half-hour further on and part of the Big Pocono State Park. Camelback offers a variety of trails and attracts a pleasant crowd. 25 slopes, 11 lifts. This 2,100 ft. mountain is the largest in the area.

    LOCATION: Tannersville, Pa. Rte. 80 Exit 45.
TELEPHONE: 717-629-1661

New York State Ski Areas

HUNTER MOUNTAIN: For ski groups and more advanced skiers Hunter is very popular. A goodly drive away, but the mountain here offers a 1,600 foot vertical drop and a large variety of trails include plenty for beginners, intermediates and those who really want to hone their skills. Ten chairlifts, six tows, 45 trails, and all services available. Variety of eateries. Daytime only. Crowded.

    LOCATION: Take Garden State Parkway to New York Thruway, then exit 20 to Route 32 for 19 miles.
TELEPHONE: 518-263-4223

SKI WINDHAM: 7 miles west of Hunter, perhaps a little less crowded. Two peaks, 33 trails, 7 lifts. Includes restaurant, cafeteria, ski school, nursery. Daytime skiing only.

    LOCATION: Windham, NY (Take NYS Thruway to Exit 21).
TELEPHONE: 518-734-4300

STERLING FOREST SKI AREA: Really close at hand, in fact it is right over the border in Tuxedo. Once the site of a popular garden, this ski area now services families and is pleasant for beginners and intermediates. Four double chairlifts, six trails, 450 ft. vertical drop. Cafeteria, warming hut, lessons, rentals and snowmakers.

    LOCATION: Route 17 north to 17A north, just above Tuxedo, New York
TELEPHONE: 914-351-2163

Note: Unless otherwise noted, snowmaking is available. Prices and number of trails (and trails available) change all the time. The number of chairlifts may be upgraded from one season to the next. It is always best to call first.

THE JERSEY SHORE

There are 127 miles of beach along the coast of New Jersey which offer swimming, boating and fishing. But for most people going to the shore means visiting one particular portion of that lengthy coastline. Here's a roundup of the various types of shore resorts that await the newcomer or oldtimer.

First of all, the beaches. Some are narrow, some are wide but few are free. Sandy Hook (government run) charges a small parking fee, but can become so crowded that cars are turned away by noon. Atlantic City and the beaches of the Wildwoods are free. Island Beach State Park (State run) charges a per-car admission. Most other beaches require beach badges (which you buy from a man sitting there selling them), or admission through a private bathhouse which charges per-day admission. The price of badges varies from $2 per day to as little as $20 per season, depending on the town. If you stay at a hotel which owns its own beachfront, you don't have to bother with all this. And then there are a few select beaches which are accessible to residents only.

Cottage and beach house rentals vary according to size, closeness to beach and the social status of the town. Guest houses remain the cheapest accommodation especially if you don't mind walking a few blocks to the beach. Most motels offer efficiency apartments for those who want to cook in, but still have motel convenience. Motel rates compare well to other beach areas along the Atlantic Coast. Major amusement areas are found at Asbury Park, Point Pleasant, Seaside Heights, Atlantic City and Wildwood. (See chapter on Amusement Parks.)

The Upper Shore:
Sandy Hook to Island Beach State Park

The closest and most accessible to the crowded urban and suburban areas of northern New Jersey, the upper shore is naturally very popular for daytime and weekend trips as well as the two-week vacation. **Sandy Hook** beach is part of the Gateway National Park and is run by the Department of the Interior. The beach is free but there are parking fees. Besides the several beaches, Sandy Hook offers the oldest operating lighthouse in the U.S., a nature center, a visitor's center, tours of Fort Hancock and surf fishing.

Below Sandy Hook there begins a string of beachfront communities, each with a slightly different personality. Some, like **Belmar** and **Manasquan**, cater to a young, singles crowd who share cottages and guest houses.(Although Belmar has recently cracked down on "groupers".) Others, like **Deal**, are quiet and rich and interested only in full-time residents and full-summer rentals. You can find **Spring Lake** with its turreted late-Victorian homes and little old lady customers plus a good smattering of singles. Just hotels in the old tradition, rental homes and guest houses.

Asbury Park is a changing area with a wide beach, and many special events. One of the "old" resorts, it now has big rock concerts at the convention hall and the Paramount — quite different from its heyday. The large *Berkeley-Carteret* has been renovated and re-opened in the hope of rejuvenating the area. And there is still some boardwalk amusements. Separated from Asbury by a canal, **Ocean Grove** is quiet, reserved and primly Victorian. The stick style houses here remain from the early camp meeting days and are now being bought up by Yuppies.

Further on are **Brielle** and **Point Pleasant**, towns with a large fishing fleet and many summer cottage rentals. And a bit down the strip come more reasonable rentals. At **Seaside Heights** and **Seaside Park** there are over 1200 cottages, many of them minimal comfort types with just two rooms and a couple of screened windows. Hundreds of guest houses and almost 100 motels service the many vacationers who come to this popular area, with its large amusement center. Neighboring Island Beach State Park with its State-run beach and nature area gets the daytime visitors. Parking at this popular public beach runs $4 on weekends. Even so, the lot is filled early.

Long Beach Island

For many middle executive families the place to go is Long Beach Island only an hour and a half away from North Jersey's affluent suburbs. A long, narrow strip of beach that extends from Barnegat Light to Holgate, the island is actually a series of little towns connected to the mainland by a bridge. Here you will find closely quartered beach houses and a few motels leading up to the dunes. The friendly small-town atmosphere and spanking clean air remind one of Cape Cod. Since most people rent cottages or apartments for at least two weeks, there is an air of leisure and permanence about Long Beach Island.

Courses in art, photography, Yoga and such are offered at both the *Foundation of Arts and Sciences* and at *St. Francis Center*. A dinner theater assures visitors there's more to summer life than basking on the beach. A small amusement park called **Fantasy Island** caters to the kids while a boutique shopping center across the street attracts teenagers and families. All this at 9th St. in Beach Haven.

Of course a trip to Long Beach Island would not be complete without a visit to "Old Barney" which is the main attraction at **Barnegat Lighthouse State Park**. The park allows swimming (although the waves are rough), picnicking, surf fishing and a view of the panorama from the red and white 122 year old lighthouse. It only takes 217 steps to climb. The beach area is closed for dredging now.

The only access to Long Beach Island is the one road, Route 72 from the mainland to the center of the island. For the **Atlantic City** area (see separate chapter) you must return to Route 9 or the Garden State Parkway.

The Cape: Ocean City to Cape May

Like Atlantic City, this last strip of coastline is considered Philadelphia's shore as well as New Jersey's. However, people from all over come to these beaches, especially Canadians. **Ocean City**, the first down the line, bills itself as America's oldest family resort. It has never allowed liquor to be sold in its environs, the beach is wide and clean and the long boardwalk is filled with stores and arcades. Right now, the town is experiencing a building boom.

Among the Wildwoods, **Wildwood Crest** may have the advantage of getting the biggest family crowd but the beaches all along this area are very wide and kept quite clean despite the huge crowds that come on weekends. The surf is definitely milder down here and shallow enough for a toddler to wade a little without fear of imminent drowning. Both Wildwood and the Crest are solid motels from start to finish with guest houses and rental houses a block behind. **Wildwood** has the nightclubs, the amusement park and the swinging crowd, while the Crest is more kiddie centered (although these things change from year to year). **Stone Harbor**, a bit above, is rich and quiet with lovely homes and just a few very good motels.

Twenty minutes down the coast and at the very tip of New Jersey lies **Cape May City**. Here is a beautiful Victorian town with whitewashed gingerbread houses and green lawns set against a placid shore. Compared to Wildwood with its many rectangular motels, Cape May presents a 19th Century dream. Quaint guest houses offer bed and breakfast and a turn-of-the-century ambience. What they don't offer is swimming pools and instant everything, although there are several hotels in town that offer at least a pool.

Young couples and older folks seem to love the environment here. The beach in town, however, is brown and narrow and a poor relation to the neighboring wide swaths. Also, Cape May town has recently had a big splash of publicity so the narrow streets are now getting crowded and the automobiles are getting to be a nuisance.

As mentioned earlier in this book, one center of attraction here is the "Victorian Town," a series of renovated houses, quaint boutique shops, gaslight lamps and brick walkways. The shops lining Washington Mall offer an evening's entertainment in themselves with their art & crafts. Parking is a problem and the local Acme charges for a space so get there early and look for a "free" space.

Beyond the town, **Cape May Point Beach** offers a wide beach, a picturesque lighthouse you cannot enter, and those little pieces of quartz known as Cape May Diamonds. And at the very tip of the county, the line begins for the **Cape May-Lewes ferry**, a three hour boat ride that takes you to Delaware the slow but pleasant way.

HIKING

There are any number of County Parks which offer both easy and more difficult hiking trails. Popular among these are the trails in the Watchung Reservation in Union County, the South Mountain Reservation in Essex County, the Lenape Trail in Nutley, the Mahlon Dickerson Reservation in Morris County. Almost all State Parks include hiking trails and you will find the complete list of State Parks at the end of the chapter. There are, furthermore, two areas of extreme interest to outdoor enthusiasts in New Jersey — the **Pine Barrens** and the **Delaware Water Gap National Recreation Area**. Both of these include or neighbor state parks.

Information on hiking trails and other events at Delaware Water Gap is available at the Kittatinny Point Station right off of Route 80 as you travel toward the Pennsylvania border. Among the many activities sponsored by the Recreation Area are: the **Peters Valley Craftsmen** — a summer place where you may watch master potters, weavers, jewelry makers, at work; the **Walpack Art Center** (basically an art gallery); and **Slateford Farm**, an 1800's farmhouse over on the Pennsylvania side. **Millbrook Village**, a restored 19th Century town is mentioned separately in this book. The **Kittatinny Point Center** is also a staging area for canoeists (who bring their own) and includes picnic area, restrooms and lots of leaflets, including hiking trail guides. Whether you hike or take the car to an outlook point, a view of the Delaware Water Gap (which is a deep gorge cut by the river between two sets of mountains) is probably the most spectacular view in New Jersey. It should not be missed.

Stokes State Forest which is right nearby in the northern section of the State includes 17 named and marked trails plus a nine-mile stretch of the Appalachian Trail that transects the area. Here you will find Tillman Ravine. The 10,000-year-old ravine is preserved exactly as it was found with a host of natural wildflowers and trees. Five bridges have been installed to gain a better perspective for the hiker. The trails here are for the more experienced hiker.

The **Pine Barrens** offer a completely different experience. The terrain is practically flat but the flora and fauna of the region are unusual. Trails and old sand roads wind through the pines and swamps. The Batona Trail is the longest, extending from Carpenter Spring in Lebanon State Forest to Batsto in Wharton Forest, for thirty miles. Another, shorter trail in the Pine Barrens is called the Absegami. Since trails in the Pine Barrens can be confusing and people have gotten lost, it is best to start your hike at Batsto where you can talk with the Rangers at the visitor's center and obtain hiking guides.

Those interested in hiking can obtain further information by writing to the *New Jersey Division of Travel and Tourism*, P.O. Box 400, Trenton, NJ 08625. Another good place to contact, especially if you are interested in joining group hikes is: **The Sierra Club**, 360 Nassau Street, Princeton, NJ. Telephone 609- 924-3141. Although this club is primarily devoted to environmental protection, their hikes and canoe trips are graded according to difficulty and led by a responsible hiker. They are very knowledgeable in the area of New Jersey trails.

FISHING

Most people think of fishing in New Jersey as off-shore fishing. Indeed, there are fleets of boats from Atlantic Highlands to Cape May, just waiting to take customers out. Party boats go out seven days a week during the summer either for half or full day excursions. They come complete with tackle, bait, food and drink although you pay for the extras, of course. These boats can handle over a hundred people and are sturdy enough to go well out into the ocean in their quest for bluefish, weakfish, tuna, fluke, and striped bass.

176

Charter boats are hired by groups for the day and in the busy season must be reserved weeks in advance. **Brielle**, on the Manasquan Inlet is one of the largest centers of party and charter boats in the state. Check the Sports Section of your daily newspaper (the Friday edition, especially) for the names and rates of party and charter boats.

Fresh-water fishermen have several favorite spots in New Jersey, two of them in State Parks. **Round Valley** is deemed to have the best sport fishing with 22 species of fish, including rainbow and lake trout and largemouth and smallmouth bass. The Round Valley Reservoir is part of the State Park about one mile south of Lebanon in Hunterdon County. It was created by two dams and is stocked by the State. In **Swartswood State Park** both Big and Little Swartswood Lakes are known for their fishing quality. This is a beautiful area high in the mountains of Sussex County.

The Pine Barrens is a magnet not only for hikers but for campers and fishermen as well. The **Bass River** in the State Forest of that name, the Batsto River and many lakes and inlets are dotted with fishing camps, both public and private.

While boating ramps are available at most of these state parks you must bring your own boat along. Anyone over 14 years of age must have a license for fresh water fishing. You may buy your Fishing License at any sporting goods store.

CAMPING

New Jersey has many state parks that offer beautiful, clean and well equipped campgrounds. All you have to do to enjoy them is to bring your own camping equipment, a minimum cash entrance fee, and to survive the state's registration and reservation rigamarole. Best to call the campgrounds for details (a listing of state parks can be found at the end of this chapter.)

Bass River and **Swartswood State Parks** are excellent for family outings. Camp sites are adequately sized. Facilities include flush toilets and showers, and they are kept fairly clean. Swimming, boating and picnic areas are close to the sites. At Bass River, the shallow lake allows for canoeing and paddle boating. Swartzwood Lake is good for sailing as well. Canoes, rowboats and paddle boats can be rented.

The problem with these two attractive grounds (and many other state parks) is their popularity. For good weather weekend camping, reservations are essential and they must, unbelievably enough, be made in person. There's just no calling ahead for reservations by Ticketron (as it's done in New York State.) Campsites fill quickly — often before noon on Friday. To beat this system, one family I know sends a scout up on Friday morning to reserve a site. Only one site per registrant, by the way. Group sites though, can be reserved in advance. If you try for a site during mid-week, it's a lot easier. You may also reserve ahead if you plan to stay for a full week.

Waywayanda and **Worthington Parks** are definitely more primitive. Waywayanda is especially suitable for group camping and day trips to the beach or for fishing. The group camp sites are served by outhouses. Flush toilets and bathhouses are located by the beach. No flush toilets are to be found at Worthington on the Delaware. Outhouses or bring your own potty have to suffice. Using the port-a-potty turned out to be the best amusement of the weekend for the six-year-old son of friends who tried this spot. Located a few hundred feet from the Delaware, this large open site will appeal to those who choose to fish, raft, or canoe on the river. There is no bathing beach.

For the truly hardy, scenic **Round Valley Reservoir** offers real wilderness camping. Campers must hike or boat to the sites. The key interest here is sailing, boating and fishing. (Round Valley's popular bathing beach with its excellent facilities is in a separate part of the reservoir.) **Spruce Run**, with facilities for boating, fishing and swimming, takes camping out of the woods and puts it in the sunshine, where, in the heat of summer, it doesn't belong. Sites are on a hill and there is no shade. Again, there is a beach for swimming with the usual facilities. During summers with low rainfalls, these sites may sometimes be closed.

At all parks, (remember, Worthington has no formal facilities), swimming, boating and fishing are open daily in season for noncampers. Check the parks to learn boat limits.

Aside from the camping facilities in the State parks, you can also find hundreds of sites in the many private campgrounds around the State. The Pine Barrens and the southern portion of New Jersey abound with these camps which usually offer more sophisticated facilities than the State-run sites (higher rates too, of course). For a listing of both public and private campgrounds write for "Your Campsite Guide". It is available, free, from: *N.J.*

ADVENTUROUS OUTINGS

For those who like to add the element of adventure to their summer activities, there are a number of options available. You don't have to live in California to surf, skydive, parachute or raft down a river. Here are a few of the places where you can jump into action:

1. Skydiving/Parachuting: If you want to learn how to skydive and parachute (well, if you expect to land safely, you had better learn both) there is an outfit in New Jersey where they teach you both in one day. You get jump training on the ground, then they take you up and out. *Contact:* **Skydive East**, Sky Manor Airport, P.O. Box 84, Pittstown, NJ 08867. They are open weekends from Mar. 1- Dec. & weekdays, June 1-Sept. 1. Closed Tues. & Wed. *Telephone:* 201-996-6262.

2. Windsurfing: All you need for this one is wind, water and a surfboard with a sail attached. Popular areas are the lakes at such state parks as Round Valley and Spruce Run. The bay side of the Jersey shore also affords windsurfing territory for experienced practitioners. Sandy Hook is popular and you can find windsurfing rentals (along with rowboats & motorboats) on Long Beach Island and other shore resorts.

3. White Water Rafting: Rafting can run the gamut from lazy tubing down the Delaware to the more exciting white water stuff on the Lehigh River in Pennsylvania. New Jerseyans who want to try the Lehigh River can use either **Whitewater Challengers** which operates out of Whitehaven, PA (Tel. 717-443-9532) or **Pocono Whitewater** in Jim Thorpe, PA, (Tel. 717-325-4097). These outfits offer guided trips (the guides accompany the rafts on kayaks) and have graded outings ranging from easy to more challenging. Call for reservations and information on what to bring and what can be rented (wet suits, etc.).

Kittatiny Canoes in Dingman's Ferry, PA, (Tel. 717-828-2338) is not only one of the biggest of the canoe renters along the Delaware River, they also offer rafting and tubing trips. Further south you can find **Point Pleasant Canoes** which offers canoeing, leisure rafting, and river tubing. They operate out of three

179

Rafting down the Delaware has become a popular sport.

places: Point Pleasant in Bucks County, PA (Tel. 215-297-TUBE); Upper Black Eddy, PA (Tel. 215- 982-9282); and Martins Creek Base (215-252-TUBE). Picnic facilities are available at the bases, since the amount for food and drink allowed on trips is limited.

4. Hot Air Ballooning: For those of you who want to go back in time, hot air ballooning offers fancy flights (often with champagne included) over Hunterdon, Mercer and Somerset counties. Some of the outfits currently operating are: The Flight Fantastic (908-479-6850), The Rainbow Express (908-359-2600) and Alexandria Balloon Flights (908- 479-4878).

5. Plane Gliding: You soar in a glider (which is pulled by an airplane) over the Delaware Water Gap, the Kittatinny Ridge and other scenic areas. Good picture taking possibilities. *Contact:* Eagle Ridge Soaring, 36 Lambert Road, Blairstown Airport, Blairstown, Warren County. *Telephone:* 908-362-8311.

STATE PARKS AND FORESTS

Following is a listing of the State Parks and Forests of new Jersey. Many of these, especially if they have swimming and boating facilities, levy a charge per car (no matter how many or few people are crammed inside). Recently the price has been $4.00 for weekends, $3.00 for weekdays. This charge is only operational from Memorial Day to Labor Day. Tuesdays have been free for the last few summers, and may remain so. Some of these parks with historic sites or beaches, have been mentioned in greater detail elsewhere in this book.

State Parks

ALLAIRE STATE PARK, Monmouth County — 2,620 acres. Historic Howell Works and restored Allaire Deserted Village. Picnicking, hiking, nature study, horse trails, fishing, camping, old-time narrow gauge train rides. Lively calendar of events. *Telephone:* 908-938-2371.

ALLAMUCHY MOUNTAIN STATE PARK, Warren County — picnicking, camping, fishing. *Telephone:* 908-852-3790.

ATSION STATE PARK, Burlington County — Swimming, picnicking, food pavilion, boating. *Telephone:* 609-268-0444.

BARNEGAT LIGHTHOUSE STATE PARK, Ocean County — 172-foot lighthouse with 217-step spiral staircase. Swimming, picnicking, fishing. *Telephone:* 609-494-2016. Beach closed for some time.

CAPE MAY POINT STATE PARK, Cape May County — fishing, picnicking, guided nature tours and tours of ruins of defense installation. *Telephone:* 609-884-2159.

CHEESEQUAKE STATE PARK, Middlesex County — swimming, picnicking, fishing, camping, hiking. *Telephone:* 908-566-2161.

CORSON'S INLET STATE PARK, Cape May County — bathing, boating, fishing, hiking. Free.

DELAWARE & RARITAN CANAL STATE PARK, Somerset County — Kingston or Bull's Island sections. Canoeing, fishing and hiking. *Telephone:* 908-873-3050. Free.

FORT LEE HISTORIC STATE PARK, Bergen County — spectacular view; picnicking permitted, historic sites. *Telephone:* 201-461-3956.

FORT MOTT STATE PARK, Salem County — fishing, picnicking, playground. *Telephone:* 609-935-3218. Free.

HACKLEBARNEY STATE PARK, Morris County — picnicking, hiking, fishing. *Telephone:* 201-875-4800.

HIGH POINT STATE PARK, Sussex County — 220 ft. monument, swimming, picnicking, hiking on Appalachian Trail, fishing, camping, nature tours. *Telephone:* 201-875-4800.

HOPATCONG STATE PARK, Morris County — on Lake Hopatcong, New Jersey's largest. Picnicking, swimming, fishing, boating. *Telephone:* 201-398-7010.

ISLAND BEACH STATE PARK, Ocean County — beach, ocean bathing, surf fishing, picnicking, wildlife sanctuary. *Telephone:* 908-793-0506.

LIBERTY STATE PARK, Hudson County — nearby ferry to Ellis Island and Statue of Liberty. Picnicking, special events. *Telephone:* 201-435-8509. Free.

MONMOUTH BATTLEGROUND STATE PARK, Monmouth County — Visitor Center, picnicking. *Telephone:* 908-462-9619. Free.

PARVIN STATE PARK, Salem County — campsites, bathing, boating, hiking, picnicking, fishing, cabins. *Telephone:* 609-692-7039.

RINGWOOD STATE PARK, Passaic County — historic mansions, botanic gardens, swimming, fishing. *Telephone:* 201-962-7031.

ROUND VALLEY STATE PARK, Hunterdon County — fishing, bathing, boating, wilderness camping. Second largest "lake" in New Jersey. *Telephone:* 908-236-6355.

SANDY HOOK STATE PARK, Monmouth County — beach, swimming, picnicking, fishing, nature and military tours. *Telephone:* 908-872-0092.

SPRUCE RUN, Hunterdon County — fishing, small boating, bathing and picnicking. Reservoir area. *Telephone:* 908-638-8572.

STEPHENS STATE PARK, Warren County — *Telephone:* 908-852-3790.

SWARTSWOOD STATE PARK, Sussex County — excellent fishing, boating, camping, hiking, swimming. *Telephone:* 201-383-5230.

VOORHEES STATE PARK, Hunterdon County — picnicking, camping, nature study. *Telephone:* 908-638-6969. Free.

WASHINGTON CROSSING STATE PARK, Mercer County — museums, nature center, picnicking, outdoor theater during summer. *Telephone:* 609-737-0616.

WASHINGTON ROCK STATE PARK, Somerset County — picnic facilities, views of Watchung Mountains. Free.

WAWAYANDA STATE PARK, Sussex County — fishing, boating, swimming, picnics, camping.

State Forests

ABRAM S. HEWITT STATE FOREST, Passaic County — hiking and hunting.

BASS RIVER STATE FOREST, Burlington/Ocean Counties — bathing, picnicking, hiking, nature study, hunting, fishing. Cabins and campsites. *Telephone:* 609-296-1114.

BELLEPLAIN STATE FOREST, Cape May/Cumberland Counties— bathing, picnicking, camping, hunting, fishing. *Telephone:* 609-861-2402.

JENNY JUMP STATE FOREST, Warren County — picnicking, camping, nature study, hunting. *Telephone:* 908-459-4366.

LEBANON STATE FOREST, Burlington County — bathing, picnicking, hiking, hunting, camping. *Telephone:* 609-726-1191.

NORVIN GREEN STATE FOREST, Passaic County — hiking, hunting.

PENN STATE FOREST, Burlington County — bathing, picnicking, hiking, hunting, fishing.

STOKES STATE FOREST, Sussex County — bathing, picnicking, hiking, camping, fishing, hunting.

WHARTON STATE FOREST, Burlington County — bathing, camping, picnicking, fishing, boating, hiking, hunting. Batsto Historical Area. Canoeing. *Telephone:* 609-561-0024, 609-561-3262.

WORTHINGTON STATE FOREST, Sussex County — hunting, fishing, hiking, picnicking, camping. *Telephone:* 201-841-9575.

THE GARDEN VARIETY

Photo: Courtesy N.J. Travel & Tourism

In This Chapter You Will Find:

Longwood Gardens, PA
The Duke Gardens, N.J.
Brooklyn Botanic Gardens, N.Y.
New York Botanical Gardens, N.Y.
Wave Hill, N.Y.
Hershey Rose Garden, PA.
Colonial Park, N.J.
Buck Gardens, N.J.
Branch Brook Park, N.J.
Skylands, N.J.
Frelinghuysen Arboretum, N.J.
Presby Iris Gardens, N.J.
Reeves Reed Arboretum, N.J.
Leaming's Run Gardens, N.J.
Well Sweep Herb Farm, N.J.

LONGWOOD GARDENS

Without a doubt the most extensive formal gardens in the area (and considered among the best in the United States), this impressive display by the Dupont family offers an amazing variety. The gardens are open all year round and there is always something of interest whatever the weather. Altogether 350 acres are open to the public, including some beautifully laid out conservatories, so bring good walking shoes.

You enter through the main Visitor's Center which looks like a standard institutional building from the front, but like an underground house from the back — it's cleverly concealed under a hillock of green. At the Center you purchase your tickets and watch a four-minute continuous film which introduces you to the highlights of the gardens and points out seasonal displays. There's a gift shop chock full of books and plants where you'll want to stop on your way out. But for now, be sure to get the brochure guide and map at the information desk — you'll need it to find your way around. Here are some of the highlights you will probably choose:

The *Conservatories* are huge glass-enclosed rooms that surround a patio. Inside there are hanging basket mobiles sprouting flowers; stone herons in a pond surrounded by azaleas and acacias; a ballroom featuring organ concerts spring and fall; and the hot and humid Palm House with its banana, breadfruit and traveler trees. There is one room for insect-eating plants another just for orchids. The main conservatory displays change four times a year. (The Christmas display alone, with its poinsettias and line of Christmas trees, attracts more than 100,000 people a year.) A new *Children's Garden* here allows a hands-on experience for kids.

Outside, directly in front of the conservatories (and below, because you watch from the terrace) is the main water fountain area. The fountain display, with its many spouting water jets is framed by trimmed boxwood. Certain nights during the summer, colored lights and music from the *Carillion* make a spectacular *"Son et Lumiere."* There are even fireworks added to the fountain displays on special Saturday nights — these must be reserved in advance. The carillion, by the way, is beyond the fountain area in its own little romantic nook. A high cascading waterfall, a rock garden and the stone carillion tower look like something out of a 19th century painting. Further on, on this west side of the gardens are the *Idea Garden, Heaths of Heather,* the *"Eye of God"* (a low, circular water sculpture), a topiary and a rose garden.

The right side of Longwood boasts the flower walk — a sort of main drag bordered by seasonal flowers, and the open air theater — a stage surrounded by sculptured trees and using a curtain of water fountains. You will also find the *Peirce-DuPont* House, open to visitors for an extra fee. This 1730 home has had only two owners — the original Mr. Peirce, who owned the basic park from which Longwood Garden was born, and the DuPonts, who saved the property from becoming a sawmill in 1906.

Further on there are wisteria and rose gardens, forest walks and meadows, a lake with gazebo and ducks, and last of all, a complete (though miniature) *Italian Water Garden* in the manner of the Villa D'Este. Luckily there are many benches and shaded spots at which to rest along the way.

The Terrace Restaurant, located near the conservatories, offers both regular dining and cafeteria-style buffet, and a nice view. No smoking is allowed at the gardens, and no food can be brought in, but there is no prohibition on strollers and children are welcome.

HOURS: Daily. April - Oct., 9-6; Nov. - Mar. 9-5. Extended hours for special events.
ADMISSION: Adults: $8.00, Children: $2.00, Under 6, free.
LOCATION: Route 1, Kennett Square, Pa.
TELEPHONE: 215-388-6741

THE DUKE GARDENS

Open from October to May, one of New Jersey's foremost attractions, the Duke Gardens, features a series of interconnecting hothouses with an amazing variety of plants. They are part of the Duke Estate in Somerville. Indeed, from the moment you board the little van in the parking lot that takes you through a winding road bordered by tall spruces you are aware you are in Rich Man's country. The administration building where you get your tickets and wait for the tour is an English style gardener's cottage replete with rich woods and carpets. From here the guide takes you across to the hothouses where you enter a different world.

Each hothouse contains a shortened version of an international garden. The layout, the flowers and the walkways are all planned to reflect the atmosphere of that particular garden. The first one you enter is the *Italian Romantic garden*. Here you find statuary amid overgrown plants, standing orchids, and the type of Mediterranean setting that threw nineteenth century poets into ecstasy.

Each garden is controlled for climate and humidity. As you move from one to the other you find yourself shedding coats and sweaters according to the climate. Enter the *Edwardian Conservatory* and it's warm. Here, in a hothouse with tropical plants such as sego palms and elephant ears, the English gentleman would propose to his lady love (or at least he did in all those old movies on late night television). He would probably clip an orchid and hand it to her. For there are enough big, fat orchids in here to send an entire graduating class to the Senior Prom.

The long *English garden*, on the other hand, is temperate. A brick walkway takes you through sedate rows of hollyhocks, primroses and manicured boxwoods. A small herb garden is here also. The *French garden* is formal, with flowers set out in greenery shaped in a fleur-de-lis pattern. Lattice work covers all, and a far statue of a goddess reminds you that this is a small version of what you might find at Versailles.

The *Chinese garden*, with its overhanging willows, stone walkway and arched bridge over a goldfish pond is for serene meditation. The scent of the fragrant tea olive permeates the air. Among the other gardens you will find an Arizona desert with succulents and tall cacti; a Japanese rustic style meditation garden; a Persian with decorated tiles and fountains; and the lush foliage of a tropical rain forest with its banana trees and large ferns.

Twenty-five gardeners attend the plantings, so the Duke Gardens changes the flowers on display often, but the overall scheme remains intact. It is a favorite destination of garden clubs, but individuals enjoy the gardens as well. Advance reservations are required however. Cameras and high heels are not permitted (you'll understand why when you walk on those arched stone bridges).

HOURS: Oct. - May, 12-4 Daily, by reservation.
ADMISSION: Adults: $5.00, Children, Seniors: $2.50, Under 6 free.
LOCATION: Route 206, south of Somerville Circle.
TELEPHONE: 908-722-3700

BROOKLYN BOTANIC GARDENS

New Jerseyans often combine a trip to these gardens with one to the Brooklyn Museum (which is right next door) since parking in the museum lot can serve for both places.

The Brooklyn Gardens are known for the cherry blossom walk — a wide swath of lawn with Japanese double blossoms, white and pink, that come out in mid-April. Another other famous display is the *Japanese Gardens* which were originally designed and built in 1914, then reconstructed in 1960. Here a pagoda rises from the calm waters. The quiet meditation walks, the willow trees and the stone turtles create a duplication of a Kyoto scene set down incongruously in the midst of urban high-rises. The latest stellar attraction at the gardens are the brilliant new conservatories which house a variety of greenhouse plants.

The Brooklyn gardens follow the natural cycles: daffodils in March, then the lilacs, then the cherry blossoms, then the wisteria and rhododendrons in May. The rose garden is fenced off and opens only in June, so it's best you visit at the time of your favorite flower.

However, there are a number of attractions that are practically seasonless — the formal prospect that greets you as you enter from Eastern Parkway, the herbal gardens, the fragrance garden, the rock garden and of course all the desert cacti and tropical trees you will find in the new conservatories.

There are 50 acres to the gardens and plenty of benches to sit on and brooks to walk by. A Terrace cafe offers interesting sandwiches and drinks (it is open only in good weather) and the gift shop has a wide assortment of flower related items. The administration is fairly strict about behavior here — no picnicking, no bicycles, no dogs, no sitting on the grass (except in the Cherry Esplanade) and no children under 16 unless accompanied by adults — and there are patrols to enforce these rules. Perhaps that is why the Brooklyn Botanic Gardens has remained a verdant oasis throughout the years. Free. (Fee for Conservatories).

> **HOURS:** May-Sept.: Tues.- Fri. 10-6; Weekends and Holidays: 10-6; Sept.-Apr.: Tues.- Fri. 10-4:30; Weekends and Holidays: 10-4:30.
> **LOCATION:** Eastern Parkway and Washington Ave., Brooklyn, N.Y.
> **TELEPHONE:** 718-622-4433.

NEW YORK BOTANICAL GARDENS

These gardens are a disappointment to some because much of these 250 acres are in such a natural state you might as well be in Central Park. Still, the gardens contain several areas of interest to garden clubs and plants lovers.

One is the imposing museum building which contains a library of 400,000 books and journals plus a herbarium of 4,000,000 plant specimens for staff and scientists. The museum also offers a first rate shop which sells plants, garden books, tools and related items.

The large conservatories, within easy walking distance of the parking lot, have been restored to their original 1901 crystal-palace look. Eleven galleries include the *palm dome, Old World* and *New World* deserts, an orangerie and one acre reserved for seasonal displays of lilacs, orchids, poinsettias, etc. These conservatories are the focal point for interesting and imaginative displays.

Outside, there are many pockets of flowering displays during the spring and summer. A rose garden with a succession of blooms from June to late autumn; a herb garden; a rhododendron slope; Daffodil Hill, Azalea Glen, and a flowering rock garden with many alpine plants are scattered about the extensive acreage.

The Bronx Gardens as they are often called, have much the look of a large, well-tended city park rather than a formal garden. On the day I visited, there were people walking dogs, joggers, and what looked like picnickers, all unusual in a garden atmosphere. Since areas of interest, such as flowering displays, the pine hill and the virgin hemlock forest, occur sporadically among the many acres, be sure to arm yourself with visitor's guide. And although the gardens are across the street from the Bronx Zoo, anyone who hopes to do both in one day is either an incurable optimist or has legs of steel.

HOURS: Daily. 10-7 in summer, 10-6 in winter. Conservatory open Tues. - Sun. 10-5.

ADMISSION: Free to grounds. $4.00 parking lot fee. Conservatory: Adults: $2.50; Children & Seniors: $1.25. Under 6 free.

LOCATION: George Washington Bridge & Cross Country Express- way east to Exit 4B, to Bronx River Parkway North. Take Bronx Zoo exit.

TELEPHONE: 212-220-8777

718 - 817 - 8705

191

WAVE HILL

A public garden located in the upper reaches of the Bronx in a quiet section called Riverdale, Wave Hill still gives the sense of a private estate filled with beauty and serenity. There are lovely vistas of the Palisades and the Hudson from the many stone benches and balustrades on the "hill". There are greenhouses filled with tropical plants and desert cacti and there are outdoor gardens devoted to herbs and seasonal flowers. A small lake and many flowering trees dot the landscape.

Two houses stand on the estate. The one called Wave Hill, now sparsely furnished was once rented to such notables as Mark Twain, Theodore Roosevelt and Arturo Toscaninni. The building is currently used for Administration offices, a gift shop and a place for groups to enjoy a luncheon. French doors lead out to a stone terrace with yet another view.

While Wave Hill was built by William Morris in 1840 it later became home to several millionaries. The gardens and conservatories, under constant restoration by horticulturists, allow the plebian tourist a feel for the ambience of a private home landscaped for leisure and gracious living. Groups, families, mothers with children and adult hikers all come to enjoy these pleasant grounds.

> **HOURS:** Daily 10-4:30.
> **GREENHOUSE**
> **HOURS:** 10-12 and 2-4.
> **ADMISSION:** Weekdays free. Weekends: Adults $2.00; Seniors, students $1.00. Under 6 free.
> **TELEPHONE:** 212-549-2055.

HERSHEY ROSE GARDENS AND ARBORETUM

Not far from the Hershey Hotel, the Rose Garden and Arboretum began as a small 3 1/2 acre plot devoted to roses and now covers over 23 acres with flowers, trees, lakes and shrubs. Individuals take a self-guided tour through terraces of roses and past a man-made lake filled with goldfish, ducks and swans and the statue of a *Boy with a Leaking Boot*. A holly collection, one hundred varieties of herbs, rhododendrons, and evergreens are part of the display all season long. Other major flowerings are: mid-April to mid-May — daffodils, tulips and early azaleas; May 15 — June 1 — azaleas, rhododendrons, peonies. Then, from June 1 to September 15, 27,000 rose plants bearing 1200 varieties of roses are in bloom. From September 15 to November 1 — chrysanthemums. Tapes available. Picnic area and sale shop.

HOURS: April 1 - Oct.: 9-5.
ADMISSION: Adults: $3.50; Seniors: $3.00; Children 4-18: $1.00.
LOCATION: Hershey, Pa. on Route 322.
TELEPHONE: 717-534-3492

COLONIAL PARK ROSE GARDEN

The original garden, once part of the Mettler Estate, was re-developed and expanded by a horticulturist so that it now covers an acre and displays a wide variety of roses. 275 species, 4,000 bushes form a formal display garden which exhibits the A.A.R.S. Award Winning Roses each year. Included here are the original York and Lancaster roses, tearoses, floribunda, and more. They are all labeled to show type and date of introduction into the horticultural world. A flagstone walk makes for easy ambling.

Behind the rose garden is the new *Fragrance Garden for the Blind* which provides both braille plaques and a handrail for the handicapped. Both gardens are set inside of Colonial Park, one of those beautiful county parks that one comes upon so often in New Jersey. An arboretum and meandering stream border the gardens. Beyond that there are tennis courts, paddle boats and picnic tables for family get togethers. A lilac garden and wedding gazebo are popular picture-taking spots.

Garden clubs, school classes and other groups can arrange for guided tours for a fee. Otherwise the gardens are free. Major bloomings are the first week of June and the first week of September.

HOURS: Daily, 10-8 Mem. Day - Labor Day. Then 10-4:30 to Oct. 31.
LOCATION: Franklin Twp., Somerset County. Take Rte 206 to 514 (Amwell Rd) then left to Mettler's Rd.
TELEPHONE: 908-873-2459.

BUCK GARDENS

Only recently opened to the public, Buck Gardens is quickly becoming a major attraction in Somerset County where some of New Jersey's most interesting horticulture exists.

The former estate of Leonard J. Buck, a Far Hills millionaire, the tract is informal, grassy and treed, with many rock gardens (which were Mr. Buck's specialty) along the trails. The Buck mansion still stands atop a winding, hilly path but is not open for viewing. There's plenty of walking here, with stops at various benches for the vistas. Terrain varies from low lying swamp to steep hillsides. The gardens are best seen in the spring when thousands of tiny flowers peek out from designed rock formations. There are many other plantings and unusual trees plus a pleasant lake that provides the ducks with a picturesque swimming area. Pick up a walking map at the visitors station. Free.

HOURS: Mon.- Sat.: 10-4; Sun.: 12-5. Winter: Sun.: 12-4.
LOCATION: R.D. 2, Layton Rd., Far Hills, Somerset County.
TELEPHONE: 908-234-2677

BRANCH BROOK PARK

More than 2,000 cherry trees in bloom in the middle of April beautify this Essex County Park which stretches from Newark to neighboring Belleville. The cherry blossom area covers 2 miles in length but only about a quarter mile in width. Originally donated by Caroline Bamberger Fuld, these pink and white, single and double flowering trees now outnumber those in Washington, D.C. Many special events are planned to coincide with the cherry blossom festival, in particular, a major foot race.

CONTACT: Essex County Dept. of Parks, 201-482-6400 for events and special bus tours.

SKYLANDS

A popular springtime attraction is the Skylands preserve flowering around the mansion in one section of **Ringwood Manor State Park**. A half-mile alley of crabapple trees, 400 varieties of lilacs, azaleas and peonies and a small formal garden surround the castle-like 44-room home. In the back of the house there are interesting terraced gardens with greenery and statues. There are signs pointing out flowering sections and you can also pick up a map when you pay your entrance toll. For location check Skylands Manor entry.

HOURS: Daily
PARKING: $3 Weekdays; $4 Weekends, in summer.
TELEPHONE: 201-962-7031

FRELINGHUYSEN ARBORETUM

Tulips, azaleas, rhododendrons, a rose garden and a wealth of flowering trees are part of the display at this 127 acre tract that was once the home of the Frelinghuysens. Cherry trees, crabapple and magnolia blossoms along with a lilac garden and a dogwood copse bring color and contrast to the many evergreens in the collection. Run by the Morris County Park System. At the Administration Building there is a botanical library and a meeting room where lectures, concerts and other activities take place. Free.

HOURS: Daily: 9-4:30.
LOCATION: 53 E. Hanover Ave. (Route 511) Morristown, Morris County
TELEPHONE: 201-326-7600

PRESBY IRIS GARDEN

From the last week in May to the second week in June, an outstanding display of irises can be found in this lovely suburban park in Upper Montclair. Hilly terrain and gracious homes are the setting for this local park where a Mr. Presby began his iris beds many years ago. Every color in the rainbow is reflected in irises. The 4,000 varieties are planted in beds that line a long walk. Free.

HOURS: Daily. Display runs approximately 3 weeks, beginning May 24.
LOCATION: Mountainside Park, 500 Upper Mountain Ave., Upper Montclair, Essex County
TELEPHONE: 201-744-1400

REEVES-REED ARBORETUM

A small 12 1/2 acre estate is the setting for this arboretum, hidden by tall trees on one of Summit's stately old streets. You follow a winding path down to the parking lot which has room for about fifty cars. The stone and shingle manor house on the rise above the lot was built in 1889 and is surrounded by trees, shrubs and flowering plants. But the major part of the gardens are out back, behind the house. It is rather like visiting the house of a rich old aunt and being allowed to wander through the backyard yourself.

You can follow the nature trails through oaks, maples, walnuts and beeches. The open area of this hilly site is devoted to both flower and herb gardens. A deep depression (called a kettle hole in geological terms) is the setting for a spectacular flowering of daffodils in April, followed by summer field flowers. Azaleas, rhododendrons and a small rose garden are also to be found along the walks.

The main house offers a variety of classes and free Sunday lectures. You can pick up literature there. Among the brochures is a garden guide to help identify the species in the arboretum. Free.

HOURS: Grounds: Daily, daylight hours. Office: Mon., Tues., Thur.: 9-3.
LOCATION: 165 Hobart Ave. Summit, Union County. Take Route 24 to Hobart Ave. Exit.
TELEPHONE: 908-273-8787

LEAMING'S RUN GARDENS

Before the Garden State Parkway was completed, Route 9 was the only way to get to Cape May County, the southernmost section of New Jersey. When the parkway opened up, development slowed on the older Route 9. And that's just fine with Jack April, who created Leaming's Run Gardens as a bulwark of quiet woods and colorful plantings against the encroachments of motels and gasoline exhaust fumes.

This is one place that can transport you back to your childhood. Everyone has probably explored a forest at least once, felt the crackling of pine needles underfoot and heard the whipoorwill above. That's the sort of woods that covers twenty acres of sandy soil here, all interspersed with colorful gardens. You come across the gardens at a bend in the road. Many are assemblages of color. The yellow garden mixes gourds, gladiola, banana peppers and taller plants. Another garden is a medley of oranges. The English garden and reflecting pool typify a particular form. There are over twenty gardens here, each planted to provide color and texture during the entire season from late spring to early fall.

One large area, (about an acre), is set aside for a Colonial farm. Here you will find the traditional log cabin (actually copied from the Swedish type used by early settlers in Salem County) and a fenced-in kitchen and herb garden. Beyond the farm there are other nooks and crannies — with snapdragons, pinks, a cinnamon walk and plenty of benches where you can sit and enjoy the view.

At the end of the one mile walk, you come to *"The Cooperage"*, a shop where you can buy a variety of dried flower arrangements and other gifts. There are a few rules for the gardens, by the way. No smoking, no pets, no drinks and no radios. During August, the Audubon Society conducts hummingbird tours here.

HOURS: Mid-May to mid-Oct.: 9:30-5.
ADMISSION: Adults: $4.00; Children 6-12: $1.00. Annual ticket available.
LOCATION: Route 9, Swainton, Cape May County. Take Exit 13, GSP to Route 9, then go north one mile.
TELEPHONE: 609-465-5871

WELL SWEEP HERB FARM

A commercial herb-growing farm that is well known to buyers in the area, Well Sweep is a nicely laid out organic farm located way out in the hinterlands. Purchasers of herbs may browse the rectangular beds of rosemary and sage at any time, but special tours by the owner are reserved for groups. However, owner Cyrus Hyde does open up his farm twice a year to the general public. It is during these "Open Houses" that hundreds of people converge on Well Sweep Farm to sample homemade refreshments and watch craftsmen work. Rosemary chicken salad and herbed lemon bread are popular. But most popular of all are Mr. Hyde's lecture tours of his gardens.

Did you know that horsetail grass can be used for fine sanding? Or that tansy, planted next to the door, will keep ants away?

Want the recipe for rose geranium sugar? No wonder this tour is popular with garden clubs and other women's groups. Of course the principal activity here is growing and selling herbs so there is always a wide selection at reasonable prices.

Group tours are available to twelve people or more on a reserved basis and are given during the growing season (May-October). The Open Houses are usually on Saturday in June and September, and are free.

HOURS: April-Oct.: Tues.-Sat., 9:30-5. Call before visiting. These hours are for selling herbs. Group tours must be booked.
LOCATION: 317 Mt. Bethel Rd., Port Murray, Warren County.
TELEPHONE: 201-852-5390

See Also: Formal gardens and landscaped lawns are often attached to the historic houses treated elsewhere in this book. For outstanding examples, see in particular, *Winterthur* (Restored and Reconstructed Villages, Homes, etc.) *Nemours, Lyndhurst,* and the *Vanderbilt Mansion* (Homes of the Rich and Famous) and *Buccleuch Mansion* (Where Washington Fought).

FLEA MARKETS AND OUTLETS

Photo by Linda Kimler

In This Chapter You Will Find:

OUTLETS

Reading, PA
Flemington, N.J. Outlets
Secaucus, N.J. Outlets
Franklin Mills Mall, PA

FLEA MARKETS

Englishtown Auction Sales, N.J.
Chester, N.J.
Lambertville, N.J.
Lahaska, PA
Other Flea Markets, N.J.
Antique Centers, N.J.
Indoor Markets, N.J.

READING, PENNSYLVANIA

Reading is a rather grim looking factory town of red brick and wood tenements. Yet every day, busloads of people pour into Reading. Why? For the outlet stores that dominate the center of town. And although buses and cars always make several stops at the major outlets, the common complaint is that there just aren't enough hours to go through all those seconds.

One reason there isn't enough time is that not all outlets are equal. A true outlet sells a manufacturer's overruns and seconds (those slightly imperfect articles that cannot be sent to the department stores). Some of the "outlets" in Reading are simply discount houses and the bargains you find are no better or worse than those in the local discount emporiums. So time is lost in running from one store to the other as you try to sort the true bargain from the not-so-great buy.

The Reading Outlet Center, at 801 N. 9th St., is a huge red brick ex-factory building that was the pioneer in the outlet business. It not only contains a host of coat and clothing stores but also owns several new, air-conditioned small buildings on neighboring Windsor and Oley streets, such as Liz Claiborne, the Bass/Van Heusen outlet and Leslie Fay.

Another popular store is the *VF Outlet* (which is actually in neighboring Wyomissing at Hill Ave. & Park Rd.). This huge complex includes several buildings and features not only Vanity Fair robes and nightgowns, but Lee jeans and Kay Windsor dresses all at 50% discount. Other names within the complex are Black & Decker tools and Oneida silver, L.L. Bean and Oxford shirts, and many more, although these offer smaller discounts than fifty percent.

Other large complexes in the Reading area are: *Heister's Lane*, which includes the Sweater Mill and the Burlington Coat Factory; and *The Big Mill* at 8th & Olney which also offers a number of clothing stores. One has to take note, though, that while overruns are usually of good quality, seconds and irregulars may have a visible defect in the cloth. Always check for loose threads and zippers. Seconds should be marked, and usually are. One shirt I bought had "Imperfect" stamped on the inside collar. It's nice finding a $15.95 shirt for $4.95, but my son had to spend the year not only with ring around the collar, but "Imperfect" around the neck as well.

If you visit Reading a few helpful hints are in order:

1. Take a bag lunch with you. It saves time and time is of the essence here.

2. Checks are acceptable in most places only if you have major credit cards (Visa, Mastercharge, Exxon, etc.) to show that you're honest. Many outlets will not accept credit cards themselves, although a majority of them now do.

3. Check local prices before you take the trip. Only when you become as expert as the contestants on "The Price Is Right" will you be sure you have a bargain.

4. The peak season for bus tours is October, November and early December. If you're not shopping for Christmas, avoid these times.

5. There is no clothing tax in Pennsylvania.

> **HOURS:** Most stores open Mon. - Sat., 9:30-5:30 or 9:30 and Sun. 12-5 (except Jan. & Feb.)
> **LOCATION:** Rte. 78 to US 222 to 422W to Reading, Pa. VF Outlet is on Park & Hall Roads, Wyomissing.

FLEMINGTON OUTLETS

A few years ago Flemington offered a mix of outlet stores and boutiques; *Turntable Junction* boasted specialty stores; and next door you could watch the colonial craftsmen at *Liberty Village*. But as the economy changes so do the towns. Thus, Flemington, while still a quiet country town of Victorian homes, and still the seat of rural Hunterdon County, is now very heavily an outlet town.

Liberty Village, which never did too well as a colonial restoration, now has outlet shops inside those authentically restored 18th Century shells. Instead of craftsmen there are bargains, bargains, bargains. New outlets open here every day. Some of the bests are at the *Van Heusen Shop* (a true outlet) with men's shirts galore, and the Corningware outlet. *Coat World* offers London Fog and other name labels at one-third off but not all the stores offer the same quality or discount. It is always important to know your merchandise.

A new mall on the south side of Liberty Village is called *Feed Mill Plaza*. This is a modern enclosure with a bevy of small shops that include Izod and Gant stores.

If you walk back to Turntable Junction and cross the tracks you'll find a few good outlets such as Pfaltzgraeff. In this huge shed there are clearly marked sections of "firsts" and "seconds" of this popular dinnerware manufacturer. Nearby are Revereware and George Briard barware.

Going north of Turntable Junction you come to the Flemington Cut Glass Factory which seems to be sprouting smaller outlets like a spider plant putting out sprigs. Besides the usual selection of ordinary glassware in the regular building, there is the separate Mart for decorative items, the China Closet for dishes and a pewter specialty store.

Other outlet stores are dotted along the area bounded by Main, Mine and Church Streets. The Flemington Fur Company has a huge building at 8 Spring St. And up near Flemington Circle (where Routes 202, 31 and 12 meet) some popular stores are: *Dansk Factory Outlet* (modern cookware and some furniture), *The Shoe Factory* and the *Ladies Factory Outlet* for Ship 'N Shore blouses. Another large outlet mall is on the circle itself.

> **LOCATION:** Route 78 to 31 south, or Route 202. From Flemington Circle follow signs for "business district."

SECAUCUS OUTLETS

Set in one of the busiest areas of New Jersey, just the other side of the Meadowlands Sport Complex, the outlets here are dispersed over a huge area in between warehouses, office buildings, streets and flat open spaces. You will definitely need a map. Fortunately you can pick one up at the first outlet mall you hit (Outlets at the Cove) which is conveniently placed on Meadowlands Parkway. This small enclosed mall features air-conditioning, clean rest-rooms, and designer outlets such as Harve Bernard. At one of the stores here you can pick up a Secaucus booklet which not only includes a map but often offers discount coupons as well.

As you progress further to streets with names like Enterprise Avenue and Hartz Way, you will find the large outlet stores devoted to a single name which has made this complex so popular. Mikasa China and Glassware, Liz Claiborne clothes and accessories, Schrader sports clothes, and Oleg Cassini all have their own buildings, chock full of merchandise at 20% to 30% discount. Of course if you hit a sale you will get even further reductions, and many people put themselves on the mailing list to take advantage of sales. You will also find a number of discount chains (such as HBO and Linens 'N Things) in the complex. Syms Clothing (of TV commercial fame) takes up a full square block.

The Harmon Cove Outlet Center (20 Enterprise North) is a large enclosed mall with a variety of discount shops of varying value. But it also contains the International Checkerboard food counter where you can rest your feet and partake of pizza, chicken, ice cream and other examples of fast food.

The Castle Road Section, at the end of the parkway, is the newest area. Here small individual stores, which feature housewares, food and clothing stand side by side. Of particular interest here is Junior's restaurant and Passport Foods. Passport Foods is that rarity - a discount gourmet emporium. Although the discounts are only 10% to 20% off, people will drive for miles to stock up on Perugina chocolates and other goodies.

Although the drive to Secaucus and the hunting for bargains can be exhausting, once you have found the store that fits your needs, or carries the name brand you usually buy, the trip is certainly worth it.

HOURS: 7 days a week. Individual stores vary.
LOCATION: Secaucus. Take NJ Tpke to Exit 16W to Route 3 East to Meadowlands Parkway.
TELEPHONE: 201-795-8970

FRANKLIN MILLS MALL

While many outlet centers evolved from nearby factories or the conversion of unused buildings, Franklin Mills is a huge, super-planned, hi-tech mall designed as a magnet for shoppers from Philadelphia and New Jersey. It combines the convenience of an indoor mall with the bargain prices of discount stores and outlets.

Inside the 1.8 million square foot complex, you will find hundreds of stores, food courts (this is square of tables ringed by numerous fast food eateries), entertainment and resting courts plus an amusement center called the 49th St. Galleria which offers bowling, roller skating and video arcades for teenage mallies. Each section of the mall is color coded and everything is on one level. The planners seem to have thought of everything, except, (since they undoubtedly were men) enough ladies rooms!

Some of the best prices here are found at the department store outlets - Sears, J.C. Penny's and Ports. Many of the bargains are clearly marked seconds, but if you're looking for bargain sheets for the guest room or curtains for the basement - this is the place. You can also find a Levi Strauss outlet in the mall plus chain discount shops such as Marshalls and Flemington Fashion among the many clothing stores.

Babysitting is available (at $3.00 a hour) but serious shoppers who come from afar may find it easier to leave the kids at home and simply lose themselves among the inlets and outlets of this futuristic mall.

> **HOURS:** Mon.-Sat.: 10-9:30. Sun.: 11-6.
> **LOCATION:** Northeast Philadelphia. Take I-95 to Woodhaven Road Exit, turn right onto Franklin Mills Blvd.
> **TELEPHONE:** 215-632-1500

FLEA MARKETS

The term supposedly originated in the Middle Ages when peddlers gathered at the marketplace to sell old clothing and assorted junk which came already infested with fleas. Nowadays the term covers a wide variety of sales, none of which have anything to do with insects. At Flea Markets you might find:

1. NEW MERCHANDISE from manufacturers overruns or seconds. Some "Flea Markets," such as the one outside of New Brunswick on Route One, are almost completely new merchandise. They are housed inside of defunct supermarkets or chain stores and the same dealers remain there all year round. Actually these are almost giant conglomerations of pushcart peddlers. Bargain hunters jam these places, especially as inflation rockets higher. But you get no guarantees of the merchandise and it's *caveat emptor* in all cases.

2. ANTIQUE AND COLLECTIBLES DEALERS. Both indoor and outdoor markets create a buying and selling arena for dealers of older merchandise. Traditionally, antiques must be 100 years old to be considered such and pieces dated before 1840 (the watershed date for the Industrial Revolution) are counted more valuable. Collectibles, on the other hand, include fairly recent items that have been discontinued or are considered desirable. Bubble gum trading cards, old postcards, Avon bottles in a series, Depression glass (nothing fancy — just those cheap dishes they handed out at movie theaters in the 30s), old orange juice squeezers enter this category. Prices vary drastically according to what's in and what's out.

3. GARAGE SALE ITEMS. Since many outdoor flea markets rent their tables for the day and often for as little as 4 or 6 dollars, it is not unusual for local people to simply hold their garage sales at a popular market. Anything goes here!

4. CRAFT DEALERS. Generally craft people do better at Craft Fairs than at flea markets, since bargain hunters balk at the prices for new, hand-made items. However, at certain flea markets you might find someone selling seashell decorations or duck decoys, especially if the dealer has staked out this territory for himself.

5. FARMER'S MARKETS. Especially in Monmouth and Ocean Counties, summer markets include a food section where fresh corn, watermelons, beans and squash are on hand in quantity and at much better prices than at the supermarket.

6. ANTIQUE CENTERS. Sometimes they abut a flea market; other times they are in the center of town; but an Antique Center can be a barn, a mall, a house, a reconverted factory. Inside the structure, you might find a series of rooms, stalls, niches or even huge quarters rented by individual dealers. Some centers are collectives with all dealers contributing to the rent, upkeep, etc. More often one dealer owns the building while the others rent. They take turns minding the store, however.

THE ENGLISHTOWN AUCTION SALES

It's advertised as the world's largest flea market, this vast dusty field set in the midst of Monmouth County's farm country, and it probably is. However, the term "flea market" is changing these days and anyone expecting acres of antiques on sale will be disappointed.

Right now, Englishtown Auction Sales consists of about 70 percent dealers in new discount merchandise and 30 percent dealers in collectibles. What you find is something like 300 garage sales going on side by side with 700 New York street hawkers all set up on tables covering a huge field. Add to that a farmer's market with tables of fresh corn, tomatoes, melons, apples and pumpkins. And then add four buildings filled with discount clothing booths, kielbasa stands, knish stands, booths selling hot dogs, hamburgers and oriental food and a complete bar and grill. Then add a cast of thousands worthy of a Cecil B. DeMille movie and you have some idea of the immensity of the place. In fact, Englishtown Auction Sales has everything but an auction — that term refers to the old days when cows were sold off too.

The Flea Market is open weekends only, but traditionally the day for "antique" bargains is Saturday, the earlier the better. The market actually opens at 5 a.m. However, chances of your finding the missing teapot to Catherine the Great's silver tea service is about the same as your chance of hitting the jackpot at Atlantic City. Even less. What you will find is a mass of memorabilia, knick-knacks, new shoes and old tires — practically anything in the world can be discovered here. A new bell for your bicycle, a collection of porcelain doorknobs, a reproduced stone plaque or garage sale "junque" all mixed in with bargain basement clothing and cosmetics.

Those who search for collectibles can certainly find something of interest. Depression glass, comic books, paper-weights and German World War I helmets and medals were some that I noticed the day I visited. More collectibles (along with food stands) can be found in the buildings called Red, Green, Blue and Brown. One dealer told me that in the old days hundreds of antique dealers would unload their goods early and that it was possible to find excellent values among the junk. Nowadays, he noted, the proliferation of new discount sales people has driven many antique dealers away.

Still in all, Englishtown Auction Sales offers you a chance to buy that elusive whatnot you could never find anywhere else. Perhaps it will be a kitchen sink faucet or a car seat cover that's just right, a beat-up plant-stand or the missing Avon bottle to your set. A craft table pops up here and there also — I found candles molded in the form of Venus De Milo, conch shell lamps and personalized birthday cards.

Outdoor tables in seasonable weather (well into fall). Lots of dust and dirt so dress appropriately. And they charge extra for parking.

HOURS: Sat.: 5 AM - 5 PM. Sun.: 9 AM - 5 PM all year.
LOCATION: Garden State Parkway to Exit 123. Route 9 South to Texas Road. Right on Texas Road to Route 527 for 3 miles to 90 Wilson Ave., Englishtown, Monmouth County.
TELEPHONE: 908-446-9644

CHESTER FLEA MARKET AND ANTIQUE STORES

Chester has been trying to be a quaint Revolutionary town for years now, but what finally put it on the map was the Chester Flea Market. Run by the Lions Club in a field right outside the main hub of town, the Flea Market now brings hundreds of dealers and thousands of visitors every Sunday from late April to October.

Tables are spread out on a dusty field and the mix of new merchandise to collectibles is about 70/30. Baseball cards for collectors and beach towels at discount prices are piled side by side on carts that stand row by row in the field.

Vendors here tend to book for the whole season, so there is some stability. Hot dogs and funnel cakes are available for snacking. Don't expect to find high quality antiques but there is a nice assortment of souvenir type collectibles.

As for the town of Chester: a combination of specialty boutiques and antique shops has the streets bustling here in spring and summer. On East Main Street, stores with cutesy names like *Karen's Koop* and the *Country Mouse* offer a mix of antiques, quilts, coverlets, cookware, etc. *Woodcock's Gourmet* and the *Factory Fudge Shop* make your mouth water with their food specialties before you even enter. P.S. Now that the flea market is really popular they are talking of moving it somewhere else. Check before going.

HOURS: (For Flea Market): Sundays only, April - Oct. Antique Shops: Weekdays, Saturdays, and in most cases Sundays from 11 AM
LOCATION: Route 24, Chester, Morris County

LAMBERTVILLE

This is another town that has benefited greatly from the presence of flea markets. Over the years it has become a genuine antique center. For years, Lambertville looked like a poor relation of its neighbor across the river, New Hope. But now the antique shops have brought a certain panache to this old canal town. The *Pork Yard Antique and Art Center*, for instance, not only has classy antiques and Delaware Valley artists, but a cute French restaurant attached to the main building. It's open for lunch only on weekends, though. Both Bridge Street, the main thoroughfare through town, and Union Street have a number of antique stores worth looking at. And The *People's Store*, in this area, offers many interesting dealers under one huge roof.

As for flea markets, they are located outside of town, on Route 29 going south. This is where you will find both the *Lambertville Antique Market* and *Golden Nugget Antiques* side by side and causing traffic jams every summer weekend. The indoor sections of the market are extensive and some carry rather nice 19th Century items. The indoor part is open all year round, while the outdoor tables only last as long as the weather is good. One nice thing about the Lambertville market is there is hardly any new merchandise, so you do not have to contend with tables of jeans and sneakers.

LOCATION: Routes 179 and 29, Hunterdon County.

LAHASKA FLEA MARKET

Across from the boutiques and restaurants of Peddlers Village, and rivaling them in popularity, is the Lahaska Flea Market. Actually, there are two markets — the outdoor tables of collectibles and antiques and the new indoor market where better quality awaits.

The outdoor flea market here is very much like the one at Lambertville (in fact I suspect that the same dealers run over to different markets on the same weekend). The indoor market includes stores that specialize in old sheet music, records and posters plus several antique furniture places. The indoor market runs weekends while the outdoor tables are open Wed. through Sunday if weather permits.

Lambertville and Lahaska are two popular stops for antique enthusiasts.

OTHER FLEA MARKETS

NEW EGYPT MARKET: Again, a mix of old and new, with everything from foundry type to bicycle parts available. There are inside buildings which, though old, host plenty of dealers and in good weather over 100 outside tables are filled with garage sale items. Once in a while a real "find" is discovered among the junque. Antique day is Sunday when the market opens at 7 AM. Auctions at 1 PM Sunday. Open Saturday, Sunday and Wednesday. New Egypt is located 6 miles west of Great Adventure in Ocean County (take Route 528). *Telephone:* 609-758-7440.

HOWELL ANTIQUE VILLAGE AND FLEA MARKET: Another popular market that attracts large crowds and bus tours. Open all year on Friday, Saturday and Sunday. Located on Route 9, Howell, Monmouth County, between Freehold and Lakewood. *Telephone:* 908-367-1105.

COLUMBUS MARKET: A well-known farmer's market that is also a flea market. The Thursday morning market sells produce and "anything legal." The Sunday "Family Yard Sale" is for used items only — no new merchandise or produce. 70 inside stores here. Located on Route 206, Columbus, Burlington County. *Telephone:* 609-267-0400.

NEWTON FLEA MARKET: Outdoors in the Newton Drive-In Theater, Route 206, one mile north of Newton in Sussex County. Open Sat. & Sun. 9-5 from May through October. *Telephone:* 201-383-3066.

NESHANIC FLEA MARKET: Neshanic Station, Somerset County. This was considered very good, then dropped out of sight for a while. It is operating again on weekends, but call first. *Telephone:* 908-369-3660.

MEYERSVILLE GRANGE FLEA MARKET: A change of pace since this market is indoors and runs only in the cold weather. The building is small, but there are almost 30 tables inside. Glassware, china, urns, posters and one or two craft tables that feature duck decoys or handmade quilts. On Meyersville Road, Passaic Twp., Morris County. Sundays only, Oct. - May. *Telephone:* 201-832-7422.

ARCHIE'S: A little farther down the road is Archie's Resale Shop — a glorified junkyard that has become an institution because of Archie's Santa Claus appearance. The 3,000 ice skates in Archie's Ice Skate Exchange are a boon to local mothers. Old sleighs, roomsful of old chairs (not in the cleanest condition), everything but the kitchen sink and probably that too. In Meyersville Center, Passaic Twp., Morris County.

FLEMINGTON FAIR FLEA MARKET: Except when it is used for the county fair in the fall, the large rural fairgrounds are fair game for flea market dealers and buyers. Tables operate on Wednesdays and weekends during the warm weather. Call 908-782-7326 for exact times. Located on Route 31, a few miles north of Flemington Circle, Hunderdon County.

ANTIQUE CENTERS

For those who do not relish the trudge through the dusty fields, there are plenty of antique stores and centers where you may browse in comfort — even air-conditioned comfort. There are over two thousand antique stores in New Jersey alone. Here is a short run-down on some of the better known centers.

The Antique Center at **Red Bank** hosts about 100 dealers in four large buildings within walking distance of one another. The shops are open daily from 11-5 and are located on Front Street and the 200s block. Take Garden State Parkway to Route 109, Monmouth County.

The Antique Mall in the Chestnut Ride Shopping Center, 30 Ridge Road, **Montvale**, in northern New Jersey has a collection of quality shops in comfortable surroundings. Take Exit 172 from Garden State Parkway.

A new enclave in north Jersey is *The Mill Market* in the quaint town of **Lafayette**, Sussex County. Forty dealers run a cooperative effort in a reconverted 1842 mill. The mill is on Route 15 in the center of town and is open Friday to Monday only. There are some other interesting antique shops in Lafayette also. Both Sparta and Andover are other Sussex County towns with a good collection of antique stores.

Hunterdon and Somerset counties have a gaggle of loosely strung out country-store type antique marts. Some of these are individual dealers and some are centers that include over a dozen dealers. A few of the well-known names are: *Whitehouse Manor*

212

Antiques Center, Route 22 West, **Whitehouse Station**, *Kitchen Caboodle* in **Mountainville**, Tewksbury Township, *Melody Cottage* in nearby **Oldwick**, *River Edge Farm, Smoke House* and *Yesterday's Barn Antiques* in **North Branch**, Somerset County and *Country Antiques* in **Pluckemin**. The town of **Summit** has several good antique stores such as *Kane Galleries* plus the *Summit Antique Center* open Friday to Sunday.

In southern Jersey the village of **Mullica Hill** hosts several antique centers. Among them are shops with quaint names like *The Eagles Nest, King's Row Antiques* and *Farm House Antiques* all on Main Street. And visitors to the shore can always find antique shops open during the season, from *The Pink House Antiques* in **Cape May** to several shops on **Long Beach Island** that specialize in nautical antiques. One of the largest enclaves in the state is now at the *Point Pleasant Antique Emporium* at Bay and Trenton Aves. at the shore resort. One hundred dealers, under one roof, offer furniture, quilts, dolls and collectibles, all in a beautiful air-conditioned building in the center of town. And close to Atlantic City in the Historic Towne of **Smithville**, the large antique filled building that once housed the Quail Hill Inn is now a genuine antique center with lots of good quality furniture and smaller pieces.

As I mentioned several pages before, towns like **Chester** and **Lambertville** and **Lahaska** have a full complement of antique and specialty stores besides their well-known flea markets. For neophytes, the best way to track down the antique marts is to pick up a copy of one of those free antique newspapers at the local flea market or antique dealer.

INDOOR MARKETS

This is a growing group of markets that is fast taking over a big share of the bargain hunters brigade. Huge indoor marts, usually abandoned supermarkets, are divided into hundreds of stalls where entrepreneurs sell everything from bells to belts. Instead of *Two Guys* you get three hundred guys all touting discount merchandise. Market days are Friday, Saturday and Sunday.

The best known is probably the U.S. *#1 Flea Market and Antiques* situated on Route #1, New Brunswick (Telephone: 201-846-0900). This one still attempts to have an antique and collectible section. Another biggie is the *Route 18 Indoor Market*, 290 Route 18, East Brunswick (Telephone: 201-254-5080) which is almost completely new merchandise. *The Union Market*, Springfield Ave., Union, and the *Watchung Market* on Route 22, are both examples of this new type of market where the fleas have all but disappeared from the flea market scene.

Often customers find good buys at these places. Whether the alligators on the Izod shirts and the swans on the Gloria Vanderbilt jeans are real or fake is a question that bothers the manufacturers a lot more than the customers. It is by no means the norm, but once in a while, a pirated item ends up at a flea market or an indoor market.

OTHER OUTINGS

Photo: N.J. Travel & Tourism

In This Chapter You Will Find:

Planetariums, N.J.
School Tours, N.J.
U.S.S. Ling Submarine, N.J.
Miniature Kingdom, N.J.
Black River & Western Railroad, N.J.
Other Excursion Railroads
Excursion Boats
Twin Lights Lighthouse, N.J.
Bushkill Falls, PA
Renaissance Festival, N.Y.
Medieval Times, N.J.
Culinary Institute of America, N.Y.
Renault Winery, N.J.
Other Area Wineries
The Meadowlands, N.J.
Other N.J. Racetracks
Other N.J. Arenas and Auditoriums

PLANETARIUMS (NEW JERSEY)

Aside from the planetariums you find within major museums, (such as The American Museum of Natural History, the Newark Museum, etc.) there are a number of places star-seeking New Jerseyans can visit for sky programs. Children under six are usually not admitted to programs for good reason — once those doors shut in darkness, there is no escape. Luckily, many planetariums feature special "Stars for Tots" shows. Here's what is available.

OCEAN COUNTY COLLEGE: College Drive, Toms River. Robert J. Novins Planetarium. Outside the main hurly-burly of Toms River on a large campus, this planetarium not only schedules public shows all year round but has a special astronomy curriculum for school grades 1-6 during the public school year. (And this attracts students from outside counties as well.) Public shows are on weekends. They do shut down every once in a while to prepare a new show, (although *not* when the college does) so call first. The planetarium holds 117 people and is quite modern. Admission: Adults $3.00; Children and students: $2.00. Under 6 not admitted. *Telephone:* 908-255-0342.

TRAILSIDE PLANETARIUM: Coles Avenue and New Providence Road in Mountainside, Union County. Part of the Watchung Reservation's Trailside Nature and Science Center, this simple "down home" building is worth tracking down (it's just down the hill from the big Nature Center). Although it seats only 35 people, it is rarely overfilled and offers the same slide presentations, manufactured by a scientific company, that you see anywhere else, plus their own local star show. Sundays at 2 and 3:30 pm. Weekly after-school shows for groups — such as scouts — who reserve in advance. *Admission:* $1.00. *Telephone:* 908-232-5930.

RARITAN VALLEY COLLEGE: Lamington Road and Rte. 28, Branchburg, Somerset County. The newest planetarium in New Jersey seats 100 people. Many school shows plus public showings on Saturdays at 1, 2 & 3 p.m. Special pre-school shows on Sunday. Uses both the "canned" slide shows, and their own give -and - take lecture style sky show. Reservations required. *Telephone:* 908-231-8805.

MORRIS COUNTY COLLEGE: Route 10 & Center Grove Road, Randolph. This automated 80-seat planetarium offers not only several programs to the local citizenry but also courses for those who really want to delve into the subject. Shows for school and scout groups are scheduled during the week and early Saturday. Public showings are every other Sat. evening while the college is in session. Reservations suggested. *Admission:* Adults: $4.00; children, seniors, students: $3.00. *Telephone:* 201-328-5755 or 5075.

SPERRY OBSERVATORY, UNION COLLEGE: 1030 Springfield Ave., Cranford. Not a planetarium but an observatory with large telescopes that is run by Amateur Astonomers, Inc., in conjunction with Union College. Fridays from 7:30 to 10:30 pm (except the third Friday of the month) everyone is welcome to shoot for the stars. Children should be accompanied by parents. *Telephone:* 908-276-7827.

SCHOOL TOURS

Almost any museum, zoo, historic house or park mentioned in this book is open to reserved guided tours for school groups, scout groups and members of adult schools. Here are a few more places, popular with school groups, that did not fit in the above-mentioned categories:

NEW JERSEY STATE HOUSE: Due to a long-term renovation, the gold-domed State House will be closed, and all tours canceled for the next few years. However, the office that books the tours for grade-school children may have some alternate sites to offer. Contact: School Reservation Service, N.J. State Museum, 205 W. State St., Trenton, N.J. 08625. *Telephone:* 609-292-6347.

ST. HUBERT'S GIRALDA: An animal shelter set up by Mrs. Geraldine Rockefeller Dodge which still has its quarters on the Dodge Estate. The education program for schools and scout groups includes movies, slides, handouts and a tour of the kennels. There are 16 different program that range from pre-school to eighth grade. Free. Location: Woodland Road, Madison, Morris County. *Telephone:* 201-377-2295.

THE U.S.S. LING SUBMARINE

The U.S.S. Ling is only 312 feet long and 27 feet wide, and when you consider that ninety-five men and twenty-four torpedoes were aboard during its short career as an active sub in 1945, you realize that this is no place for someone with claustrophobia. Nowadays, most of the torpedoes and many of the berths have been removed to allow for tour groups to move about. Indeed the inside seems surprisingly spacious compared with the outside.

Tickets are bought at the outside trailer museum which also houses pictures and paraphernalia — including the periscope of a Japanese sub. Tours leave about every 15 minutes and last about 45 minutes, depending on your guide.

You begin in the torpedo room where there are still two of these sleek weapons left. (No, they are not active). I learned that torpedoes do not go off by accident since they are activated only after they leave the tube. They also had to be aimed right, since a miss would give away the sub's position to an enemy ship.

I also learned that much of the time on the sub was devoted to eating and cooking. Besides three meals a day and night for all shifts, sailors could raid the refrigerator at any time. When the Ling first left port, space was so dear that fresh fruit and vegetables were stacked in one of the showerheads.

Since it was hot and cramped in the sub, showers were popular, as was Lifebuoy soap. And a huge laundry room throbbed night and day, cleaning the sailor's clothes. Smoking was allowed, surprisingly, until the air became so stale that the cigarette would not light.

Tours include the Control Room, Maneuvering Room, Main Engine Room, sleeping quarters and more; but the Conning Tower with its periscope is off limits. You are allowed to handle certain equipment, including the wheels and gauges, and the guide does sound the diving signal (memorable from a host of old war movies starring Cary Grant and John Garfield).

While modern submarines are larger and sleeker, this black, fleet-type vessel is a memorial to the World War II submariners who must have been a hardy lot. An interesting place, both for older children and ex-servicemen.

HOURS: 10 AM - 5 PM Daily except major holidays. May be closed Mon. - Tues. in winter.
ADMISSION: Adults $3.00, Children: $2.00
LOCATION: Court & River Streets, Hackensack
TELEPHONE: 201-342-3268

MINIATURE KINGDOM

When you approach this white concrete structure with its flags flying from the battlements you tend to expect an amusement park for children. Instead, what you find, once you enter the huge dimly lit room of the "kingdom", is a world of Lilliputian replicas of castles and harbors. For these are scale models of some of Europe's most famous landmarks.

Among the more spectacular exhibits is the shining white castle of Mad Ludwig of Bavaria, the major buildings and churches of the Kremlin, a German Festhaus, and a complete replica of an 11th Century fortress under seige. There are 10,000 miniature hand-painted hyacinths in one Dutch scene and thousands of cheeses in another. A model railroad chugs around the exhibits and serves to keep children interested while their parents explore the nooks and crannies of these miniature architectural wonders.

As you walk in you are handed a sheet which describes the history and background of the exhibits. Lots of interesting reading here. Did you know that the towers of the Kremlin contained a secret escape route for the Czar? (Too bad he was someplace else when the Revolution broke out). Did you know that the scale at the Cheese Market in Alkmaar, Holland, was once used to determine whether or not a woman was in cahoots with the devil? If she weighed less than 150 pounds she was declared a witch and was burned at the stake. Gory, yes, but that piece of information alone is worth the price of admission for any number of dropouts from the Weight Watchers Club.

All in all, an interesting place for homesick Europeans, Americans who have lived in Europe, history buffs, architectural students and children, too, (although they are not allowed to touch). The price is a bit high, and the kingdom is out of the way, but its cheaper and closer than the miniature kingdoms of Holland and Denmark.

HOURS: Tues. - Sun.: 10-5. Closed winter.
ADMISSION: Adults: $4.50; Seniors: $4.00; Children: $3.50; Under 5: $1.50.
LOCATION: Route 31, Washington, Warren County. Take Rte. 78 to Clinton Exit, then north on 31.
TELEPHONE: 908-689-6866

Photo: Courtesy Miniature Kingdom

The Miniature Kingdom features scale models of European landmarks, including castles, cathedrals and forts.

BLACK RIVER AND
WESTERN RAILROAD

Here is an old-fashioned train ride that runs through the pretty countryside between Flemington and Ringoes in Hunterdon County. The trip takes about an hour and includes a twenty-minute stopover at Ringoes. For kids and adults who have never ridden a steam-driven train (with its resulting soot and nostalgia) this is the only full-scale excursion train now operating in New Jersey. The train leaves from Turntable Junction in Flemington.

> **HOURS:** Weekends from April to December 1st. Several trips a day.
> **ADMISSION:** Adults: $5.00; Children 5-12: $2.50; Children 3 & 4: $1.00.
> **LOCATION:** Mine St. at Turntable Junction, Flemington, Hunterdon County.
> **TELEPHONE:** 908-782-6622.

OTHER EXCURSION RAILROADS

A popular attraction at *Allaire State Park* in Monmouth County is the **Pine Hill Railroad** which runs a ten-minute trip. The train ride and a railroad museum are part of the several attractions at this large park. The ride operates on weekends during the summer season. Check the *Allaire Village* listing for further information.

Another train ride, this one well into Pennsylvania Dutch territory (and therefore, technically, beyond the periphery of this book) is the **Strasburg Railroad**. Located on Route 741, Strasburg, in Lancaster County, Pennsylvania, the ride is so well known that it attracts tourists from across the border. The 45-minute ride offers a steam train with pot belly stoves in the coaches and an observation car straight out of "Hello, Dolly!". It operates on weekends during March, April, November and December. Weekdays on May 1 through October 31. Call 717-687-7522 for time schedules.

As for the **Morris County Railroad** in Newfoundland, which used to run a scenic ride complete with holdup men, please be advised that this train ride is not operating at this time. However, there is a small museum dedicated to railroad memorabilia, toy trains, models and such back at the original site for this train ride. You can find it at the Morristown and Erie Railroad Depot, Route 1 and Whippany road, Whippany, N.J., where it is lovingly tended on weekends in season. Call 201-887-8177 for details.

EXCURSION BOATS

Although there have always been sightseeing boats, they seemed, in the old days, to be secondary to the more popular fishing excursions. Nowadays, there is an increased popularity of the excursion type vessel, whether it is a motor launch or a re-created sidewheeler. These boats will offer entertainment, narrated tours, lunch, dinner or simple cruising depending on the time of year, and the place. Here are a few:

The *"Spirit of New Jersey,"* leaves from Weehawkin and sails into the Hudson River and New York Harbor. The trip may include brunch, lunch, cocktails and Broadway style entertainment. A similar excursion boat called *"The Spirit of Philadelphia"* leaves from Penn's Landing to circle around the Philadelphia harbor. Food is buffet style and the waiters turn into the entertainers after they clear the dishes. And as mentioned in the write-up of South Street Seaport, there are two 19th century style paddle-wheelers leaving from there that offer 1 1/2 hour narrated tours of New York Harbor.

At the Jersey shore you will find several versions of sightseeing and excursion boats. *"The River Queen,"* a simplified version of a Mississippi River paddle boat, cruises for lunch, afternoon sightseeing, etc. The River Queen, which sails from Bogan's Basin in Brielle, and its sister ship the *"River Belle"* which leaves from Point Pleasant Beach are both popular with groups, especially senior citizens groups. The boats cruise the inland waters of the Manasquan River and Barnegat Bay so the water is calm and sightseeing is mostly of the docks and patios of shore homeowners plus an occasional bridge. Some cruises have narration, but there is no entertainment except for the special Dixieland band cruises that run on Wednesdays during the summer. *Telephone:* 908-528-6620.

Over at Atlantic City, Harrah's Marina Casino Hotel operates a paddleboat called *"Harrah's Belle"* during the summer. This one hour cruise of the Absecon waterway allows customers a change from the smoke-filled casinos. Adults: $5.00, Children: $3.00.

Further down at Wildwood Crest, there is *Captain Sinn's*

Sightseeing Center (609-522-3934) which runs sightseeing cruises as well as whalewatching trips and dinner cruises. And the *Cape May Fishing & Sightseeing Center* (609-898-0055) in Cape May operates whale and dolphin watching cruises plus a shorter wine and cheese harbor cruise. Of course the whale-watching trips go out into the ocean but whether or not they actually spot any whales depends on the time of year. There are a number of other short sightseeing cruises that leave from Otten's Harbor in Wildwood and the Cape May Yacht Basin in Cape May, most with narration (although the evening trips usually favor band entertainment).

All these excursion boats are available for group charter as well as weddings, bar mitzvahs, company picnics and whatever else you can think of.

TWIN LIGHTS LIGHTHOUSE

An unusual brownstone building that looks more like a castle than the lighthouse it once was, Twin Lights is perched on a mountainous bluff in Atlantic Highlands and affords a sweeping view of the ocean and coast. The "twin" lights, (one is square and one octagonal) are towers on either side of the main building. The first Fresnel lights were used here in 1841. The present fortress-like structure was built in 1862 and was the scene of many "firsts".

The museum inside includes exhibits on early life-saving equipment, a replica of the first rowing skiff to cross the Atlantic and displays concerning Marconi's first demonstration of the wireless in America.

Naturally part of the enjoyment of visiting a decommissioned lighthouse is making the climb up the stairs. The ascent up the spiral staircase involves only 167 steps and leads to an excellent view of Sandy Hook and the ocean. Downstairs, there is a small gift shop and outside you will find a picnic area and several historical markers. A look at the original Fresnel lens which is housed in a separate area, is also available. Free.

HOURS: 10-5. Closed Mon. & Tues.
LOCATION: Atlantic Highlands, Monmouth County,
Take Route 36E make right turn just before Highlands Bridge, then another right. Follow signs.
TELEPHONE: 908-872-1814

BUSHKILL FALLS

For families who wish to avoid the hurly-burly of amusement parks there are many scenic attractions which offer a day in the country with the simpler amusements of an earlier day. One of these is Bushkill Falls, set in a primeval forest in the foothills of the Poconos. The forest is cool in the summer and colorful in the fall, and while the main waterfall is nowhere near Niagara in width or grandeur, it does present both photographers and easy hikers with a pleasant outing. For Pocono tourists and visitors to the Delaware Water Gap area, the Falls have long been a standard attraction. A small fishing pond, miniature golf and paddle boats offer extra recreation.

You first enter through a "nature" museum, then a pathway through a hushed forest near the top of the falls. Although you get a good view of the cascading water from up top, it is more impressive to see it from below. That however, requires a climb up and down a "natural" log stairway. The Main Falls drop over the edge of a 100-foot cliff to a deep pool below. From that point the water now drops another 70 feet through a large gorge strewn with gigantic boulders. The falls are fairly narrow, but the drop is spectacular.

There are three routes to follow to the falls. The short route, with a green trail marker, takes only 15 minutes to walk. It is the "chicken" trail to a lookout where you can drink in the vistas, take a picture then sit down. The second or "popular" route takes 45 minutes and is for those who want their money's worth. This takes you down and around the bottom of the main falls, where from a bridge across the creek you get a full view from below of the majestic spill of white water.

The third route takes one and a half hours. Here you pass the series of three pretty, mist-laden falls on your trek. Following this path you also come upon a lookout where you can enjoy a panoramic view of the Delaware Valley. It is absolutely necessary for one to wear good walking shoes. Wedgies, Dr. Scholls, clogs and such are a disaster on these paths.

When visiting the Falls be sure to check the map in the brochure you receive with your ticket. It clearly marks the trails to follow. Senior Citizens and young children could probably do without the huffing and puffing on the longer trails. Food service and beer is available for those who need rest and relaxation after their exertions. Picnic tables also.

HOURS: April - Oct.: Daily, 9 to dusk.
ADMISSION: Adults: $4.50; Seniors: $3.75; Children 6-12: $1.00;
Under 6, free.
LOCATION: Bushkill, Pa. Take I-80 to Exit 52, then 209 N. Fol-
low signs.
TELEPHONE: 717-588-6682

RENAISSANCE FESTIVAL, N.Y.

This festival has been running for several years now and has become quite popular. For eight weekends — from early August to mid-September — , the greenery at Sterling Forest in New York (close to the Jersey border) is taken over by knights in shining armor, ladies, peddlers dressed in motley, jugglers and mimes. A joust on horseback is the big attraction here, but it takes place during the last hour of the festival (5 to 6 P.M.) so allow time for that one. Otherwise a series of "shows" depicting outlaws, queens and jesters are part of the festival. However, the mud wrestling, juggling, Wagnerian puppets and other attractions are operated by free-lancers who expect the customers to come up with some coin of the realm so bring extra change along. Rides (some simple ones) and games (such as axe-throwing) are extra too. The main attractions - such as the Living Chess Game, the Queen's Feast and the Joust, take place at particular locations at specific times - so it's really necessary to buy a program in order to enjoy everything.

There is plenty of food and drink here, but there is no pro-hibition to bringing your own. Veterans carry their own canteens or goatskins because there's plenty of hiking over the greensward. There are also gift "shops" which are set up in tents and offer such unusual items as brass rubbings and flower circlets for milady's hair. An Equity production of a different Shakespeare play is put on each year in the Festival's own Globe Theater — which has seating on a rustic hill and is about as comfortable as the original Globe.

HOURS: Weekends, 11-6, Aug.-mid-Sept.
ADMISSION: Adults: $12.50; Seniors: $10.00; Children 6-12: $5.00;
Under 6 free
LOCATION: Sterling Forest, Tuxedo, N.Y. Take Route 17N, look
for signs.
TELEPHONE: 914-351-5171

MEDIEVAL TIMES

Combine a horse show, a night club, a dinner theater and a Renaissance Festival, put it all in a circus-like arena inside of a huge stucco castle and plunk it down near one of New Jersey's busiest intersections (right near the Meadowlands) and you have the northern version of Medieval Times. Here you get not one, but six jousts, a steady narrative by a Master of Ceremonies and a chance to eat dinner without any utensils!

First you enter the cavernous castle, where you buy your tickets and are handed a paper hat with a special color. This color will determine which section you sit in and which knight you root for. These colored hats are a great gimmick, for it is in cheering on a particular champion that the audience becomes part of the show and gets to act as silly as they want. But that comes later. You are first ushered into a greeting room where you pose for a picture with the king and queen. Then you go into a larger room where you have a chance to buy a drink and any number of medieval accoutrements including wooden swords and shields. Hungry yet? Well, you should have had a snack at home, because although drinks are readily available, there are no munchies around.

Then you are herded into a reception room where the Master of Ceremonies regales you with jokes. Finally you are ushered into the arena itself where chairs are set against long banquet tables. These are all set in tiers so that everybody in the huge oval arena does get a chance to see the show.

And now, the menu. As the serving wench will tell you, there is soup (served in a porringer which you lift up and drink from), assorted raw vegetables, chicken, potato and ribs served in a steaming foil package, dessert, coffee or punch. You also get a huge napkin which is best tucked into your collar in standard Henry the Eighth style. Afterwards, the wetnap for sticky fingers.

And now for the show! First a presentation by a magician and some fancy stepping by a trained horse and his Saracen rider. Then its on to the jousts. The various knights not only fight on horseback, but engage in choreographed swordplay after being unhorsed. This goes on for all six knights until the final victor is announced. All this while, the wenches are either serving supper or selling you pictures, banners, wines or whatever.

After the jousts, many couples stay on to dance at a small nightclub set up in the anteroom. Families often hang around until their knight shows up to autograph the picture, shield or whatever else their kids have bought. An interesting evening.

HOURS: Closed Mondays. Weekdays: 7:30 p.m.; Fri., Sat., Sun. Call for hours. (2 pers. some months)
ADMISSION: Sun.-Thurs.: Adults, $33.00; Children, $23.00; Weekends: Adults, $35.00; Children, $24.00.
LOCATION: 149 Polito Ave., Lyndhurst, Bergen County. From Route 3, take 17 S to Lyndhurst.
TELEPHONE: 800-828-2945; 201-933-2220

CULINARY INSTITUTE OF AMERICA

Any organization that wants to run a day trip and be assured of a well-filled bus, has only to mention the Culinary Institute of America and the seats fill up fast. The trick is to find a suitable date — for group bookings must often wait eight to twelve months for reservations. If you go on your own, with just two or four in tow, you may find it easier to reserve a table at this school where budding chefs cook, clean and serve in the ever-expanding restaurants on the first floor.

What makes CIA so popular? Well prices are reasonable for a seven course meal for one thing. And since many of the graduates go on to found chic, ultra-expensive restaurants there is the feeling of getting in on the ground floor of a good thing. But if the cooking is done by seniors, the waiters must be freshman, because the service can vary from efficient to inept. The food, however, is always good, if not necessarily in the sublime category.

Set high on a hill overlooking the Hudson Valley, the red brick Institute includes student dorms, several restaurants and a well-stocked bookstore. **The Escoffier Room**, which specializes in the formal, seven course European meal includes a large window which allows patrons to watch the chefs at meal preparation. (All we ever saw, however, was someone making butter curls). A typical formal meal might include a light hors d'oeuvre, a soup, a main course such as medallions of veal, a molded rice pilaf, and a handful of vegetables cooked *al dente*. This would be followed by salad, a sorbet, and then a handsome dessert table — a movable feast of tortes, tarts and eclairs — that winds its way around the room very slowly. The **American Bounty Room** offers faster service and includes such staples as roast beef and American pies.

Other eating areas include **St. Andrew's Cafe** which offers an informal atmosphere and does not require reservations, and the new Italian room called the **"Caterina de Medici"** for formal fare. Although tours of the CIA are available, most people are content with a meal and a browse through the bookstore. If you are combining a trip to the Institute with a visit to the neighboring historic houses at Hyde Park or Vanderbilt Mansion, be sure you allow plenty of time, as lunch is leisurely affair here.

       HOURS: Tues.- Sun., lunch & dinner, except cafe.
  ADMISSION: Prix fixe for Escoffier; A la Carte for other rooms.
   LOCATION: Hyde Park, NY (3 miles north of Poughkeepsie).
TELEPHONE: 914-471-6608

RENAULT WINERY

Let's face it, a winery tour is just about the most popular kind of industrial tour there is. The art of winemaking is so ancient, the slightly fermented air in the cellars so heady and the little old winemaker is usually so jolly that there is always a party air about these tours. And since wine-tasting is involved, no wonder everyone seems to have a good time.

Historic Renault Winery calls itself the best little tour-house in New Jersey and for good reason. It's fun! Yes, you learn about the early wine presses and dosage machines, but the tour leader also plays to the crowd, threatening to send the women in to stomp the grapes or the men in to clean the barrels. The tour includes a sip of wine and some history of the place. The winery is not run by the Renault family, by the way, but by the third family to buy this thriving business. It is situated way out in the Pine Barrens about 16 miles northwest of Atlantic City. Apparently this sandy soil lends itself well to grape production.

There are various stops in rooms full of antique winemaking equipment and small wine-tasting rooms. Then it's into the cellars where giant vats store the wine. These oak and redwood vats are fifty and sixty years old and would have to be replaced today by stainless steel as the old cooper's craft is lost. The guide explains how the wine is poured off and facts of vineyard life. If I learned one salient fact here it was to never-more buy cooking wine at the supermarket. It seems that food companies buy the wineries' rejects, then add salt to the already bad wine (that's a law), bottle it and sell it. It's best to use your leftover open bottles for your cooking. As the tour leader mentioned — no cookbook every says to add cooking wine to your recipe.

Before your tour, you are invited to inspect the glass museum which is a collection of fanciful wineglasses, many from the 16th and 17th Centuries and some from Venice. After the tour there is, of course, the gift shop where you can buy wine and accoutrements. Many vineyards make at least one third of their sales from the tours so the last stop is a most important one to them. For the best view of winemaking the optimum months to visit are in September and October when the grapes are harvested and processed.

Aside from regular tours, Renault Winery also serves lunches, and of course a good number of the dishes are "au vin". There is also a weekend gourmet restaurant, open to the public by reservation.

> **HOURS:** Daily. Tours are Mon. - Sat.: 10-5; Sun.: 12-5
> **ADMISSION:** $1 for tours. Under 18 free.
> **LOCATION:** Bremen Ave., Egg Harbor City, Atlantic County. Take Garden State Parkway exit 44 (if coming from north only!) and right onto Moss Mill Rd., then 6 miles to Bremen Ave. From Atlantic City: Route 30 to Bremen Ave.
> **TELEPHONE:** 609-965-2111

OTHER AREA WINERIES

Another Atlantic City sidetrip is the one to **Gross' Highland Winery**. Champagne tanks and equipment a specialty. Gift shop includes a wide selection of glassware. *Hours:* Mon. - Sat.: 9-6. *Location:* Absecon Highlands. Take Route 9 to Route 561 (Jim Leeds Road) look for winery on left. *Telephone:* 609-652-1187.

In New York State, about one-half hour north of West Point you can find the **Brotherhood Winery** which bills itself as America's oldest and most historic winery. The $3.00 guided tasting tours last about 1 1/2 hours, and include lots of walking. *Hours:* 10-4 daily except major holidays. Take Route 17 to Exit 130, then right onto Route 208 into town. *Telephone:* 914-496-9101.

Wineries are a fast growing segment of New Jersey's agricultural scene and they seem to be popping up all over. While some emphasize tours more than others, they are always open to group tours and usually to individuals who call ahead. Here are a few of the names:

A recent addition to New Jersey viticulture is the **Tewksbury Wine Cellars**, tucked in the Hunterdon County hills. Started only a few years ago, this small vineyard hopes to produce "estate bottled" wines. Tours are available on Saturdays 11-5 or Sunday 1-5 and are $2.00 (refundable with wine purchase). Located at Burrell Road, Lebanon. Take Rte. 78 to Oldwick exit, then 517 north to Sawmill and then to Burrell Road. *Telephone:* 201-832-2400.

Another recent New Jersey vineyard is called **Alba** and is located near the border of Warren and Hunterdon counties, close to the Delaware River. Grapes are harvested from 35 acres of vines and then processed. Public tours are conducted Wed.-Fri., 1-5; Sat., 11-5; and Sun., 12-5. There is a picnic area on the grounds and of course wine is for sale. The **Alba Vineyard** is located on Route 627, Finesville, Warren County. And the **Four Sisters Winery** in Belvidere hosts tours if you call first (201) 475-3671. The **Tamuzza Vineyards** in Hope is another winery interested in having people come and look especially during special festival days. *Telephone:* 908-459-5878.

A new custom is for several regional wineries to get together and hold a weekend festival of wine-tasting, food and hayrides. These are held most often in the fall, but there is usually at least one or two in the spring. A different vineyard hosts each time, but all the wineries show their wares, and for the single price (usually $7.50) you get cheese, crackers, craftsmen, and a tour of the host's winery.

THE MEADOWLANDS

You have only to drive through the battle-scarred South Bronx on your way to Yankee Stadium to realize what a stroke of genius it was to build the Meadowlands Sports-Arena Complex in the middle of a wide open area. It may have been a wasteland once, but now the sports-entertainment complex is breaking all box-office records. In fact, the biggest problem now is traffic tie-ups, especially when all three buildings are holding events. The complex consists of:

1. THE RACETRACK: Both harness and flat racing have their season at this modern, sparkling facility. The glassed-in, climate controlled Grandstand can hold up to 35,000 people. There are several restaurants here for those who want to combine a night out with dining out. The Tracksider restaurant offers good though unexciting food at moderate prices. The tables are set on tiers so you can watch the race while you eat. The Handicapper also provides food, while the Pegasus restaurant, up on the top level of the track, gives you a bird's eye view of the race and a fancier place to eat with its two buffets, sitdown section and high prices.

For those watching the race from the grandstand a large 15 x 36 foot video matrix screen allows you to watch the action on the far side of the field and also flashes the results almost immediately. The Meadowlands Racetrack has now become the number one track in harness racing and is among the top ten in thoroughbred racing in attendance and wagering.

2. GIANTS STADIUM: So named because the football team of that name makes its home there. The stadium has a seating capacity of 76,000, color coded seats and a video matrix scoreboard that delights the kids. The stadium is used not only for sports events for special concerts, antique shows and other extravaganzas as well.

3. THE ARENA: (Officially the Byrne Arena). The third addition to the Meadowlands Complex boasts a striking modern design that arches eleven stories high. The arrangement of seats (approximately 20,000) allows good viewlines. However, a shortage of personnel often closes off the lower concourse so you may have quite a hike if you go for snacks. The Arena hosts the N.J. Nets, college basketball games, ice shows, Ringling Brothers Circus, rock shows and many other entertainments that New Jerseyans used to travel to Madison Square Garden to see.

FOR THE MEADOWLANDS COMPLEX

PARKING: Fee varies. Come early to avoid jamups.
LOCATION: East Rutherford, Bergen County.
DIRECTIONS: From N.J. Turnpike northbound - take Exit 16W for direct access. From Turnpike south - take Exit 18W. From Garden State Parkway northbound - Exit 153A to Route 3 East. From G.S.P. south-Exit 163 to Route 17S to Paterson Plank Road East.
TELEPHONE: 201-935-8500; Racetrack: 201-460-4092

OTHER NEW JERSEY RACETRACKS

MONMOUTH PARK: Oceanport, Monmouth County (Use GSP Exit 105). *Telephone:* 908-222-5100. Thoroughbred racing at this track close to the Jersey shore runs from May through September.

FREEHOLD RACEWAY: Park Avenue, Freehold, Monmouth County (Take Route 9 to junction of Route 33). *Telephone:* 908-462- 3800. A beautiful new track with flags flying, right in the heart of horse breeding country. Harness racing continues from January through December. Thursday is ladies day.

ATLANTIC CITY RACE COURSE: Junction of Route 40 and Route 322, Atlantic County (Atlantic City Expressway Exit 12). *Telephone:* 609-641-2190. Thoroughbred racing June 1 - September 30.

OTHER NEW JERSEY ARENAS & AUDITORIUMS

GARDEN STATE ARTS CENTER: A beautiful white concrete ampitheatre designed by Edward Durell Stone is the setting for nightly concerts and loads of special events throughout the summer. The "shell" is covered and offers seating for 5,000 while an additional 4,000 people can be accommodated on the lawn. The lawn people, however, must bring their own blankets and chairs and risk the weather.

The shell is open on all sides so that there is easy access to seats and a delicious breeze from the nearby seashore wafts through the auditorium. Shows at the Garden State range from pop singers to symphony orchestras with a few ethnic festivals thrown in. The season runs from late June to early September.

> **LOCATION:** Holmdel, Monmouth County. Take Exit 116 off Garden State Parkway, follow signs.
> **TELEPHONE:** 908-442-9200

OCEAN GROVE AUDITORIUM: A cavernous 7,000 seat auditorium built in the late Victorian age is one of the attractions of this quiet camp-meeting town right next to Asbury Park on the shore. The Great Auditorium, with its majestic organ, has recently been refurbished and restored. It is now home to many familystyle entertainments plus a lecture series. Typical attractions are singers (including pop singers) choral groups and festivals. Again, this is for the summer season only.

LOCATION: 54 Pitman Avenue, Ocean Grove, Monmouth County.
TELEPHONE: 908-775-0035

WATERLOO VILLAGE SUMMER MUSIC FESTIVAL:
Mentioned in the chapter on Restored Villages, this festival has plans afoot to build a permanent shell next to the historic village. As of now, concerts are given under a huge tent, and picnickers often arrive early. Classical music, jazz, pop, and bluegrass are featured here. There have been some "soft" rock stars of late, and these concerts are held in the huge field nearby. A food pavilion provides an alternative to picnics for visitors to the festival.

LOCATION: Waterloo Village, Stanhope, Sussex County.
TELEPHONE: 201-347-4700

INDEX

C

D

E

H

P

R

REGIONAL INDEX

NEW JERSEY

ATLANTIC COUNTY
Atlantic City
  Casinos and boardwalk
  Atlantic City Race Course
  Historic Gardners Basin
Brigantine National Wildlife
  Refuge
Gross' Highland Winery
Lucy, Margate Elephant
Noyes Museum, Oceanville
Renault Winery
Smithville, Historic Town of
Pine Barrens
Somers Mansion
Storybook Land

BERGEN COUNTY
Aviation Hall of Fame, Teterboro
Bergen Museum
Bergen County Wildlife Center
Campgaw Ski Area, Mahwah
Flat Rock Brook Nature Center
Fort Lee Historic State Park
Hackensack Env. Center
The Hermitage
Lorimar Nature Center
Meadowlands Sports Complex
Medieval Times
Montvale Antiques
Schoolhouse Museum, Paramus
U.S.S. Ling, Hackensack
Van Saun Park
Von Steuben House

BURLINGTON COUNTY
Atsion State Park
Bass River State Park
Batsto Village
Bordentown Tour
Burlington Tour

Columbus Flea Market
Lebanon State Forest
Mount Holly Tour
Penn State Forest
Pine Barrens
Rancocos State Park
Wharton State Forest

CAMDEN COUNTY
Barclay Farmstead
Camden
  Camden County Historical
  Society
  Campbell Museum
  Walt Whitman House
Clementon Lake Park
Greenfield Hall, Haddonfield
Indian King Tavern, Haddonfield

CAPE MAY COUNTY
Belleplain State Forest
Cape May Bird Observatory
Cape May County Museum
Cape May County Park Zoo
Cape May-Lewes Ferry
Cape May Point State Park
Cape May (town)
Corson's Inlet State Park
Historic Cold Spring Village
Leaming's Run Garden
Ocean City
Ocean City Historical Museum
Stone Harbor
Stone Harbor Bird Sanctuary
Wetlands Institute
Wildwood
Wildwood Crest

CUMBERLAND COUNTY
Belleplain State Forest
Bridgeton Tour
Cohansic Zoo, Bridgeton

Pine Barrens
Wheaton Village, Millville

ESSEX COUNTY
Center for Environmental Studies
Grover Cleveland Birthplace
Edison Labs/Glenmont
Force House, Livingston
Hartshorn Arboretum
Montclair
    Israel Crane House
    Montclair Art Museum
    Presby Iris Garden
Newark
    Ballantine House
    Branch Brook Park
    New Jersey Historical Society
    Newark Museum
Riker Hill Geological Museum
Turtle Back Zoo

GLOUCESTER COUNTY
Gloucester County Tour
Hunter-Lawrence House,
    Woodbury
Mullica Hill Antiques
Red Bank Battlefield Park

HUDSON COUNTY
Hoboken
Jersey City Museum
Liberty State Park
    Ellis Island
    Statue of Liberty
Secaucus Outlets

HUNTERDON COUNTY
Black River & Western Railroad
Clinton Historical Museum Village
Flemington Fair Flea Market
Flemington Outlets
Hunterdon Art Center, Clinton
Lambertville Antiques
Marshall House, Lambertville
Round Valley State Park

Spruce Run State Park
Tewksbury Wine Cellars
Twp. of Lebanon Museum
Voorhees State Park
Windmill Museum

MERCER COUNTY
Belle Mountain Ski Area
Hopewell Museum
Kuser Farm Mansion
Howell Living History Farm
Princeton
    Bainbridge House
    Morven
    Princeton Art Museum
    Princeton Battlefield
    University Tour
    Squibb Headquarters
Trenton
    New Jersey State House
    New Jersey State Museum
    Old Barracks
    William Trent House
Washington Crossing State Park

MIDDLESEX COUNTY
Cheesequake State Park
East Jersey Olde Towne
Edison Memorial Tower
Middlesex County Museum
New Brunswick
    Buccleuch Mansion
    Rutgers Geology Museum
    Zimmerli Art Museum

MONMOUTH COUNTY
Allaire State Park
Allen House
Asbury Park
Belmar
Brielle
Deal
Englishtown Auction Sales
Freehold
    Covenhoven House

248

Monmouth Battlefield State Park
Monmouth County Historical Society
Freehold Raceway
Garden State Arts Center
Howell Antique Flea Market
Keansburg Amusements
Longstreet Farm, Holmdel
Marlpit Hall
Monmouth Museum, Lincroft
Monmouth Park Racetrack
Ocean Grove
Owl Haven
Poricy Park Nature Center
Sandy Hook
Spring Lake
Spy House Museum
Twin Lights Lighthouse

MORRIS COUNTY

Archie's Resale Shop, Meyersville
Chester Flea Market
Cooper Mill
Craigmeur Ski Area
Fosterfields
Frelinghuysen Arboretum
Great Swamp Outdoor Center
Hacklebarny State Park
Historic Speedwell
Hopatcong State Park
Meyersville Grange Flea Market
Morris County College Planetarium
Morris Museum of Arts and Sciences
Morristown
    Acorn Hall
    Ford Mansion
    Jockey Hollow
    Macculloch Hall
    Schuyler-Hamilton House
Museum of Early Trades and Crafts
St. Hubert's Giralda

OCEAN COUNTY

Barnegat Lighthouse State Park
Great Adventure
Island Beach State Park
Lebanon State Forest
Long Beach Island
New Egypt Flea Market
Ocean County College Planetarium
Ocean County Historical Museum
Point Pleasant
Popcorn Park
Seaside Heights
Seaside Park

PASSAIC COUNTY

Abram S. Hewitt State Forest
American Labor Museum
Dey Mansion, Wayne
Fairy Tale Forest
Norvin Green State Forest
Paterson
    Great Falls
    Lambert Castle
    Paterson Museum
    Paterson Tour
Ringwood Manor State Park
Skylands
Van Riper-Hopper House, Wayne

SALEM COUNTY

Fort Mott State Park
Hancock House
Parvin State Park
Salem Tour

SOMERSET COUNTY

Buck Gardens
Colonial Park Rose Gardens
Delaware and Raritan Canal State Park
Golf House, Far Hills
Great Swamp

Neshanic Flea Market
Raritan Valley College Planetarium
Scherman-Hoffman Sanctuary
Somerset Environmental
   Education Center
Somerville
   Duke Gardens
   Old Dutch Parsonage
   Wallace House
Washington Rock State Park

SUSSEX COUNTY
Action Park
Delaware Water Gap
Franklin Mineral Museum
Gingerbread Castle
Great Gorge Ski Area
Hidden Valley Ski Area
High Point State Park
Millbrook Village
Old Monroe Schoolhouse
Newton Flea Market
Space Farms Zoo
Stokes State Forest
Swartswood State Park
Vernon Valley Ski Area
Waterloo Village
Wawayanda State Park
Worthington State Forest

UNION COUNTY
Bell Labs Exhibit
Bowcraft Amusement Park
Boxwood Hall, Elizabeth
Cannonball House, Springfield
Dr. Robinson Plantation
Drake House, Plainfield
Miller-Cory House
Ogden Belcher Mansion
Osborn Cannonball House
Reeves-Reed Arboretum
Sperry Observatory
Terry Lou Zoo
Trailside Nature Center
Trailside Planetarium

WARREN COUNTY
Alba Vineyards
Allamuchy State Park
Delaware Water Gap
Doll Castle Doll Museum
Four Sisters Winery
Jenny Jump State Forest
Land of Make Believe
Merrill Creek Reservoir
Miniature Kingdom
Pequest Trout Hatchery
Stephens State Park
Tamuzza Vineyards
Well Sweep Herb Farm

NEW YORK

HUDSON VALLEY AREA
Boscobel
Brotherhood Winery
Culinary Institute of America
Hunter Mountain Ski Area
Hyde Park
Lyndhurst
Philipsburg Manor
Renaissance Festival
Ski Windham
Sterling Forest Ski Area
Sunnyside
Van Cortlandt Manor
Vanderbilt Mansion
West Point

NEW YORK CITY

MANHATTAN
American Museum of Natural
   History
Chinatown
Circle Line Tour
Cloisters, The
Empire State Building
Forbes Galleries
Frick Collection

Lincoln Center Tour
Metropolitan Museum of Art
Museum of Modern Art
NBC TV Tours
N.Y. Stock Exchange
Soho Tour
South Street Seaport
U.N. Headquarters
World Trade Center

BROOKLYN
Brooklyn Botanic Gardens
N.Y. Aquarium

BRONX
Bronx Zoo
N.Y. Botanical Gardens
Wave Hill

STATEN ISLAND
Staten Island Zoo

PENNSYLVANIA

BRANDYWINE VALLEY AREA
Brandywine Battlefield State Park
Brandywine River Museum
Longwood Gardens

BUCKS COUNTY
Andalusia
Green Hill Farm
Lahaska
Mercer Mile, Doylestown
New Hope
Pennsbury Manor
Sesame Place
Washington Crossing Park

PHILADELPHIA AREA
Barnes Foundation (Merion)
Fairmount Park Houses
Franklin Institute

Franklin Mills Mall
Independence Mall
Pennsylvania Academy of Fine
   Arts
Philadelphia Museum of Art
Philadelphia Zoo
United States Mint
University of Pennsylvania
   Archeology Museum

POCONOS AREA
Big Boulder Ski Area
Bushkill Falls
Camelback Ski Area
Delaware Water Gap
Jack Frost Ski Area
Shawnee Mountain Ski Area
Shawnee Place

OTHER PENNSYLVANIA AREAS
Dorney Park -
   Wildwater Kingdom
Hershey Rose Gardens
Hersheypark
Reading Outlets
Strasburg Railroad
Valley Forge

DELAWARE
Cape May-Lewes Ferry
Hagley Museum
Nemours
Winterthur

Can't find a copy of NEW JERSEY DAY TRIPS in your local bookstore? Want to send a copy to a friend in another state? Just photocopy the coupon below and send, with check or money order, to:

THE WOODMONT PRESS
P.O. BOX 108
GREEN VILLAGE, N.J. 07935

Please send me _____ number of copies of NEW JERSEY DAY TRIPS @ $10.95 a copy. Postage and handling are $1.50 extra.

I am enclosing ....$ _____
Postage $1.50

TOTAL ....$ _____

Send book to:

NAME _____

ADDRESS _____

CITY/STATE/ZIP _____

*For 2 or more copies add .50 to postage for each additional copy.